Aviation Infrastructure
Performance

Aviation Infrastructure Performance

A Study in Comparative Political Economy

CLIFFORD WINSTON
GINÉS DE RUS
editors

BROOKINGS INSTITUTION PRESS
Washington, D.C.

Copyright © 2008
THE BROOKINGS INSTITUTION
1775 Massachusetts Avenue, N.W., Washington, D.C. 20036
www.brookings.edu

All rights reserved. No part of this publication may be reproduced or transmitted in any form or by any means without permission in writing from the Brookings Institution Press.

Library of Congress Cataloging-in-Publication data
Aviation infrastructure performance : a study in comparative political economy / Clifford Winston and Ginés de Rus, editors.
    p.   cm.
   Summary: "International transportation experts compare and contrast how different nations have managed their airports and air traffic control systems to address congestion and delays, carrier competition, and air travel safety and how well they are meeting the needs of their people"—Provided by publisher.
   Includes bibliographical references and index.
   ISBN 978-0-8157-9394-6 (cloth : alk. paper) — ISBN 978-0-8157-9395-3 (pbk. : alk. paper)
   1. Airports—Economic aspects. 2. Airports—Traffic control. 3. Air traffic control. 4. Aeronautics—Safety measures. I. Winston, Clifford, 1952– II. Rus, Ginés de. III. Title.

HE9797.4.E3A95 2008
387.7'36—dc22
                                        2008002979

9 8 7 6 5 4 3 2 1

The paper used in this publication meets minimum requirements of the
American National Standard for Information Sciences—Permanence of Paper for Printed Library Materials: ANSI Z39.48-1992.

Typeset in Minion

Composition by R. Lynn Rivenbark
Macon, Georgia

Printed by R. R. Donnelley
Harrisonburg, Virginia

Contents

1	Introduction *Clifford Winston and Ginés de Rus*	1

PART ONE THE UNITED STATES AND CONTINENTAL EUROPE

2	Delayed! U.S. Aviation Infrastructure Policy at a Crossroads *Steven A. Morrison and Clifford Winston*	7
3	The European Union: Evolution of Privatization, Regulation, and Slot Reform *David Gillen and Hans-Martin Niemeier*	36

PART TWO AUSTRALIA, NEW ZEALAND, THE UNITED KINGDOM, AND CANADA

4	Airport Policy in Australia and New Zealand: Privatization, Light-Handed Regulation, and Performance *Peter Forsyth*	65
5	Airport Planning and Regulation in the United Kingdom *Anne Graham*	100
6	Airport Policy in Canada: Limitations of the Not-for-Profit Governance Model *Michael W. Tretheway and Robert Andriulaitis*	136

PART THREE CHINA AND DEVELOPING COUNTRIES

7   Airport Policy and Performance in Mainland China
    and Hong Kong   159
    Anming Zhang and Andrew Yuen

8   Air Transportation Infrastructure in Developing
    Countries: Privatization and Deregulation   193
    Kenneth Button

9   Synthesis and Conclusions   222
    Clifford Winston and Ginés de Rus

Contributors   225

Index   227

Aviation Infrastructure
Performance

CLIFFORD WINSTON *and* GINÉS DE RUS

1
Introduction

The increasing interdependence of firms and individuals throughout the world—popularly defined as globalization—has been greatly facilitated by air transportation. In 2005 the world's airlines carried roughly 2 billion passengers, more than one-third of whom were traveling for business or pleasure to another country. For the next several years, the world's air traffic is expected to grow about 6 percent annually.[1]

Globalization can enable a nation to develop and benefit from its comparative advantage in commodities and services including tourism, but a nation must have adequate infrastructure to realize its comparative advantage. For example, a country must have a network of airports that are capable of handling operations by large jets safely and efficiently as well as an air traffic control system that uses the latest technology to optimize routings and prevent accidents.

Accordingly, many countries have made substantial investments in aviation infrastructure. Currently some 49,000 airports are operating in the world, with 3,500 of them providing scheduled passenger service. The United States has 19,000, or 40 percent of the world's airports; of those, 663 provide scheduled passenger service. Radar-based air traffic control systems have been implemented to guide aircraft, especially in heavily used domestic and international air space, and some countries are planning to shift to satellite-based technology over the coming decades.

1. These figures and others presented below were obtained from the Air Transport Association, Washington.

Investments in aviation infrastructure have undoubtedly contributed to the long-run improvement in airline safety. During 2005 the world's scheduled airlines experienced only 0.02 passenger fatalities per 100 million passenger-kilometers. But if air travel safety is to continue to improve, aviation infrastructure must be able to accommodate the growing demand for air travel. In fact, this concern has motivated certain countries to begin development of a satellite-based air traffic control system, which is capable of safely handling more aircraft than radar-based systems can.

At the same time, the continuing failure of policymakers to implement efficient pricing of and investment in airports and air traffic control has generated significant costs in those parts of the world where air transportation is heavily used and means that travelers and carriers can expect to incur longer and more irritating delays to prevent safety from deteriorating. An additional concern is that the benefits of global liberalization of airline ownership and economic regulation will not be fully realized if airline entry at major airports is impeded by a lack of available gates and takeoff and landing times. For example, in its recent negotiations with the European Union to liberalize the trans-Atlantic airline market, the U.S. government raised concerns about capacity constraints at the EU's major hub airports.

The purpose of this book is to assess how different regions around the world make investments and operate airports and air traffic control systems to address congestion and delays, carrier competition, and air travel safety. The assessment amounts to a study in comparative political economy because countries have established different institutional arrangements—public versus private ownership, light versus heavy regulation—to tackle these issues. Hence, the study is able to provide an initial indication of how institutions affect aviation infrastructure performance.

Among the countries included here, the United States is generally thought to be a bastion of free markets and at the forefront of airline deregulation, but its airports and air traffic control system are publicly owned and operated. Airports and air traffic control systems in continental European countries (which excludes the United Kingdom) are, for the most part, also owned and operated by the public sector. In contrast, Australia, New Zealand, the United Kingdom, and Canada are experimenting with various ways of privatizing their airports and air traffic control systems. And even mainland China and some developing counties are allowing the private sector to participate in airport ownership.

Commercial users (airlines) and some economists have traditionally regarded privatization with skepticism because they believe airports and air traffic control have market power. But the initial findings from various countries' efforts to privatize their airports and air traffic control systems give cause for optimism about the social desirability of private sector involvement in aviation infrastructure. The evidence also suggests that the performance of privatized (and quasi-privatized) airports, in particular, has been compromised by inappropriate government regulation. Broader and less restrictive experimentation with privatization may reveal substantial benefits from the policy, but such dramatic institutional change faces formidable political opposition.

The book is divided into three parts that group assessments of aviation infrastructure policy: countries that predominantly have publicly provided aviation infrastructure—the United States and continental Europe; countries that are experimenting with some form of privatization of their infrastructure—Australia, New Zealand, the United Kingdom, and Canada; and countries that are exploring a limited amount of private sector participation—China and some developing countries. The final chapter synthesizes the assessments and draws policy conclusions.

The material in this book is drawn from a series of papers that were presented at a conference sponsored by and held at the Rafael Del Pino Foundation in Madrid, Spain, in September 2006. The revised papers benefited from useful comments by Dorothy Robyn, David Starkie, and an anonymous reviewer and careful editing by Marty Gottron.

PART ONE

The United States and Continental Europe

2

STEVEN A. MORRISON *and* CLIFFORD WINSTON

Delayed!
U.S. Aviation Infrastructure Policy at a Crossroads

In the aftermath of the September 11 terrorist attacks, travelers' fears of flying have given way to their anxieties about delays they may encounter when going through airport security, leaving the departure gate and taking off, flying to their destination, and landing and disembarking from the aircraft. In 2005 in-flight delays and earlier airport arrivals for security screening were estimated to cost passengers and airlines in the United States $40 billion annually.[1]

Of course, delays are hardly a new concern with airline travel. As shown in figure 2-1, travel times have been increasing for the past three decades. Forecasts by the Federal Aviation Administration (FAA) call for more than 1 billion passenger enplanements by 2016, indicating that landside and airborne delays and their associated costs will become significantly worse unless the nation's aviation infrastructure—airports and air traffic control—improves the efficiency with which it helps passengers get to their destinations.[2]

Currently responsibility for basic aeronautical services in the United States—including terminals, gates, taxiing areas, and runways—lies with local

---

1. Total delay costs for 2005 are obtained as follows. The U.S. Department of Transportation (2006) estimated that aircraft delays cost passengers $9.4 billion. This figure is likely to be an underestimate because the delays to passengers are inferred from delays to aircraft. Passenger delays are likely to be greater than aircraft delays because delays to passengers may cause them to miss connections. Using Federal Aviation Administration delay data, the Air Transport Association in 2006 estimated that the additional operating costs to airlines from delays were $5.9 billion. Finally, a one-hour earlier arrival at an airport for security purposes valued at $50 an hour (obtained by applying Transportation Department guidelines to determine the value of time in 2005 for airline travelers) for roughly 500 million trips resulted in an additional cost of $25 billion.

2. FAA (2006).

Figure 2-1. *Changes in Components of Actual Flight Time since 1977*

Change in flight time (minutes)

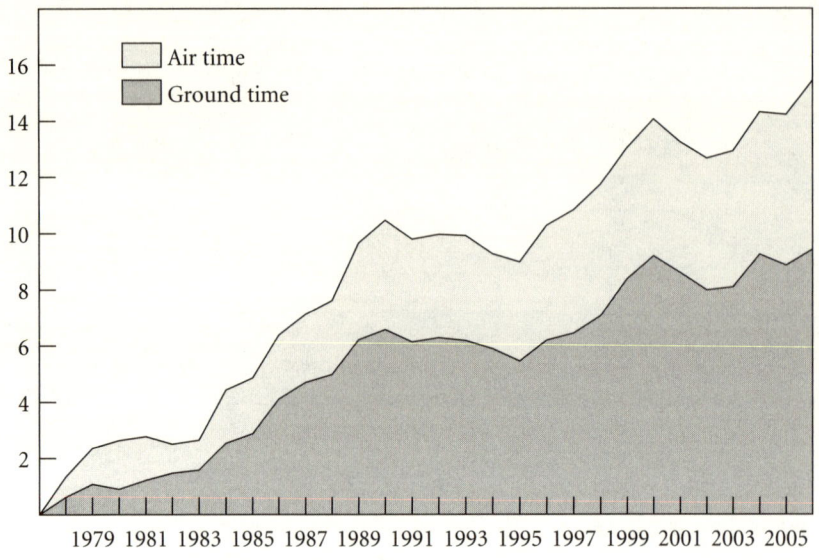

[Chart showing Air time and Ground time from 1979 to 2005]

Source: Authors' calculations from data in U.S. Department of Transportation, Service Segment Data and Schedule T-100, Data Bank 28DS, Domestic Segment Data. The data in the graph are based on a fixed set of flight segments (that is, all domestic segments in the Service Segment and 28DS databases for which data were available for all years 1977–2006). Changes in flight time at the segment level were aggregated using 1977 passenger weights.

governments that operate airports either directly, as in the case of small airports, or through airport authorities, as in the case of medium and large airports. The Transportation Security Administration (TSA) is responsible for airport security, and the FAA provides air traffic control. In 2004 the FAA's air traffic control function was reorganized into the Air Traffic Organization (ATO), a "performance-based" organization. Nonetheless, the ATO remains an agency within a civil aviation administration that is funded by annual budget appropriations from Congress.

Congress has repeatedly criticized the FAA for the excessive delays and cost overruns it has experienced in trying to develop a technologically up-to-date air traffic control system that would reduce U.S. airborne delays by expanding usable airspace capacity. Some members of Congress have characterized the TSA as a bloated bureaucracy whose screening tasks could be performed better and more efficiently by private screeners. Congress has not singled out airport authorities for criticism, but before September 11, Rudolph Giuliani, then the mayor of New York City, advocated privatization of the airports managed by the Port Authority of New York and New Jersey. Despite complaints by elected officials and an increasingly frustrated flying public, delays seem to be an inescapable part of air travel. Finally, in September 2007, President George W. Bush invited aviation officials and U.S. Department of Transportation secretary Mary Peters to the Oval Office to discuss solutions to air travel delays, proclaiming, "We've got a problem, we understand there's a problem, and we're going to address the problem."

In our view, excessive travel delays are—to a significant extent—a manifestation of the failure of publicly owned and managed airports and air traffic control to adopt policies and introduce innovations that could greatly improve the efficiency of the U.S. air transportation system. Given little economic incentive and saddled with institutional and political constraints, major airports and the air traffic control system have not exhibited any marked improvement in their performance for decades despite repeated assurances that they would do so, and they have provided little reason for policymakers and travelers to expect such improvements to ever occur.

Some observers believe that delays would be reduced if the nation invested more money in airports and air traffic control. However, the returns from such spending would be compromised by the system's vast inefficiencies. Thus, the key to reducing delays efficiently is to rid the system of its major inefficiencies. We believe that can be accomplished only by privatizing the nation's aviation infrastructure. The aim of this chapter is to argue that by operating in a less constrained and a more competitive environment, privatized airports and air traffic control would have the potential to improve service to travelers and reduce the cost of carrier operations while maintaining the nation's outstanding record of air travel safety in the face of an ever greater volume of traffic. In addition, privatized airports could facilitate greater competition among airlines that would lead to lower fares.

We recognize that privatization of public aviation facilities does not guarantee that monopolies will not be formed. Thus, we call for carefully designed privatization experiments to preview the extent of competition that is likely to develop among airports and the resulting economic effects and to alleviate concerns that public airports will be replaced by private monopoly airports. We also recognize that privatization faces strong resistance from entrenched interests who benefit from current policies. At the same time, as indicated by President Bush's recent attention to the problem, policymakers cannot ignore the political costs of periodic crises related to increasing travel delays. It is our view that the impasse in reforming aviation infrastructure policy would be broken if experiments reveal that the flying public would realize large benefits from privatization.

Congress enacted legislation in 1996 to create a federal airport privatization demonstration program, but barriers to participation have discouraged significant experiments. As discussed in other chapters in this book, during the last several years countries such as Australia, New Zealand, and the United Kingdom have privatized their airports, and countries such as Canada and the United Kingdom have explored ways to enable private entities to provide (at least in part) their air traffic control services. We hope U.S. policymakers will intensify their efforts to encourage the private sector to participate in addressing growing concerns that the nation's air transportation system is inexorably headed toward longer delays and potential threats to safety.

In what follows, we provide institutional background on U.S. aviation infrastructure; assess the economic efficiency of current public policy toward airports, air travel security, and air traffic control; and outline the case—including experiments to produce hard evidence—for privatizing these services.

An Overview of U.S. Aviation Infrastructure and the Evolution of Current Policy

The federal government has shaped the development of aviation infrastructure through congressional funding of—and the FAA's allocation of those funds for—airports and air traffic control. It also has a major presence at airports through the Transportation Security Administration's screening of passengers and luggage. Different regulations and funding sources govern the operations of these services, so it is useful to discuss the evolution of current policy toward them separately.

Airports

The Civil Aeronautics Act of 1938 is notable for instituting economic regulation of fares, entry, and exit in the U.S. airline industry, but it also paved the way for federal funding of airports by authorizing funds to build additional airfields.[3] Previously, states and local governments had sole responsibility for airport planning and issued general obligation bonds that were supported by taxes to pay for runways, terminal construction, and improvements in these facilities. The Federal Airport Act of 1946 created an intergovernmental grant program, providing federal matching funds to states and local governments for airport projects. The program lasted until 1970 when it was replaced with the Airport Development Program, which increased federal funding for con-

---

3. Dilger (2003) provides a complete discussion of the major federal legislation toward airports and air traffic control.

struction and improvements at large public airports. Federal funding for airport projects is currently provided under the Airport Improvement Program (AIP), which provides grants to enhance public-use airport safety, capacity, security, and environmental concerns. AIP funds are drawn from the Airport and Airway Trust Fund, which is supported by excise taxes, fuel taxes, and other similar revenue sources, and are distributed to airports of all sizes by the FAA on the basis of national priorities.[4]

As shown later, the majority of AIP funds are allocated to airports that account for a small share of commercial enplanements. In addition, because the demand for AIP funds exceeds availability, the FAA typically apportions the funds into major entitlement categories such as primary, cargo, and general aviation. Any remaining funds are then distributed at the discretion of the FAA.

Airports continue to issue bonds to help pay for terminals and runways, and they cover bond payments for projects approved by the FAA with the passenger facility charge. Airports also meet expenses with revenues generated from parking fees, retail store rents, and advertising display charges. Finally, airports raise revenues by renting terminal facilities such as counters and gates to airlines and by charging landing fees based on an aircraft's weight subject to guidelines set by the FAA. Runway landing fees vary widely, but currently a typical fee is $2.00 per 1,000 pounds of weight. For example, landing fees for a Boeing 757-200 aircraft, with a maximum design landing weight of 198,000 pounds and a capacity of about 186 passengers, would be somewhat less than $3 a passenger for typical passenger loads. During the 1950s and 1960s, as a quid pro quo for airlines' agreeing to pay off billions of dollars in airport bonds for expansion projects, airlines obtained exclusive-use gate leases (that is, gates leased exclusively to one airline) at many large and mid-size airports.

Airports and airlines either use a residual or compensatory charging system to establish rents, landing fees, and passenger facility charges.[5] Under a residual charging system, airlines pay the remaining costs of running the airport after commercial and nonairline sources of revenue are taken into account. The airlines guarantee that the level of charges and rents will enable the airport to break even. Under a compensatory charging system, the airlines

---

4. Currently, the trust fund is composed of revenue from a 7.5 percent ticket tax plus a fee of $3.30 per passenger for each flight segment flown, a fee of $14.50 per passenger for each international departure and arrival, a 6.25 percent cargo waybill tax, a 7.5 percent frequent flier tax on third parties (such as credit card companies) that sell frequent flier miles, and a fuel tax of 4.3 cents a gallon. As of 2007, the trust fund's uncommitted balance was $1.6 billion, a ten-year low and well below its uncommitted balance of $7.4 billion in 1999.

5. Graham (2004).

agree to pay charges that allow the airport to recover the costs of the facilities that the airlines occupy and use. The airport is responsible for covering the remaining costs such as parking and concessions. In practice, negotiations between airlines and large and midsize airports have not resulted in a clear preference for one system over the other. Some of the contracts detailing the charges airlines pay to airports contain "majority in interest" clauses that give the airlines signing the contract the right to approve certain capital expenditures, especially spending on terminals and gates.

Given a variety of funding sources, airports have generally been able to maintain their financial health even in the period after September 11, 2001, when the airline industry lost billions of dollars. To increase their airline tenants' operations, some airports (among them, Detroit, Philadelphia, San Francisco, and San Jose) have directly cut fees and charges or offered discounts to carriers that serve additional cities or expand existing service—or taken both steps.

Currently, more than 19,000 public and private airports operate in the United States, some 3,300 of which have been identified by the FAA's National Plan of Integrated Airport Systems as significant to national air transportation and therefore eligible to receive federal grants under AIP. Table 2-1 classifies these airports by size and presents their share of commercial enplanements and federal grants. Although the nation's large and medium hub airports serve 89 percent of the nation's passengers, they receive only 41 percent of federal airport grant dollars. The 31 large hub airports account for two-thirds of commercial air travelers, but only one new large hub airport has been constructed since 1973. Built in Denver in 1995, that airport has advantages that are difficult to replicate elsewhere—a flat, largely uninhabited site that is fewer than thirty miles from downtown. More than half of the nation's large hub airports are on sites that were chosen in the 1920s, 1930s, and 1940s and were later significantly expanded.[6] These airports and others built more recently have expanded available aircraft capacity by building new runways, but adding capacity in this fashion takes considerable time because airports must account for communities' input, especially their opposition to proposed projects. As of 1970, such projects also must satisfy Environmental Protection Agency environmental impact standards.

Airport Security

Before the September 11 terrorist attacks, airlines were responsible for providing passenger screening, and the FAA was supposed to promulgate performance and training standards. The airlines hired roughly 19,500 screeners from private

6. Altshuler and Luberoff (2003).

Table 2-1. *Distribution of Federal Airport Grants, by Airport Size, 1996*

Airport type[a]	Number of airports	Share of grants (percent)	Share of scheduled commercial enplanements (percent)
Large hub	31	24	67
Medium hub	42	17	22
Small hub	70	18	7
Nonhub	272	15	3
General aviation, relievers, and other commercial service	2,981	27	0

Source: Altshuler and Luberoff (2003), from original data in U.S. General Accounting Office (1998).

a. A large hub handles at least 1 percent of national enplanements, a medium hub from 0.25 percent to 1.0 percent of enplanements, a small hub from 0.05 to 0.25 percent of enplanements. A nonhub has more than 10,000 annual enplanements but less than 0.05 percent of the national total. General aviation, reliever, and other commercial service airports do not provide regularly scheduled commercial flights, although some house air taxi services.

security companies to perform screening procedures at U.S. airports.[7] After the attacks, some have claimed that reliance on private screeners was disastrous, but it should be noted that the screeners were subject to government regulation. In any case, the Transportation Security Administration was created, and in February 2002 it assumed responsibility for screening at virtually all U.S. airports. By the end of 2002 TSA deployed a workforce that, accounting for temporary employees, had grown to more than 50,000 screeners.

Passengers pay $2.50 for each leg of their flight, up to a maximum of $10 per round trip, to help pay for security screening. Airlines then remit the fees to the TSA to support its annual budget of roughly $5.5 billion. To facilitate flexibility in staffing that can respond to changes in airline service, airports have been given the option to replace federal screeners with screeners from private companies. But private screeners are still overseen by federal employees and are required to be paid at least as much as federal ones and to have undergone the same training. Not surprisingly, only a handful of (small) airports have applied to the government to switch back to privately employed screeners.

In response to air travelers' complaints about the excessive delays created by TSA screening at major airports, a "registered traveler" program was initiated

7. U.S. Government Accountability Office (2005).

to create special, speedier airport security lines for people who are willing to pay an annual fee of $50 to $100 and undergo background checks. However, TSA has failed to implement the program nationwide; in fact, as the final draft of this paper is being written, the program is operational at only eight airports—Orlando, where it was pilot-tested; three major airports, New York Kennedy, Newark, and San Francisco; and four smaller airports. Airlines, such as Southwest and United, have tried to expedite screening at certain airports by building separate terminals to accommodate their passengers or instituting special security lines for travelers who are elite members of their frequent flier programs.

Air Traffic Control

Federal provision of air traffic control was spurred by a series of fatal midair collisions and thousands of near misses during the mid-1950s. Concerned that the negative publicity about air safety would sharply curtail passenger demand, aviation interests supported the creation of a centralized federal agency to oversee air traffic control and other safety issues. Thus, in an atmosphere of crisis, Congress passed the Federal Aviation Act of 1958, which gave responsibility for managing the nation's navigable airspace to the new Federal Aviation Agency (renamed the Federal Aviation Administration in 1967, when it was brought into the newly established Department of Transportation).

In practice, the FAA operates en route and terminal facilities to ensure that air travel is safe and to prevent the system from becoming congested. En route facilities include air route traffic control centers (ARTCCs) that provide air traffic control service to aircraft operating under instrument flight rules within controlled airspace.[8] Terminal facilities include radar towers at airports and terminal radar approach facilities (TRACONs) within a fifty-mile radius of an airport; both provide service to aircraft that are arriving, departing, and transiting the controlled airspace. Currently, the FAA system includes roughly 150 radar towers, thirty-five TRACONs, and twenty-one ARTCCs. The FAA is also responsible for hiring air traffic controllers and other air traffic control personnel and for supplying terminal and en route facilities with new equipment.

Air traffic control is supported by the Airport and Airway Trust fund as well as by general revenues. Commercial airlines pay for more than 90 percent of the costs of the system, while private business jets pay the small remaining share. In addition, the military provides as well as uses air traffic control.

---

8. ARTCCs may also assist with aircraft flying under visual flight rules.

Given that they account for two-thirds of all flights, the commercial airlines contend that they are overpaying for air traffic control services.

An ongoing challenge for the FAA has been to adopt and implement the latest technological advances to expand the airspace where planes can fly safely and to reduce controller error and aircraft encounters with dangerous weather that contribute to accidents. For example, during the early 1980s the FAA announced plans to develop an advanced automation system to provide flexible, computer-oriented air traffic control capable of handling greater traffic volumes at reduced manpower. The system also included significant improvements in detecting wind shear, the primary cause of several crashes, including two major ones in the 1980s.

Although some progress has certainly been made in implementing that system, ongoing assessments by the U.S. General Accounting Office (GAO) indicate that delays and inefficiencies have characterized its development.[9] Scheduled to be completed by 1991 for $12 billion, the fully upgraded system is more than a decade late, billions of dollars over budget, and still nowhere in sight. As of 2007, the cost of the modernization was expected to climb to $51 billion.

Moreover, by the time the FAA's upgrade is complete, the system will be approaching technological obsolescence. Air travel can become even safer and faster if air traffic control replaces its ground-based radar systems with more accurate and reliable satellite communications. The satellite-based system, known by the acronym ADS-B (automatic dependent surveillance-broadcast) would allow pilots and controllers to be cognizant of the planes in the vicinity as well as their speeds, headings, and flight numbers. Travel times would be reduced because pilots would be able to fly closer together and take the most direct routes to their destination using signals from global position satellites to navigate. Pilots would also be able to operate in cloudy weather much as they do on clear days. Radar is imprecise—it typically updates aircraft positions every 4.8 seconds, while ADS-B does it every second—and forces controllers to separate aircraft by several miles to avoid collisions. The FAA has recently proposed a rule for airlines to equip all aircraft operating in controlled airspace with ADS-B-compatible avionics by 2020.

Managing the next generation air traffic control system, referred to as NextGen, would be much simpler and less costly than managing the current system because it would require a few dozen facilities dispersed throughout the country. Much of the current system of radar towers, TRACONS, and en

9. The GAO issued a series of reports in the late 1990s that critically assessed the FAA's progress in modernizing the air traffic control system (GAO 1998a, 1999a, 1999b). More recent critical assessments include Dillingham (2003) and Mead (2003).

route centers would be eliminated. The remaining facilities would be consolidated and kept as a backup in case the satellite system faltered; they would also be used to help detect planes with defective ADS-B devices and planes whose pilots were trying to avoid detection.

Key components of the system are moving forward and being tested in Alaska. The FAA reports that since satellite communications were first deployed in aircraft, the fatality rate for general aviation in Alaska has dropped roughly 40 percent.[10] The system's technology is also being used by UPS at its air cargo hub in Louisville, Kentucky. The FAA plans to switch from today's radar-based to satellite-based air traffic control, but the timetable, as outlined by the Joint Planning and Developing Office that is coordinating the effort, calls for NextGen to take twenty-five years to complete at a cost estimated to be at least $30 billion.[11]

In sum, the federal government has shaped the nation's aviation infrastructure through its long-term strategic planning and design, allocation of funds, project approval process, and specific policy guidelines on runway charges, air traffic control charges, and the like. We now consider how the government's highly interventionist role has affected the air transportation system's performance.

An Economic Assessment

The value that travelers place on air transportation reflects its convenience, price, and safety. In theory aviation infrastructure policy should enhance these attributes by efficiently reducing travel delays, facilitating greater airline competition, and using the most effective technology to keep flying safe. In practice, the evidence indicates that current policy could be significantly improved in all these areas.

Airport Performance

Airport policy encompasses charging aircraft for their use of the runways, investing in runways, leasing gates, and screening passengers and luggage. We draw on scholarly and anecdotal evidence to assess the efficiency of these policies.

10. Del Quentin Wilber, "Overhaul of Air Traffic System Nears Key Step," *Washington Post*, August 27, 2007.
11. Jennifer Oldham, "Nation's Air Traffic Control Again Nearing Obsolescence," *Los Angeles Times*, June 3, 2006; Barbara Peterson, "End of Flight Delays?" *Popular Mechanics*, August 2007.

RUNWAY PRICING. As noted, airports charge airlines landing fees that are based on the weight of the aircraft and that are consistent with the terms of the residual or compensatory contract that the parties negotiate. Generally, the fees do not vary by time of day in accordance with the volume of aircraft traffic. But congestion—which delays travel—does. Beginning with Levine and Carlin and Park, researchers have called for airports to reduce delays by replacing weight-based landing fees with efficient landing *and takeoff* tolls based on an aircraft's contribution to congestion.[12]

Weight-based landing fees were probably a reasonable way to allocate airport costs and raise revenue when airports were uncongested, but today, the principal cost that an aircraft imposes when it takes off or lands is that it delays other aircraft. (Runway damage caused by most aircraft is small.) Based on a sample of aircraft operations at thirty-one of the most congested airports in the United States, Morrison and Winston found that this delay can be substantial.[13] For example, the elasticity of average departure delay, defined as the percentage change in average departure delay caused by a 1 percent change in aircraft departures, is 2.9 for commercial carriers and 2.5 for general aviation. Thus, current weight-based landing fees, which charge large planes much more than they charge small planes but account for a small share of large planes' operating costs, have little effect on congestion because a plane waiting to take off or land is delayed at least the same amount of time by a small private plane as by a jumbo jet.[14]

We estimated that replacing weight-based landing fees with efficient marginal cost takeoff and landing tolls could generate nearly $6 billion (expressed in 2005 dollars) in annual benefits to the nation. Travelers reap $5.3 billion in reduced delay costs and carriers gain $1.8 billion from lower operating costs. Airports' substantial increase in net revenue from higher takeoff and landing fees is modestly exceeded by travelers' losses in consumer surplus. As discussed below, the redistribution from travelers to airports would be softened if efficient tolls were combined with efficient runway investment.

---

12. Levine (1969); Carlin and Park (1970).
13. Morrison and Winston (1989).
14. To be more precise, delay is affected by the type of lead and trailing aircraft (Ball, Donohue, and Hoffman 2006). If the lead aircraft is small, then the flight separation time for a heavy aircraft (that is, one with a maximum certified takeoff weight of 300,000 pounds or more) is 64 seconds and the flight separation time for a small aircraft is 80 seconds. These are roughly comparable. But if the lead aircraft is heavy, then the flight separation time for a small aircraft, 240 seconds, is much greater than the flight separation time for a heavy aircraft, 100 seconds.

Recently, some economists have raised doubts about the extent to which optimal airport pricing would reduce delays. Brueckner has pointed out that because an air carrier bears the cost of delay to itself, it should be charged only for delays it imposes on other carriers.[15] For example, a carrier with a 50 percent share of operations at an airport should be charged for one-half of the delay costs it creates—the delay incurred by other carriers—whereas the carrier's smaller (atomistic) competitors with a very small share of airport operations should be charged for all the delay they create because their delay is imposed virtually entirely on other carriers. Mayer and Sinai apply this idea to hub airports where dominant carriers cluster their operations to provide convenient connections for passengers (while nondominant carriers operate most of their flights at less-congested times); thus optimal tolls at hub airports should be small because most delay at hub airports is internalized.[16] However, Morrison and Winston find that setting optimal tolls along the lines suggested by Brueckner and by Mayer and Sinai would generate only a small welfare improvement over congestion tolls that assume atomistic behavior for two reasons.[17] First, a large fraction of delays is caused by commercial and commuter carriers and general aviation that behave atomistically (that is, there is more than twice as much external delay as internal delay). Second, the nature of carriers' (private) average costs and their (social) marginal costs, the two factors that account for the costs of congestion for a given level of traffic, means that the benefits from correctly charging carriers for contributing to congestion greatly exceed the costs of incorrectly charging them when their congestion has been internalized.

Instead of using the price mechanism at congested airports to curb delays efficiently, the FAA has instituted arbitrary quantity controls, namely, takeoff and landing slots, at some airports. Since 1969 limits—called slots—have been set on the number of takeoffs and landings per hour at New York LaGuardia, New York Kennedy, Washington Reagan National, and Chicago O'Hare airports. Although it is theoretically possible to design a slot system that has the same welfare properties as efficient tolls, no evidence exists that slot controls at U.S. airports have been designed optimally while evidence does exist that slots have tended to reduce competition and raise fares.[18]

Congress has acted in the past to eliminate slots, but the FAA has countered by imposing administrative controls in response to traffic growth. Recently, the FAA has dealt with congestion at O'Hare by getting hub carri-

15. Brueckner (2002).
16. Mayer and Sinai (2003).
17. Morrison and Winston (2007).
18. Morrison and Winston (2000).

ers together in a room and allowing American Airlines and United Airlines to agree to reduce flights, and it has proposed a new rule at New York LaGuardia that would discourage the use of small jets by imposing an average plane size of 105 to 122 seats for all gates at the airport. Both actions exemplify the FAA's preference for an (inefficient) administrative solution over a potentially efficient market solution.

RUNWAY INVESTMENT. During the past fifty years, public officials have attempted to keep up with growing demand for air travel primarily by building more runways at existing airports rather than by building additional large airports. But adding a runway is fraught with hurdles as airports must contend with community opposition and meet federal environmental impact standards. Indeed, the nation's thirty-one large hub airports, which account for the majority of delays, built just three new runways during the 1980s and six during the 1990s. In 1999 the Air Transport Association, representing major air carriers, and the National Air Traffic Controllers joined forces and called for "fifty miles of concrete"—the equivalent of twenty-five new runways—as an antidote to growing delays. Twelve runways have been christened since then, but the time and cost to build some of them simply cannot be justified. For example, Atlanta's new (fifth) runway has been nearly twenty-five years in the making, with an estimated cost of $1.3 billion; Boston's sixth runway was put into service at the end of 2006, thirty years after it was initially planned; and St. Louis's new runway cost $1.1 billion, while its value to travelers is being strongly questioned because the airport has excess capacity. The construction of taxiways has also been delayed. For example, Boston is scheduled to finish construction of a taxiway to reduce the danger of plane collisions in 2009—after a seven-year delay.

Runway investments often meet opposition when they are part of an airport's comprehensive plan to upgrade its facilities. For example, Los Angeles Airport (LAX) has been trying for more than a decade to develop a proposal acceptable to the surrounding residential community and the FAA that would involve building a new terminal and reconfiguring some of its runways. Chicago O'Hare has also been trying for many years to gain approval for an expansion plan that would lengthen and widen some of its runways and build new terminals and parking spaces for oversize jets and passenger jet bridges.

The impediments to building new runways should be of great concern because their potential benefits are huge. Morrison and Winston analyzed the situation where an airport owns land and is able to construct an additional runway measuring 10,000 feet by 150 feet.[19] Optimal runway capacity is

---

19. Morrison and Winston (1989).

reached when the marginal cost of an additional runway is equated with the marginal benefit of reduced delay. We found that a policy of efficient congestion tolls and optimal runway capacity could generate roughly $16 billion (2005 dollars) in annual benefits. Travelers would gain nearly $12 billion in reduced delays and also would pay lower fares because the expansion in runway capacity would reduce congestion to such an extent that, on average, landing fees would fall.[20] Carriers benefit from the lower operating costs from reduced delay, while airports' net revenues would fall slightly. But because airports are characterized by overall constant returns to scale, they would be financially self-sufficient under optimal pricing and investment.[21]

To be sure, our findings largely neglect the practical and political difficulties that many airports face when trying to expand their runway capacity. Nonetheless, the reductions in delays from additional runways at most major airports are so large and so important in softening the distributional effects of optimal pricing that federal policy has unquestionably compromised traveler and carrier welfare by helping to turn runway construction into a task that is measured in decades and billions of dollars.[22]

Federal grants under the Airport Improvement Program are used to reduce delays at airports; however, the program suffers from two inefficiencies. First, political forces cause federal funds to be distributed more broadly across airports than if they were allocated according to cost-benefit guidelines. Thus it is not surprising that table 2-1 suggests only a modest correlation between the airports that receive federal funds for projects that are primarily intended to reduce travel delays and the airports that experience the greatest delays. Second, efficient runway prices signal which airports will benefit most from additional runway investment. But the AIP program does not make decisions using this signal; instead it makes them subject to constraints on efficient runway investments just noted.

GATE UTILIZATION. Airport gates are classified as exclusive use (leased exclusively to one airline), preferential use (the airport operator may assign the

20. General aviation would face higher landing fees. But our model does not account for the greater flexibility that people who use general aviation have in their choice of airport and arrival and departure time; thus their loss is overstated.

21. Morrison (1983).

22. One federal agency, the Food and Drug Administration, recognized that the delays it imposed on the introduction of new drugs were generating large social costs. Accordingly, as part of the 1992 Prescription Drug User Fee Act, the FDA set user fees that were paid by pharmaceutical companies and used the revenues to hire additional new drug reviewers to improve the speed and efficiency of its reviews. In contrast, although the FAA has recently claimed that it is streamlining environmental reviews (see Benet Wilson, "FAA: Airport Capacity Improved with Boost in Runways Built," *Aviation Now*, September 26, 2006), it is not clear that the agency has expedited the construction of new runways.

gate temporarily to another carrier when it is not being used by the lessee), or common use (the airport authority makes all gate assignments). Gates available for use by new entrants consist of common-use gates, preferential-use gates that are made available by the airport authority, and exclusive-use gates that are made available by incumbent carriers. In a 1998 survey of forty-one major airports, the Air Transport Association found that 56 percent of the gates were exclusive use, 25 percent were preferential use, and 18 percent were common use, resulting in 25 percent of the gates' being available for use by new entrants.[23]

The prevalence of exclusive-use gates that are not made available to other carriers—a legacy of airline-airport contractual arrangements established during the 1950s and 1960s—makes it difficult for new entrants to provide service at several airports. Another problem facing nonincumbent carriers, especially at airports where most gates are exclusively leased, is that they must often sublet gates from incumbent carriers at nonpreferred times and at a higher cost than the incumbent pays.

In principle, an airport has a legal obligation to provide reasonable access to the facility. Policymakers, however, have yet to define precisely what *reasonable* means. Hence, some incumbents are able to prevent competitors from having access even to gates that are little used. For example, Delta offers just thirty-nine departures a day at Los Angeles, but still uses sixteen gates in two terminals.[24] Since 2002 JetBlue has expressed an interest in serving Chicago O'Hare, but subleasing a gate from another carrier was a difficult proposition because incumbents did not welcome the competition.[25] Finally, in 2006 JetBlue received federal authorization, which was needed because O'Hare is slot constrained, for four daily departures. In a few cases, airports have actually bought back and terminated long-term leases on their own gates. For example, the Maryland Aviation Administration agreed to pay US Airways $4.3 million to give up twenty-nine gates at Baltimore-Washington airport, enabling expansion by Southwest and AirTran.[26] And the Los Angeles Airport Commission voted to spend up to $154 million to take over several terminals at Los Angeles International Airport to free up aircraft parking spots for discount carriers and other airlines that had tried to add flights at the airport.[27]

---

23. Morrison and Winston (2000, p. 23).
24. Scott McCartney, "Fewer Travelers Routed through 'Hub' Airports," *Wall Street Journal*, February 14, 2006, p. D4.
25. Mark Skertic, "'Jet Who' Has City Blues," *Chicago Tribune*, January 8, 2006.
26. Scott McCartney, "Airports Crack Down on Games," *Wall Street Journal*, June 7, 2005.
27. Jennifer Oldham, "Panel Acts to Control LAX Terminals," *Los Angeles Times*, January 9, 2007.

In one study, we found that fares are $4.4 billion (2005 dollars) higher annually because of the limited availability of gates at many major and mid-size airports.[28] The loss to travelers reflects the competitive disadvantages that new entrants face when they are unable to acquire gates or can acquire them only at nonpreferred times and locations or at excessive cost.[29]

Airport authorities as well as federal law have also reduced competition and raised fares by preventing carriers from serving certain airports. Perimeter rules prohibit airlines from offering flights that exceed 1,500 miles at LaGuardia airport and, with the exception of six cities, that exceed 1,250 miles at Reagan National airport.

Until 2006 the Wright Amendment prohibited airlines that use Love Field in Dallas from offering flights to cities other than those in Texas, Alabama, Arkansas, Kansas, Louisiana, Mississippi, Missouri, New Mexico, and Oklahoma. Currently, travelers can fly anywhere from Love on a single ticket provided their carrier first stops at one of the nine Wright Amendment states, and in 2014 all Wright Amendment restrictions will be eliminated. Consistent with the predictions of opponents of the Wright Amendment, the number of flights and passengers at Love Field has increased since the 2006 action loosened restrictions on carriers' service from that airport, and fares at both Dallas airports (Love and Dallas–Fort Worth) have declined.[30] In 2006 King County in Washington blocked proposals by Southwest and Alaska airlines to offer flights from Boeing Field, which undoubtedly would have lowered fares for certain flights from Seattle-Tacoma (Sea-Tac) airport.

Performance of Airport Security

An efficient airport security system allocates resources based on cost-benefit considerations—that is, expenditures are directed toward detecting and preventing the greatest threats to safety from materializing. Although we are not aware of a formal economic assessment of the Transportation Security Administration's passenger screening, the Department of Homeland Security, GAO, and TSA routinely test screeners' ability to intercept weapons smuggled through checkpoints. The results are poor. Both the GAO and Homeland Security found that screening was no more effective by April 2005

---

28. Morrison and Winston (2000).

29. Private entrepreneurs are not precluded by airport authorities from building gates and leasing or selling them to new entrants. But they are subject to the airport authority's determination of what constitutes a fair and reasonable charge for the use of a gate. This regulatory arrangement has apparently dissuaded private entities from building gates at airports where new entrants face difficulties in acquiring them.

30. Terry Maxon, "With Fewer Limits, Love Field Is Soaring," *Dallas Morning News*, September 29, 2007.

than before September 11, and in 2006 screeners failed twenty of TSA's twenty-two tests.[31]

It is also clear that current screening procedures are inefficient. The annual cost of TSA security includes its budget of $5.5 billion and the several billions of dollars in time costs incurred by passengers waiting to be screened. It is, of course, difficult to assess the benefits of TSA screening because we will never know of the terrorist attacks, if any, that screening has prevented. In any case, federal screeners have intercepted some seven million prohibited items, but only six hundred were firearms while the rest were nail scissors, penknives, and the like.[32] Instead of expending billions of dollars in time and money to confiscate firearms—almost all of which were probably intended for recreational use—it was far more cost effective to put bulletproof doors on cockpits, which the airline industry did for some $300 million to $500 million.

Other inefficiencies suggest that airports could obtain the current level of security at much lower cost. For example, the large costs associated with passengers' excessive waiting times at heavily used airports could be sharply reduced if the TSA implemented a registered traveler program with technology that expedited screening. Wait times would also be reduced efficiently if TSA's labor force were flexible and could be deployed in response to the peaking characteristics of air travel throughout the day and during certain times of year. TSA's large budget has come under fire for wasteful expenditures on inappropriate or outdated technology and a bloated labor force described by critics as "Thousands Standing Around." TSA was embarrassed when a graduate student exposed the uselessness of its boarding-pass identification check by developing a fake boarding pass that would enable an individual to pass through security and get to any airport gate. Conducting basic investigation and intelligence appears to be more cost effective than performing ID checks, maintaining secret databases, and instituting no-fly lists.[33]

A more fundamental concern is whether TSA should even exist. One alternative that is likely to be superior to the TSA on cost-benefit grounds is a variant of Israel's model, where a branch of law enforcement receives additional funding and is responsible for questioning and identifying suspicious passengers. Turning to the private sector, security firms have been able to provide effective and subtle security for millions of customers at high-risk facilities in the United States, such as casinos in Las Vegas and Atlantic City and

---

31. Becky Akers, "A Better Way than the TSA," *Christian Science Monitor*, March 21, 2007.
32. Anne Applebaum, "Airport Security's Grand Illusion," *Washington Post*, June 15, 2005, p. A25.
33. Randall Stross, "Theatre of the Absurd at the TSA," *New York Times*, December 17, 2006, p. 5.

major amusement parks. Private security firms could be hired at airports, not just to replace federal screeners with private screeners, but to develop security strategies and make safety investments to anticipate and respond to potential terrorist attacks without being constrained by the federal government's regulatory oversight. As noted, private screeners that were used before September 11 were regulated by the government. Indeed, it has been claimed that government bureaucracy has discouraged research and development of new innovative solutions to combat terrorism, causing a political disagreement over whether the government or the private sector should drive the development of security technology.[34]

Performance of Air Traffic Control

Today, the probability of dying in a commercial aviation crash is at an all-time low, following a dramatic improvement in safety during the past ten years.[35] FAA expenditures on air traffic control deserve some credit for the nation's excellent safety record.[36] But the FAA's inefficient pricing of and investment in the system and its slow adoption of the latest technology have exacerbated air travel delays. In addition, some observers in industry and academia caution that air transport safety could be threatened if the air traffic control system is not expeditiously upgraded so it can handle the expected growth in traffic over the next decade.

PRICING. The relevant consideration in pricing air traffic control services is the marginal cost that a given flight imposes on the air traffic control system, including delay costs to other users. The cost clearly increases with the volume of traffic in a controller's airspace. Because the ticket tax is based on a percentage of the price of a given flight that may or may not vary with the time of day and, incidentally, with airspace congestion, it does not force a plane to account for the delays it imposes on other aircraft. In addition, because of the intensity of airline competition, real average fares have declined over time; thus, the ticket tax is not a stable source of revenue.

As air traffic controllers try to manage congested airspace near airports, delays may take the form of slower air speeds, indirect routings, suboptimal altitudes, and the like. Unscheduled aircraft (general aviation) may cause greater delays than scheduled aircraft cause because of unpredictable peaks in

---

34. Dan Luzadder, "Airports, Tech Firms in Holding Pattern on New Security Systems," *Travel Weekly*, November 8, 2006.

35. In 1997 there was one fatal crash in the United States for every 2 million departures. After ten years of improvement in air safety, that ratio in 2006 was one fatal crash for every 4.5 million departures.

36. Morrison and Winston (2008).

their demand for airspace, especially near airports, and because general aviation prefers altitude approach levels that create additional complexity for controllers. These costs are also not reflected in the ticket tax.

We are not aware of any studies that quantify the welfare effects of replacing current air traffic control charges based on the ticket tax with appropriately measured marginal-cost user fees. The Congressional Budget Office reports rough estimates of the marginal cost of services provided by air traffic control.[37] But because of data limitations, these estimates are based on the unrealistic assumption that all air traffic control facilities are optimized. Investment in these facilities, however, has not been optimal. Under efficient (marginal-cost) pricing and investment, it is likely that air traffic control operations would be designed so that they exhaust any scale economies and fully cover costs.

A fundamental problem in determining efficient charges for air traffic control services is that the FAA has had historic difficulties in establishing its costs for these services. In fact, Russell Chew, the former head of the FAA's Air Traffic Organization, which operates the air traffic system, acknowledged that after extensive work by analysts, "an understanding of air traffic control costs is only now just coming."[38] In any case, we expect the efficiency gains from marginal-cost pricing, as reflected in reduced delay for travelers and lower operating costs for carriers, would be significant given that the ticket tax bears little relationship to the costs that an aircraft imposes on the system and on other aircraft and does little to discourage planes from using airspace near airports during congested periods. In addition, marginal-cost user fees would generate revenues that cover the costs of air traffic control services.

The expiration on September 30, 2007, of the taxes and fees that support the U.S. Airport and Airway Trust Fund and the trust fund's reauthorization provide an opportunity for the FAA and Congress to reconsider how the air traffic control system should be funded. Not surprisingly, input is being provided by the system's users. Commercial airlines support user fees, instead of the ticket tax, because they believe that under this pricing scheme they will pay less for their use of air traffic control services and business jets will pay more. The private- and corporate-jet owners prefer a fuel tax and argue that they should not pay higher fees because they cost the FAA less to handle than do the commercial airlines. Instead of mediating the debate, the FAA should focus on how current pricing inefficiencies are contributing to travel delays and develop a cost-based pricing scheme. As of January 2008, Congress had been unable to

37. Congressional Budget Office (1992).
38. Matthew L. Wald, "FAA Seeks New Source of Revenue in User Fees," *New York Times*, March 7, 2006.

agree on a measure that would reauthorize the trust fund. Frustrated by these delays, Transportation Secretary Mary Peters had begun to encourage congested airports to adopt congestion pricing.

INVESTMENT. As noted, the FAA hires air traffic controllers and other air traffic control personnel and supplies terminal and en route facilities with new equipment. Personnel and equipment tend to be added to those parts of the system where traffic levels exceed a threshold. The FAA's allocation of funds is also influenced by airlines, airports, trade associations, and members of Congress, a process that may compromise the efficiency of FAA investments.

Morrison and Winston document at least one way that FAA investments could be improved.[39] Compared with the current allocation, we find that allocating expenditures at towers and TRACONs to airports where travelers incur the most costly delays would generate more than $1 billion in annual time savings to air travelers and cost savings to airlines. Under the current allocation, smaller airports get a disproportionately large share of funds, an allocation that appears to be zealously protected by representatives of the districts where the airports are located. For example, Oster and Strong point out that when the Air Traffic Organization proposed in February 2005 to close control towers between midnight and 5:00 a.m. at forty-eight lightly used airports, U.S. representatives from the airports' districts strongly opposed the action without even considering whether the tower services were needed or even used.[40]

TECHNOLOGY ADOPTION. The FAA could also reduce delays by expeditiously implementing technologies that have the capability of expanding navigable airspace around airports and en route. We have indicated that the FAA has yet to fully adopt the air traffic control technology that was envisioned when the advanced automated system was initiated during the early 1980s. Worse, the technology is no longer state of the art. By enabling pilots to be less dependent on controllers and to choose the most efficient altitude, routing, and speed for their trip, the NextGen satellite-based system could reduce air travel times and carrier operating costs, especially those related to fuel, and handle more traffic while maintaining, if not improving upon, the nation's outstanding air transportation safety record. In fact, the NextGen system would facilitate the first significant change from the air traffic routes established in the 1920s when the government was developing airmail service. Today's pilots, while flying at much higher altitudes than they did several decades ago, still follow the same routes.

39. Morrison and Winston (2008).
40. Oster and Strong (2006).

Unfortunately, the delays that the FAA has experienced with implementing experimental satellite-based systems suggest that NextGen will take more than the projected twenty-five years to become fully operational and that the current system may eventually have to impose additional delays on aircraft to handle growing traffic volumes safely. The GAO has concluded that the FAA has failed to provide the expertise to make the transition to NextGen and has urged it to seek assistance from a third party.[41] In addition, because the old equipment continues to consume vast amounts of money for operations and maintenance, it will need to be shut down to implement new navigational procedures. Eventually, all the facilities associated with the current system will be eliminated or consolidated as NextGen is managed and operated with fewer and more technologically up-to-date facilities. Such disinvestment and consolidation will undoubtedly face political resistance that slows the implementation of NextGen because members of Congress will attempt to keep navigational aids and jobs in their districts.[42]

Institutional and Political Constraints on Reform

Although many travelers and some policymakers are painfully aware of the suboptimal service provided by U.S. aviation infrastructure facilities, regulations and political forces have made it extremely difficult for would-be reformers to rid the system of its major inefficiencies. At the heart of the problem is the FAA, which lacks organizational independence and is prevented to a significant extent by Congress and the administration from using its resources—and from encouraging airports to use theirs—more efficiently.

Special interest politics has also thwarted efforts to reform aviation infrastructure policy. Joseph Stiglitz described his efforts, as part of the Clinton administration, to institute peak-period pricing for air traffic control only to find reform blocked by owners of corporate jets and small planes who opposed higher user fees.[43] The FAA and commercial airlines appear to support replacing the expired ticket tax with user fees—although commercial airlines are opposed to congestion pricing. In any case, the current funding mechanism is supported by the potent National Business Aviation Association and the National Air Traffic Controllers Association; hence, a compromise that falls far

---

41. "FAA Urged to Seek Help with NGATS," *Flight International*, August 1, 2006.
42. David Hughes, "FAA Accelerates Performance-Based Navigation, Outlines Mandates," *Aviation Week*, July 30, 2006; Dick Armey, "Fixing the Air Traffic Mess," *Wall Street Journal*, August 20, 2007.
43. Stiglitz (1998).

short of marginal-cost pricing is likely to emerge.[44] Both associations fear that any user fee is the first step to taking air traffic control out of the congressional funding process and privatizing it. Political pressure applied by air transport interests including members of Congress is the primary cause of misallocated FAA expenditures among traffic control facilities and is also behind the inertia preventing the elimination and consolidation of these facilities to implement the NextGen system.

Turning to airports, a problem with introducing congestion pricing is that existing residual and compensatory contracts between airline tenants and their airport landlords would have to be abrogated and an acceptable framework for determining all airport charges would have to be instituted. Efficient expansion of airport runway capacity is impeded by regulatory hurdles imposed by the Environmental Protection Agency and by opposition from the local community; "majority in interest" clauses permit incumbent airlines to block construction of new terminals and gates that could enable new entrants to serve the airport; and TSA's shortcomings can be partly traced to the political objective of Congress and the Department of Homeland Security to convince an anxious public that they are doing something to combat terrorism, even if their efforts are wasting resources.

Finally, the FAA, TSA, and local airport authorities are constrained by the inflexibility, shortsightedness, and conflicts that characterize most regulatory agencies and are entangled in a decisionmaking process with diffuse accountability.[45] Hence, technological advances that could improve airport and air traffic control services require an excessive amount of time and resources to be implemented, which reduces productivity in the air transportation sector.

Building the Case for Privatization

Given the vast and growing inefficiencies in the aviation infrastructure, our view is that policymakers should question the wisdom of allowing public sector airport authorities and a federal air traffic control system to continue to provide aviation services, especially when there is little indication that the efficiency of air travel will significantly improve in this institutional environment. Accordingly, we believe policymakers should explore whether privatizing airports and air traffic control could enhance the efficiency of the air transportation system.

44. Laura Meckler, "Collision Course: Why Big Airlines Are Starting a Fight with Business Jets," *Wall Street Journal*, June 1, 2006, p. A1; David Esler, "Controllers Don't Like Them Either," *Aviation Now*, May 23, 2006.
45. Winston (2006).

Political resistance to such dramatic institutional change is great. As noted, the very interests that oppose efficient pricing of air traffic control fear that it will lead to privatization. Thus, political support for privatization must be built carefully and strengthened by favorable experimental evidence of its economic effects. Here we briefly outline the conceptual case for privatizing airports and air traffic control, its likely economic effects, and important considerations in designing experiments to provide evidence of these effects.

Privatizing Airports

The central tenet of airport privatization is that travelers will experience fewer delays and airline competition will increase if airports are forced to compete with each other to attract passengers and airline service. To be sure, airport competition already exists to some extent as airports located in adjacent metropolitan areas compete for passengers through their location and the airlines that serve them. Examples of competing airports include Oakland, San Francisco, and San Jose in northern California; Boston, Manchester, New Hampshire, Providence, and Hartford in New England; Los Angeles, Orange County, and Long Beach in southern California; and Washington (Reagan), Baltimore (BWI), and northern Virginia (Dulles) in the Middle Atlantic region. In addition, satellite airports could expand and provide competition in certain major metropolitan areas; examples are Palmdale airport (Los Angeles), Stewart airport (New York City), and Gary, Indiana, airport (Chicago). The potential for competition also has been demonstrated by airports that have tried to induce carriers to offer new service or expand existing service and by airports that have lost carriers that are dissatisfied with their facilities and performance.[46] And competition among airports in different metropolitan areas even exists. For example, LAX is spending $1.2 billion to build ten new gates at an extension of its international terminal to remain competitive with San Francisco for overseas traffic.[47]

In principle, privatization would make unrestricted airport competition a reality by giving airports the freedom and incentive to compete for passengers and carriers by efficiently producing a level of service that its users value. Skeptics may counter that privatization would enable some airports to become

---

46. Airlines' dissatisfaction with airport facilities and performance is understated because airlines may be unable to serve an alternative airport in the metropolitan area (for example, although Southwest Airlines wanted to abandon service at Seattle-Tacoma airport, it was barred from offering service at Boeing Field).

47. Steve Hymon, "Council OKs 10 New Gates at LAX," *Los Angeles Times*, August 16, 2007.

monopolies, which would charge excessive prices for and have little incentive to provide high-quality services. But the economic conditions under which an airport would have monopoly power are not clear. A fundamental constraint on any airport's exercising monopoly power—even if it is the only airport serving an outlying area—is that the airport will still have to be efficiently integrated into a carrier's entire network. Thus, if an airport sets monopoly charges, an airline may not find it optimal to include the airport in its spoke routes. Or in the process of determining the routes that it will serve, an airline may be able to play off monopoly (spoke) airports against each other to reduce charges.[48]

We would expect private airports to introduce some form of rational pricing to make efficient use of available taxiing areas and runway capacity, to make efficient investments in terminals and runways to reduce delays, and to allow access to any carrier that is willing to pay the cost of using its facilities.[49] Privatized airports would also be able to allocate their resources for security toward the greatest threats to safety. To this end, they would have the choice of whether the government or the private sector provides their security without any constraints on private sector provision. In addition, airports would be free to coordinate and share their security strategies with each other. Similar to other profit-maximizing entities in the private sector, airports would have a strong financial incentive to ensure that their security is efficient and minimizes passenger and carrier inconvenience. As noted, the private sector has had considerable experience and success in providing security for facilities such as theme parks, gambling casinos, and the like.

Generally, we would expect efficiencies to accrue to the traveling public as airlines and airports develop their buyer-seller relationship without governmental interference or contractual mandates. In a more competitive environment, airlines would be more forthcoming about their preferences of the types of airport services that would reduce operating costs and improve service to passengers, while airports would have an incentive to respond to these preferences and introduce new services. It is, of course, difficult to predict what service innovations airports might offer. But deregulation of the U.S.

---

48. As shown in Grimm and Winston (2000), an analogous situation occurs in rail freight transportation when an industrial firm is served by one railroad but can draw on alternative origins served by alternative railroads to receive a product. Such geographic competition has enabled shipping firms to negotiate lower rail rates.

49. Although private airports would still have to contend with environmental regulations and local opposition to their investments, we would expect them to be more aggressive and resourceful than public airports have been in overcoming these potential obstacles.

intercity transportation system has demonstrated that consumers have substantially gained from pricing and service innovations that are introduced when firms are exposed to a more competitive environment.[50]

Although we expect privatization to have positive economic effects, we also recognize that uncertainties exist about how to manage the transition to private airports and how airport competition will evolve. Thus, we believe it is imperative for policymakers to design privatization experiments before proceeding with the policy. In 1996 Congress enacted legislation creating an airport privatization pilot program. But a major barrier for participation in the program was the requirement that a city or state had to obtain the approval of airlines representing 65 percent of the landed weight at the airport. In many cases involving hub airports, this enabled one airline to have veto power over privatization efforts.

Policymakers must be more committed to designing useful privatization experiments, especially because interest in these experiments among investors and cities is starting to develop. For example, private equity firms such as Goldman Sachs are raising billions of dollars for infrastructure investments including airports, while the City of Chicago has filed a preliminary application with the FAA to include Midway Airport in a pilot privatization program. Accordingly, policymakers should convene meetings with potential investors, airport authorities, and other major stakeholders for guidance on how to conduct airport privatization experiments.

We envision that several issues must—but can—be resolved. First, airport competition should be encouraged to develop by selling each airport in a given metropolitan area to a distinct owner. Airports serving the London metropolitan area, Heathrow, Gatwick, and Stansted, were sold to the same owner, raising concerns about the effectiveness of privatized airport service. Second, private airports should be able to finance themselves with user charges and without tax-exempt debt financing. Third, local and state governments should be able to reap sufficient financial benefits from the sale of U.S. airports but be prohibited from imposing residual regulations as a condition of a sale. Finally, policymakers must ensure that entities do not have legal grounds for blocking privatization.

Although these and undoubtedly other issues pose major challenges to formulating experiments and transitioning to a privatized system, policymakers must persevere because it is clear that they do not have the option of standing still and hoping that public airports improve their performance.

50. Morrison and Winston (1999).

Air Traffic Control

The Clinton administration recognized that the nation's air traffic control system was inadequate to meet the growth in airline traffic and sought to "corporatize" it by spinning off air traffic control operations as an independent government corporation that would be financed by user fees and be able to borrow money from capital markets. Although Congress did not support the effort, the justification for it—and an even stronger reform, privatization—is more valid than ever.[51]

In a comparison of the U.S. Air Traffic Organization with Nav Canada, a private sector air traffic control corporation established in 1996 and financed by publicly traded debt, Oster and Strong concluded that the ATO was disadvantaged by a disconnect between its source of funds and costs, the poor performance of its capital investment programs, and a lack of organizational independence that would enable it to take steps to improve its performance. The authors concluded that Nav Canada was able to overcome these problems while maintaining a high level of air safety in Canada by having the main stakeholders and users determine user fees subject to legal requirements that limit charges to full cost recovery, by undertaking modest projects that could be efficiently managed, and by having complete freedom to allocate resources and consolidate facilities when necessary.[52]

Generally, we would expect that a privatized air traffic control system would introduce some form of rational pricing for its services, allocate resources to address the greatest risks to safety and the major sources of delay, and adopt the latest and most effective technology in a timely fashion. As in the case of airport privatization, we would also expect that travelers would gain from service improvements as airlines and the control system provider develop their buyer-seller relationship. The evidence provided by Canada's privatization experiment suggests that the United States could realize significant benefits from a privatized traffic control system.

Accordingly, U.S. policymakers should explore ways to overcome the political opposition that has blocked previous efforts to reform the nation's air traffic control. An incremental approach could include an agreement to conduct an experiment to privatize the nation's air traffic control system. As in the air-

---

51. See Stiglitz (1998) on the congressional response to the corporatization proposal.
52. Oster and Strong (2006). Another recent study compared commercialized provision of air traffic control (including but not limited to Nav Canada) with the ATO's provision and found that under commercialization, safety was enhanced or unaffected, modernization of technology was greatly improved, and users benefited from improved service quality. At the same time, costs were reduced and financial stability was maintained (MBS Ottawa 2006).

port case, key stakeholders must be consulted and critical features of the experiment must be pinned down—including the selection of a private air traffic control corporation; the contractual framework within which airlines and the provider would negotiate prices and service; and the oversight role, if any, for the federal government. While formidable, the challenges to resolving these matters should not obscure the motivation for or impede the implementation of this vital experiment.

Final Comments

As shown in figure 2-1, during the past thirty years airline travel times have been characterized by cycles of sharp increases followed by modest decreases. Growth in travel times and delays have spurred promises from the FAA to address the problem; however, declines caused by recessions in the early 1980s and 1990s and by the September 11, 2001, terrorist attacks have changed the FAA's focus. On net, delays continue to mount, the flying public accepts the inconvenience without calling for a change in policy, and the performance of the nation's aviation infrastructure worsens. At some point, however, the level of delays—not the increase—may generate a public outcry that cannot be silenced by an external shock.

We have argued that travel delays are a manifestation of inefficient pricing and investment policies and the slow adoption of state-of-the-art technology by public airports and a federally managed air traffic control system. Given little reason to believe that policymakers have the determination to overcome regulatory obstacles and given the existence of political forces that preclude the introduction of efficient policies, we have argued that the private sector represents the best hope for improving aviation infrastructure. But we have also recognized that such major institutional change should not proceed without hard evidence that it will benefit the public. Thus, we have called for the federal government to initiate privatization experiments, which we expect would produce favorable evidence that strengthens the case for a change in policy.

During the past decade, periodic interest among U.S. policymakers in privatization and the implementation of it abroad have provided some hope that the policy may eventually receive consideration in the United States. With the growing realization among public officials and the public that the U.S. air transportation system is being severely compromised by its infrastructure, it appears inevitable that privatization will be thoroughly—and justifiably—explored.

References

Altshuler, Alan, and David Luberoff. 2003. *Mega-Projects: The Changing Politics of Urban Public Investment*. Brookings.

Ball, Michael O., George Donohue, and Karla Hoffman. 2006. "Auctions for the Safe, Efficient and Equitable Allocation of Airspace System Resources." In *Combinatorial Auctions*, edited by Peter Cramton, Yoav Shoham, and Richard Steinberg. MIT Press.

Brueckner, Jan K. 2002. "Airport Congestion When Carriers Have Market Power." *American Economic Review* 92 (December): 1357–375.

Carlin, Alan, and R. E. Park. 1970. "Marginal Cost Pricing of Airport Runway Capacity." *American Economic Review* 60 (June): 310–19.

Congressional Budget Office. 1992. *Paying for Highways, Airways, and Waterways: How Can Users Be Charged?*

Dilger, Robert Jay. 2003. *American Transportation Policy*. Westport, Conn.: Praeger.

Dillingham, Gerald. 2003. "Air Traffic Control, FAA's Modernization Efforts—Past, Present, and Future." Statement before the Subcommittee on Aviation, Committee on Transportation and Infrastructure, U.S. House of Representatives, October 30, 2003 (GAO-04-227T).

GAO (U.S. General Accounting Office, renamed the Government Accountability Office in 2004). 1998a. *Airport Financing: Funding Sources for Airport Development*. GAO/RCED-98-71 (March).

———. 1998b. *Air Traffic Control: Status of FAA's Modernization Program*. (December).

———. 1999a. *Air Traffic Control: FAA's Modernization Investment Management Approach Could Be Strengthened* (April).

———. 1999b. *Air Traffic Control: Observations on FAA's Air Traffic Control Modernization Program* (March).

———. 2005. *Aviation Fees: Review of Air Carriers' Year 2000 Passenger and Property Screening Costs* (April).

Graham, Anne. 2004. "The Regulation of U.S. Airports." In *The Economic Regulation of Airports*, edited by Peter Forsyth and others. Burlington, Vt.: Ashgate.

Grimm, Curtis, and Clifford Winston. 2000. "Competition in the Deregulated Railroad Industry: Sources, Effects, and Policy Issues." In *Deregulation of Network Industries: What's Next?* edited by Sam Peltzman and Clifford Winston. Brookings.

Levine, Michael E. 1969. "Landing Fees and the Airport Congestion Problem." *Journal of Law and Economics* 12 (April): 79–108.

Mayer, Christopher, and Todd Sinai. 2003. "Network Effects, Congestion Externalities, and Air Traffic Delays: Or Why Not All Delays Are Evil." *American Economic Review* 93 (September): 1194–215.

MBS Ottawa. 2006. *Air Traffic Control Commercialization Policy: Has It Been Effective?* Ontario, Canada.

Mead, Kenneth M. 2003. "Cost Control Issues for the Federal Aviation Administration's Operations and Modernization Accounts." Statement of the Inspector General of the Department of Transportation before the Committee on Appropriations, Subcommittee on Transportation, Treasury, and Independent Agencies, U.S. House of Representatives, April 9.

Morrison, Steven A. 1983. "Estimation of Long-Run Prices and Investment Levels for Airport Runways." *Research in Transportation Economics* 1: 103–30.

Morrison, Steven A., and Clifford Winston. 1989. "Enhancing the Performance of the Deregulated Air Transportation System." *BPEA, Microeconomics:* 61–123.

———. 1999. "Regulatory Reform of U.S. Intercity Transportation." In *Essays in Transportation Economics and Policy: A Handbook in Honor of John R. Meyer*, edited by Jose A. Gomez-Ibanez, William B. Tye, and Clifford Winston. Brookings.

———. 2000. "The Remaining Role for Government Policy in the Deregulated Airline Industry." In *Deregulation of Network Industries: What's Next?* edited by Peltzman and Winston.

———. 2007. "Another Look at Airport Congestion Pricing." *American Economic Review* 97 (December): 1970–977.

———. 2008. "The Effect of FAA Expenditures on Airport Delays." *Journal of Urban Economics* (March).

Oster, Clinton V., Jr., with the assista nce of John S. Strong. 2006. *Reforming the Federal Aviation Administration: Lessons from Canada and the United Kingdom*. Washington: IBM Center for the Business of Government.

Stiglitz, Joseph E. 1998. "The Private Uses of Public Interests: Incentives and Institutions." *Journal of Economic Perspectives* 12 (Spring): 3–22.

U.S. Department of Transportation. 2006. *National Strategy to Reduce Congestion on America's Transportation Network* (May).

U.S. Federal Aviation Administration, Office of Policy and Plans. 2006. *FAA Aerospace Forecasts: Fiscal Years 2006–2017*.

Winston, Clifford. 2006. *Government Failure versus Market Failure: Microeconomics Policy Research and Government Performance*. AEI-Brookings (www.aei-brookings.org/publications/abstract.php?pid=1117).

DAVID GILLEN and HANS-MARTIN NIEMEIER

3
The European Union: Evolution of Privatization, Regulation, and Slot Reform

Far-reaching changes to the aviation sector in the European Union over the last two decades have included, among other things, deregulation of the airline service sector, the formation of the EU common aviation market, the recent signing of an EU-U.S. open-skies agreement, a gradual move toward airport privatization, and a continuing evolution of airport regulation and slot allocation reform. The goal of this paper is to examine the continental EU experience with changes to economic regulatory policy and capacity allocation through slots (a slot is the right to take off or land at an airport during a specific period of time) and the effect of these changes on airport operations and economic efficiency.[1] It is difficult to assess changes to airport regulation without also examining privatization initiatives and how they have varied across European states. We therefore include a brief description and assessment of privatization plans across member states.[2]

<small>We are indebted to Christiane Müller-Rostin, Vanessa Kamp, and Haibin Huang for excellent research assistance as well as to students in Transport Economics, Bremen University of Applied Science, who assisted with data collection. We also thank David Starkie and Peter Forsyth for useful comments on earlier drafts as well as participants at the workshop on Comparative Political Economy and Infrastructure Performance: The Case of Airports, held in Madrid in September 2006. In addition we are grateful for constructive and helpful comments from two anonymous referees. The research was partially funded by the research project GAP (German Airport Performance), supported by the Federal Ministry of Education and Research, Germany, and by the Centre for Transportation Studies, University of British Columbia.

1. This chapter excludes discussion of airports in the United Kingdom; Anne Graham discusses U.K. airports in chapter 5.
2. Numerous other reforms have occurred, such as deregulation of ground handling and substantive changes in airline market structure. These have been driven by several factors</small>

The shift to more market-oriented policies in the ownership and management of airport infrastructure reflects a position that airports can improve their cost efficiency and level of service to passengers and airlines under privatization. With adoption of the green paper on fair and efficient pricing in 1995, the European Commission stated its view that airports are part of the general infrastructure that should be priced according to social marginal-cost principles.[3] Member states such as Germany have also adopted these principles in their policy papers.[4] Therefore a key objective for airport policy is efficient provision of airport services. Second, there has been a shift to considering regulation or semiregulatory processes that differ from either state ownership or rate-of-return regulation as an alternative means of governance for the airport system. Academic circles, for example, have engaged in substantial debate about the comparative merits of types of regulation—price-cap versus cost-based regulation with single- versus dual-till systems—as well as whether there needs to be any formal regulation at all. This view of relaxed or minimal regulation has been taken up by airports that depict themselves as an industry facing significant competitive pressures. Airlines in contrast criticize airports for not having achieved the cost efficiencies of the carriers. Airlines tend to see airports as natural monopolies that are not regulated effectively under current rules.

We begin with an overview of the EU airport industry and the changes in traffic over time. We also discuss legislation that affects airports, take note of the number and features of airports in member states, and briefly discuss airport privatization, which leads naturally into the topic of airport regulation. Our purpose is simply to point out what has been happening in aviation in the EU and to discuss those factors that have hindered greater privatization of EU airports. This discussion leads to an examination of the evolution of airport regulation and the distribution of differing types of regulation across member states. In this section differences in single- and dual-till price regulation are assessed. The second major topic of the paper—the evolution of slot allocation—is examined next, along with the methods of allocation. In the summary section, we take up

---

including an important policy directive by the EU on introducing policies that focus on improving economic efficiency and competition. While these issues are interesting and important, they are not discussed in this paper. The EU has twenty-eight member states, each with its own aviation sector. Despite EU dominance in aviation policy, member states still have significant influence over infrastructure policy.

3. For the green paper, see European Commission, Transport Directorate (1995); on pricing, see Frerich (2004a, 2004b, and 2006).

4. Nash (2003). We interpret the EU policy as an effort to increase economic welfare by first- and second-best marginal-cost pricing. For a more critical view, see Rothengatter (2003).

the question of social marginal-cost pricing and how and the extent to which current governance structures of the airport industry should be reformed to increase economic welfare.

The EU Airport Industry

The EU airport industry has two distinguishing features. First, many member states have a large number of airports: for example, France has sixty-eight airports; Germany, forty-eight; Greece, thirty-eight; Norway, fifty-one; and Sweden, forty-four. (A list is presented in table 3-1.) Many of these airports, however, have very little traffic. For example, 69 percent of the airports in Ireland, 58 percent in Denmark, and 54 percent in France each have less than 100,000 passengers annually. The second feature of EU airports is that many of them are connected to and compete with a well-developed rail system. The rail system has increased the substitutability among airports and serves as a connector for others.[5]

Regulatory and governance (privatization) changes have taken place at a small subset of these airports, while slot allocation governs a larger number. The large number of airports has created opportunities for entry by low-cost carriers and therefore has increased the opportunity for greater competition among airports than experienced in other countries or regions; perhaps only the United Kingdom and the United States have similar situations of broad geographic coverage and density of airports.

Traffic growth within the continental EU has been strong, buoyed by economic recovery, the addition of five new member states, a rapidly expanding and developing low-cost carrier sector with strong network links to the United Kingdom and the eastern EU states, and the growth of the legacy carriers as they adjusted their business model to focus relatively more on long-haul connecting passengers. The EU aviation market is the second-largest common aviation market in the world, after the United States, and recent growth within and between the EU and other parts of the world has been well beyond forecasts. In 2004 alone, the total number of passengers transported by air in the EU rose by 8.8 percent, to 650 million; 24 percent were carried on national (domestic) flights, 42 percent on intra-EU flights, and 34 percent on extra-EU flights.[6] This considerable traffic growth has resulted in strains in some airports, including delays, "gray" markets for slots, and pressure to expand capac-

---

5. Hubs like Schiphol in Amsterdam and Fraport in Frankfurt have increased their catchment areas and gained market power with their connectivity to the high speed rail system.
6. Eurostat (2005); figures include U.K. traffic.

Table 3-1. *EU Airports, by Traffic Level, for Selected Countries*

Country	Less than 100,000	Percent	100,000 to 1 million	Percent	1 million to 5 million	More than 5 million	Total number of airports
Austria	0	0	4	67	1	1	6
Denmark	7	58	3	25	1	1	12
Finland	10	48	10	48	0	1	21
France	37	54	20	29	8	3	68
Germany	18	38	10	20	14	6	48
Greece	16	42	15	39	6	1	38
Iceland	10	77	3	23	0	0	13
Ireland	9	69	2	15	1	1	13
Italy	11	31	14	39	9	2	36
Norway	25	49	13	25	5	1	51
Spain	4	11	16	44	10	6	36
Sweden	21	48	20	45	2	1	44

Source: Williams (2005).

ity at specific airports, most notably some of the megahubs, such as Frankfurt, which are reaching capacity limits.

The EU has five large hubs (Frankfurt with 50 million passengers a year, Charles de Gaulle with 51 million, Amsterdam with 38 million, Madrid with 38 million, and Munich with 27 million) as well as a number of regional airports that vary in size from 27 million annual passengers at Barcelona to 10 million at Hamburg, 10 million at Prague, and 7 million at Budapest (all 2004 data). As in the United States, there are multiple airport ownership groups, but unlike in the United States where no single entity owns all the airports within its territory, a group can sometimes include an entire country's airports. For example, AENA, a division of the Spanish government, owns and operates all airports in Spain; Finnish Airports (CAA) owns and operates twenty-five airports in Finland; and LFV (a Swedish state enterprise) owns and runs nineteen airports in that country. Airport groups include Aéroports de Paris (ADP), Aeroporti di Roma, and the ANA group, which manages all major airports in Portugal.

In table 3-2 passenger and freight transport numbers are listed for twenty of Europe's top airports, along with the growth in traffic from 2003 to 2004.[7] This table illustrates the remarkable and widespread growth in passenger traffic

7. U.K. airports are included for a more complete comparison.

Table 3-2. Passenger and Freight Traffic at the Top Twenty Airports in Europe, 2004

		Passenger air transport				Freight transport		
Rank	Country	Airport	1,000 Passengers	2003–2004	Country	Airport	1,000 tonnes	Growth 2003–2004
1	UK	London-Heathrow	67,110	6.2	DE	Frankfurt am Main	1,827.3	11.2
2	FR	Paris-Charles de Gaulle	50,951	6.1	NL	Amsterdam-Schiphol	1,467.0	8.4
3	DE	Frankfurt am Main	50,700	5.6	UK	London-Heathrow	1,412.0	8.6
4	NL	Amsterdam-Schiphol	42,425	6.6	FR	Paris-Charles de Gaulle	1,275.8	6.9
5	ES	Madrid-Barajas	38,155	7.9	BE	Brussels-National	660.4	8.9
6	UK	London-Gatwick	31,392	5.0	DE	Cologne-Bonn	621.9	17.3
7	IT	Rome-Fiumicino	27,160	6.6	LU	Luxembourg	616.6	2.3
8	DE	Munich	26,601	11.1	IT	Milan-Malpensa	36.6	13.3
9	ES	Barcelona	24,354	8.3	ES	Madrid-Barajas	352.8	19.1
10	FR	Paris-Orly	24,049	7.1	UK	East Midlands	277.2	16.8
11	UK	Manchester	20,970	7.4	UK	London-Stansted	239.0	17.9
12	UK	London-Stansted	20,909	11.7	UK	London-Gatwick	226.9	-2.8
13	ES	Palma de Majorca	20,363	6.5	DE	Munich	192.4	17.8
14	DK	Copenhagen-Kastrup	18,889	7.6	AT	Vienna-Schwechat	158.1	24.5
15	IT	Milan-Malpensa	18,419	5.4	UK	Manchester	153.3	21.9
16	IE	Dublin	17,032	7.9	IT	Rome-Fiumicino	139.6	-14.6
17	SE	Stockholm-Arlanda	16,467	7.7	IT	Bergamo-Orio al Serio	129.6	1.3
18	BE	Brussels-National	15,445	2.3	FI	Helsinki-Vantaa	118.0	33.9
19	DE	Düsseldorf	15,092	6.6	IT	Genoa-Sestri	111.4	—
20	AT	Vienna-Schwechat	14,711	15.7	EL	Athens	104.1	-20.8

Source: Eurostat (2005).

across Europe. Freight traffic growth has been less evenly distributed, reflecting the relative growth in cargo carried by integrators, including FedEx, UPS, and DHL among others; the significant growth at Cologne-Bonn, for example, reflects the expansion of UPS at that airport.

Each country in the EU has jurisdiction over airports within the country and can set rules and regulations. However, an airport wishing to participate in the European Common Aviation Area (ECAA) must adhere to EU aviation law. The *Guide to Community Legislation in the Field of Aviation* provides a detailed list of all EU legislation pertaining to aviation.[8] This legislation covers eight areas: economic policy, air traffic management, safety, security, environmental matters, social matters, passenger protection, and external relations. The guide notes that the EU legislation is mandatory for member countries; that there will be no exceptions; and, perhaps most interesting, that economic aspects were of particular importance in developing the policy, which applies to all air carriers, *airports,* and air traffic control services.

Article 87 of the European Commission Treaty focusing on competition issues has particular application to airports, as well as to carriers. Article 14 and Annex III of the EU agreement set out the conditions under which member countries can aid airports. Specifically such aid may not distort or threaten to distort competition by favoring agents, undertakings, or products. Aid can take the form of grants, interest relief, tax relief, state guarantees, and preferential access to state provision of goods and services or purchasing. It can also include restructuring aid and exclusive rights concessions. Subsidies may be provided under some conditions, such as a regional development program, but such aid must be available to all parties; for example, if one airline is offered discounts and payments under some conditions, such payments must be made available to all carriers provided they meet the same conditions.[9]

Airport Ownership and Privatization

Airports, like transportation infrastructure in general, have been seen as public assets, suitable for promoting economic development. They have also been

---

8. European Commission (2006).
9. The EU has made a distinction between capital and operating subsidies, allowing both under specific but limiting conditions, but it has not balanced this distinction across modes or between service and infrastructure. In aviation, subsidies can take a number of forms; in Spain (AENA Spanish Airports), where the airports are state-owned, profitable airports subsidize loss-making airports. Examples of state-owned airports that have provided financial assistance to other airports are Schiphol, Charleroi, and Strasbourg; see Cranfield University (2002); Morrell (2006).

seen as a means of protecting a country's national carrier in the face of increased liberalization. It is therefore not surprising that many airports in Europe are or have been owned by national, state, or local government. For example, the national governments of Greece, Ireland, Portugal, Spain, and Sweden each own all the airports in their countries. Germany's larger airports are owned by state or local governments, while the French regional airports are owned by the central government but are managed by local governments. This picture is changing, however, as the EU has been one of the world leaders in reforming ownership policy and regulations affecting airport infrastructure. These reforms were seen as a progressive move to improve economic efficiency and to liberalize access in the EU.[10] Although other member countries have not following the U.K. model of complete privatization, private operators hold minority shares of airports in Frankfurt, Hamburg, Rome, Copenhagen, and Zurich. Most recently, a 33 percent share of Aéroports de Paris was sold to private operators. BAA acquired a 75 percent share of Budapest airport in December 2005. But after Spain's Ferrovial acquired BAA in 2006, the British airports operator agreed in May 2007 to sell Budapest airport to Airport Holding Kft, a consortium led by Hochtief AirPort GmbH.[11]

Governments have had several motives for privatization, including a desire to stimulate more efficient performance from their airports. Airports that remain publicly owned are often corporatized, meaning that they are expected to behave more like private corporations. Privatization can be expected to alter the incentives faced by the airport's owners. Thus privatization combined with strong incentive regulation can be expected to give the owners incentives to keep costs low and achieve productive efficiency.

However, privatization is also an opportunity for governments to convert fixed assets into cash. While economists see no particular merit in this motivation, many governments see the additional cash as desirable. This motive might explain why governments in many cases in which airports will be privatized in the near future shelter them from competition and effective regula-

---

10. Only Australia and New Zealand have been more aggressive in moving to privatization and reliance on market forces to deliver airport services. In November 2007, however, the New Zealand government announced changes in its regulations to give it more direct control over airport charges.

11. Infratil, the New Zealand–based company that invests heavily in airport and other infrastructure, has recently purchased Lübeck airport in northern Germany. Other regional airports will move to full or partial privatization as the EU expands. In the new states of the EU, a growing number of airports are partially privatized; Malta International is 60 percent privately owned, while private owners hold 51 percent of Slovenia's Ljubljana airport. Similar trends are taking place in many developed and developing countries around the world.

tion, an issue discussed below.[12] Privatization in and of itself does not necessarily lead to higher airport rates and charges for aviation services; a government, for example, can choose to increase charges for any airport it owns when and if it so desires. The shift to privatization actually limits the government's ability to raise more revenue from its airports, since it involves giving up control over their pricing. Governments often increase rates and charges just before privatizing their airports, leading many to associate privatization with higher prices.

Airport privatization gained momentum in the 1990s with the first wave of privatization, which continued into 2001. As illustrated in table 3-3, the majority of cases have minority privatizations. It appears that states are reluctant to give up a major asset that they use in many cases for their own economic promotional purposes. This is at direct odds with EU policy, which is focused on improving the efficient use and investment in such infrastructure.

The crisis that hit aviation in 2001 more or less broke this wave of privatization, which has only recently begun to pick up, with the partial privatizations of the airports in Bratislava, Brussels, Budapest, Lübeck, Malta, and Paris in 2006. No major airport in continental Europe has been fully privatized without any ownership restrictions. Only for Ireland, Malta, and the Netherlands are there strong expectations that airports will be partially or completely privatized.

Although they have not been privatized, the governance structure of several public European airports has been changed. The federal government of Austria, for example, has sold not only a 50 percent stake in Vienna's airport to private owners, but also a controlling stake in several regional international airports such as Graz, Innsbruck, and Linz to regional and local administrations.[13] The Slovak Republic and a few other countries have done the same. Although ownership of public airports may not have changed radically, many

---

12. Privatization has not necessarily led to more airport competition as is shown by the examples of multiple airports that were privatized as a group under common ownership, such as BAA (once British Airports Authority) and ADP (Aéroports de Paris); the takeover of Frankfurt-Hahn airport by Fraport; and the failed takeover of Bratislava airport by Vienna airport. The privatization of Bratislava was stopped by the antimonopoly office of the Slovak Republic in September 2006 after a change in government, and the takeover was subsequently permitted under conditions set out by the Austrian cartel office. In early 2006 Erste Bank (2006, p. 1) commented that profits from Bratislava/Kosice will be low but "it is still better to pay a high price and receive low contributions than let a strong competitor grow next door." Erste Bank estimated that the purchasing price of €525.7 million included a premium of €359 million.

13. Schneider (2004, p. 150).

Table 3-3. *Airport Privatization in the European Union, 1992–2001*

Airport	Percentage privatized	Year privatized
Vienna	27	1992
Copenhagen	25 (1994), 24 (1997), 17 (2000)	1994, 1997, and 2000
Athens	45	1996
Düsseldorf	50	1997
Rome	45.5	1997
Naples	65	1997
Slovenia, Ljubljana airport	51	1997
Stockholm, Skavsta	90	2000
Florence	39	2000
Turin	41	2000
Hamburg	36	2000
Zürich	50	2000
Fraport (Frankfurt)	29	2001

national, state, and local airport owners have adopted new organizational structures over the past three decades.

Thus far privatization has not changed the nature of the airport industry in the continental EU as much as it has in the United Kingdom, but privatization has made the airports more profit oriented. This has contributed to some cost-cutting efforts, especially in ground handling, and to the development of non-aviation business, particularly retail shopping and food and beverage, within airports. Aéroports de Paris is a typical example of partial privatization that has led to the development of airport retail and real estate businesses, something that has been neglected by the public airport management. Privatization has not led to a strong tendency to increase aviation revenues by differentiated price structures and peak pricing.

Airport Regulation in the EU

In Europe the control over airport charges, meaning the charges for aviation services such as runways, gates, and apron use, varies from explicit regulation to none whatsoever. International airports with some private ownership have some form of price (airport charge) regulation. State-owned airports have no formal regulation but do have a not-for-profit mandate. Larger airports that are still majority publicly owned, such as Hamburg, generally have some form of price regulation. Privatized airports with the notable exception of Zürich are always regulated. Regional airports are not regulated because it is believed that airport and modal competition limits their market power.

When charges have been regulated, it has traditionally been on a rate-of-return or cost-plus basis. Our analysis differentiates between cost-based regulation, pure price caps, hybrid price caps, and revenue-sharing agreements; a detailed table is contained in the appendix. Many airports are subject to old-style rate-of-return regulation—essentially, cost-based regulation. More recently price-cap regulation has often been implemented when airports are privatized or semiprivatized. Price-cap regulation sets an overall limit in the allowed average price increase, whereas rate-of-return regulation seeks to regulate individual prices. Price caps can be regarded as a form of incentive regulation, although the strength of the incentives varies. The price cap can be under a single- or dual-till regime. Under a single till, all revenues are considered when the price cap is being set; in a dual-till system, only those revenues derived from aviation operations (such as landing, passenger, and parking charges) are considered; revenues from nonaviation operations are put in the second till. At some airports, the price caps are based on costs and reset at three- to five-year intervals; this form of regulation can be seen as a combination of cost-based and incentive regulation, or hybrid regulation.

The single-till principle was recommended by the ICAO (International Civil Aviation Organization) and has been widely used in Europe, but this long tradition is slowly breaking down. In 2000 the Hamburg airport became the first airport in Europe to be switched to a dual till, on grounds that price regulation should be confined to the monopolistic aspects of airport operation and that incentives for developing nonaviation business should not be stifled.[14] The Malta airport followed with a dual-till price cap in 2001; more recently, the Budapest airport adopted a dual-till price cap for the period 2006–11. The Brussels airport, currently regulated on a rate-of-return basis with some yardstick elements, is planning a step-by-step move from the single to the dual till over the next twenty years. The regulatory framework for Aéroports de Paris is a single till that also sets some mixed incentives for developing nonaviation business.

Cost-Based Regulation

A number of airport authorities regulate airport charges according to principles of cost relatedness. The charges are designed to create just enough revenue to cover total costs, including the depreciation of capital and a normal rate of return on capital. The structure of charges is supposed to be cost related, that

---

14. Niemeier (2002).

is, each charge should reflect its costs. In Europe many of the public airport systems, such as those in Finland, Greece, and Poland, set their charges in this way. Charges are supposed to be set according to ICAO principles of cost relatedness and departments of transport that operate and manage airports directly follow these principles. In the case of fully privatized airports in Germany, mostly regional airports, the regulator approves charges only if they are cost related.

The problems with cost-based regulation are twofold. First, the lack of incentives to minimize overall costs generally leads to an inefficient choice of inputs. Second, cost-based regulation leads to an *inefficient price structure*.[15] Under cost-based regulation the airport has no incentive to minimize costs because if costs go up, prices are adjusted upward to cover any cost increases. Moreover, an airport with peak traffic periods has no incentive to price efficiently by adopting peak pricing; conversely, its incentive is "to lower the price of capital-intensive peak demand in order to justify more capital assets, and charge a monopoly price at off-peak times to realize a profit that greater capital will justify."[16] In other words, the incentives at cost-based-regulated airports lead to average cost pricing with no consideration for peak and congestion pricing. These average cost prices are manifested in the form of weight-based runway charges (charges that are set according to the weight of the aircraft), and these weight-related charges are retained even if demand exceeds capacity at some points during the day or for the entire day; four of the busiest European airports, Düsseldorf, Frankfurt, Madrid, and Paris Orly, all have weight-related charges.

Price-Cap Regulation

Price-cap regulation involves setting an allowed average price increase plus or minus a value, X, that is generally some measure of expected productivity growth. The allowed average price increase is commonly set according to a widely available price index such as the consumer price index (CPI). This is referred to as the *RPI-X* formula, where *RPI* is the allowed or average price increase and X is the limiting offset. The value of X is determined by the regulator based on a range of criteria including, for example, the overall level of productivity in the industry, the performance of the firm in the previous regulated period, and whether the regulator wishes to encourage the firm to reduce costs; price caps are set for individual airports.

Unlike cost-based regulation, price caps do not regulate profits, but they do set incentives for cost reduction. The regulated airport can keep any gains it has made through cost reductions within the regulation period and might

---

15. Sherman (1989).
16. Sherman (1989), p. 241.

then pass those savings on to users through lower charges in the next period. The airport might be monitored to ensure it does not try to achieve cost reductions by lowering quality. A criticism of price-cap regulation is its short-run focus and lack of incentive to invest.

Pure and hybrid price caps differ in the way in which the X in the price-cap formula is set; a pure price cap sets X without reference to the costs of the individual airport regulated but rather according to a broadly based airport benchmarked cost. Hybrid price caps set X with reference to a regulated cost base and therefore have some elements of cost-based regulation.[17] The price caps at Aéroports de Paris, Copenhagen, and Dublin have an X factor based on regulated but forward-looking, not historical, costs.

Revenue-sharing agreements in the European airport industry often relate the level of charges to the passenger growth over a certain period. These so-called sliding scales can be combined with price-cap regulation as in the case of the Hamburg[18] and Vienna airports. At two German airports, Düsseldorf and Frankfurt, the revenue-sharing agreements are the result of a memorandum of understanding between the airports and their users, legalized as a public contract between the airport and regulator.[19] In case of disagreement, the charges are to be fixed according to cost-based regulations.

Under these contracts at Düsseldorf and Frankfurt, the average charge per passenger is determined by the future passenger growth rate. At Frankfurt airport, for example, both parties agreed that average charges could be raised by 2 percent when the projected passenger growth rate reaches 4 percent.[20] If the growth rate is higher, the airlines receive one-third of the additional revenues. If the growth rate is lower, the airport can only cover a third of its revenue losses through higher charges.

Such agreements have the important advantage that they break with the tradition of low-powered cost-plus regulation, meaning that the regulation leads to costly and weak outcomes and in some cases to overinvestment and inefficiency. Within the contract period, the airport may behave as though it is subject to a price cap, although not of the *RPI-X* form. Furthermore, these agreements offer some stability if demand fluctuates. A demand shock leads to higher charges, so the airport can cover average costs and avoid bankruptcy, which would undermine the political stability of regulation as well. However,

---

17. Hybrid price-cap regulation is superior to pure cost-based regulation because it is forward looking while cost-plus regulation relies on historical costs; however, hybrid price caps provide fewer incentives for cost reductions.
18. Immelmann (2004).
19. Klenk (2004).
20. Note that these are nominal prices, as the agreement is not related to the price level.

revenue sharing has disadvantages. First, in the cases of Düsseldorf and Frankfurt, the incentives for cost reduction and for traffic increase are rather mild because the charges are stabilized at a high level. It could be, for example, that Fraport (the part-owner and management firm operating Frankfurt airport) prefers the contract to the cost-plus regulation because the rate of return on the aeronautical assets is higher than the normal rate of return accepted by the cost-related regulation. Second, a flat linear sliding scale guarantees the airport nearly the same revenues irrespective of output. This reduces the incentives to differentiate charges and increase output. Third, the revenue-sharing contract usually creates an inefficient price structure; fast-rising demand leads to lower charges and lower demand to higher charges.

One key issue surrounding price setting at airports is the independence of the regulator and the transparency with which rates and charges are set. Only the Netherlands has a fully independent regulator. It is interesting that several countries have retained control over their airports even as they privatize portions of them. For example, the Vienna airport was privatized in three steps in 1992, 1995, and 2001. Up to the last step, the central government held a major share and regulated the airport charges. German airports are regulated by the federal states that have a minority or majority share in the partially privatized airports of Frankfurt, Hahn, Hamburg, and Hannover.[21]

A fair, accessible, and open procedure requires at a minimum a consultation process. Since the early 1990s more and more European states have implemented a consultation on airport charges, and it has become standard practice today. Still there is room for improvement—in most consultation processes, most airports do not provide the necessary information to make a decision on airport charges transparent or plausible to the airlines. An example is the recent price-cap regulation by Aéroports de Paris, in which "the value of the regulated asset base and the percentage return on capital are not disclosed by ADP or the French government."[22] This practice is in sharp contrast to rate setting in the United Kingdom, which is open even to the general public. In continental Europe, the only airport with such transparent regulation is the Brussels airport, where the regulator demands a consensus among the airport and its main

---

21. For further discussion, see Niemeier (2002).
22. Morgan Stanley (2006, p. 4). While avoiding the risk of capture might be very complicated, many of the European regulatory systems that do not separate the functions of ownership and regulation and lack transparency and fairness seem to be perfect for regulatory capture. Public ownership gives the management of the airport the rare opportunity to influence the government regulator in various ways, which may lessen the airport's incentives to operate efficiently and might create rents for management and employees.

users. To get around the lack of transparency Lufthansa recently decided to acquire a 9.1 percent share in its main hub, the Frankfurt airport, thus obtaining a seat on the airport's board of directors, which will give the airline access to information it would not otherwise receive.

Capacity Constraints and Slot Allocation

Excess demand for airport facilities is evident in the EU as elsewhere. Increasing the capacity of airports is difficult; expansions are expensive and often involve sustained environmental challenges. As a consequence, many airports face excess demand, either for part of the day, or in some cases like Frankfurt, for the entire day. In the EU, capacity at airports is rationed by means of a slot allocation process, set out in EC Regulation 793/2004.

A slot is most commonly defined as a landing or takeoff right at designated airports during a specified time period. The IATA (International Air Transport Association) scheduling process is a well-recognized means of allocating slots and managing demand at slot-coordinated airports around the world, including those in the EU; more than two hundred airports, and all international airlines, take part in the scheduling meetings, which are held twice a year before the winter and summer schedules are announced. Each participating airport has an airport slot coordinator (ASC), who may be appointed by the airport or the government, depending on the jurisdiction; in the EU the government generally selects the slot coordinator.

The process for allocating and trading slots follows:

—Each airline submits its desired schedule to the ASCs about six months before the start of the season, and the ASCs then allocate slots according to set procedures.

—The ASCs' decisions are formally announced at the start of the relevant international conference, which is also when airlines first see the planned schedules of their competitors.

—Trading starts, with airlines who did not receive their desired slots seeking to improve their allocations and ensuring that they have consistent sets of departure and arrival times both within and between airports.

—ASCs provide information showing slot mismatches and who "owns" various slots (brokerage role).

—Airlines may trade slots at the same or different airports, alter the type of aircraft flown, and change the flight origin or destination, subject to the approval of the ASCs. Trading can be complex, involving many parties in simultaneous swaps of slots.

—All trades must be reviewed and approved by the relevant ASC to ensure that there is sufficient terminal capacity and aircraft parking space to accommodate any changes.

—Any slots not used are placed in a slot pool, and the ASC allocates these slots under set rules, many governing new airlines or airlines seeking new flight routes.

Slots can be obtained from the ASC from the slot pool and through grandfather rights (see below). Slots can be also be swapped between two or more carriers. This is fairly commonplace among many carriers for scheduling and logistical reasons. Carriers can also lease unused slots, which is more attractive than selling them as the holder retains control. Leases are also useful for short-term agreements with early termination clauses. Slots can be sold, but for a number of reasons, there are relatively few outright sales. First, airlines do not hold the property rights to slots, only the right to use them, and therefore slots are treated as quasi-permanent assets with a sizable amount of risk of loss attached. Second, incumbent slot holders engage in strategic behavior based on the potential network opportunity costs and knowledge of who current and potential competitors are. This creates an incentive for hoarding and babysitting slots (babysitting is the practice of leasing slots on a short- to medium-term basis to noncompeting airlines). Third, the value of a slot is higher if it is part of a package than if it is sold individually—incumbents therefore will want the full package value of each slot, but potential buyers may not be willing to pay full package value for a single slot. Slots can also be reallocated in bankruptcy proceedings, as part of a route transfer between carriers, to redeploy slots within an alliance group, and to babysit surplus slots for the current owner.[23]

Grandfathered slot allocation means incumbent airlines that have served a market are given first rights to access airport capacity, and generally these rights are provided at no cost.[24] The grandfather rights provision was intro-

---

23. Air carriers operating in the EU typically can service new routes at congested airports only if they acquire slots through slot transfers or from slot pools. After the primary allocation of slots, airlines are allowed to transfer slots between themselves but only under the supervision of a slot coordinator and under the provisions outlined in Article 8a of EC Regulation 793/2004. Airlines also have access to the slots retrieved by slot coordinators and placed in the slot pool. The rules governing access to the landing and takeoff rights placed in the slot pool are also outlined in Article 8. However, some scholars have argued that these slots do not possess a high commercial value. In the United Kingdom a gray market in slot trading has developed; see chapter 5 in this volume.

24. The number of available slots at any given airport is established collaboratively among the airport, airlines, and air traffic control services, which examine all factors—technical, operational, and environmental—that affect the number of effective slots available. The airport has most say in the matter, but other airports may have some influence when networks

duced in the EU in 1993, when Council Regulation (EEC) 95/93 on common rules for the allocation of slots at community airports became effective. Under the rule, any air carrier that has used a slot 80 percent of the time in the previous season is entitled to the same slot in the following season.

Moreover, slot allocation is generally used only at airports where demand for capacity exceeds that which is available. However, a distinguishing feature in Europe is that the vast majority of airports, even those that are not capacity constrained, are designated as level III airports, meaning that they are slot-coordinated.[25] With the exception of the United Kingdom, EU member countries have relied for the most part on administrative measures, rather than market mechanisms, for allocating slots.[26] The 1993 EU Council Regulation has been amended only twice since it was enacted, in 1995 and in 2004, and neither amendment significantly affected the slot allocation process.

The 2004 amendment, EC Regulation 793/2004, did, however, provide for enforcement of the slot allocation system. The member states are required to designate a neutral airport coordinator qualified to supervise the allocations and to administer penalties to negligent or ill-intentioned parties (Article 4). In addition the coordinator must take into consideration other rules and guidelines, both international and domestic, conditional on their compatibility with the community law. Any slot exchanges or transfers are considered illegal if completed before they have been approved by the slot coordinator (Article 8). Further, to ensure competition, slots provided to new entrants are protected under Articles 8 and 10. For example, section 3c of Article 8a dictates that "slots allocated to a new entrant as defined in Article 2(b) may not be exchanged . . . for a period of two equivalent scheduling periods, except in order to improve the slot timings for these services in relation to the timings initially requested." Likewise, Article 10 helps ensure competition by reserving

---

are trying to be established. Once slots have been allocated, the slot coordinator ensures airlines use them under the slot rules. Establishing capacity and its use in this way generally leads to an underutilization of true airport capacity.

25. A level I airport is one at which there are no slots and no need for coordination, and infrastructure can be allocated on a first-come first-served basis; a level II airport is considered slot facilitated, meaning an airline can request the use of the airport facilities (runways and gates) at a particular time and the airport cannot deny access unless facilities are not available; a level III airport is slot coordinated, meaning an airline can request a slot but this can be denied by the airport. Clearly the property rights for airport capacity rest with the airline at level II airports and with the airport or slot coordinator at level III airports.

26. Secondary markets in slots were growing in the United States until the partial abandonment of the High Density Rule; the rule covered access to four heavily used airports—Chicago O'Hare, John F. Kennedy and LaGuardia in New York, and Reagan National in Washington.

half of the slots in the slot pool to fill requests from new entrants; the remaining slots can then be distributed to incumbent airlines.

In the EU under the 2004 regulation, a slot is defined as "the *entitlement* established under this Regulation, of an air carrier to use the full range of airport infrastructure necessary to operate an air service at a coordinated airport on a specific date and time for the purpose of landing and take-off as allocated by a coordinator in accordance with this Regulation."[27] The use of the term *entitlement* suggests that airlines have a form of property right for use of the infrastructure despite not having paid for it. The importance of this is that the airport, despite being slot coordinated, loses some control once a slot is allocated to a carrier. Furthermore, the slot refers to use of all necessary airport infrastructure. This reference effectively creates higher barriers to entry since the total slots made available at an airport are determined not just by runway capacity but also by other factors such as the numbers of available gates and apron space.

The 2004 regulation also defines a *new entrant* in terms of the number of slots held by the air carrier as a percentage of the total number of slots available on the day in question. Thus to be considered a new entrant and hence have priority access to slots in the slot pool, an airline may still have some slots at the airport and need not be a brand new entrant.

In the continental EU, slots are not allowed to be bought and sold; even in the case of an exchange or swap of slots between two carriers, no money is allowed to change hands. Values may differ to reflect the fact that one slot might be worth more than another because of the time of day. However, monetary transactions do take place in a limited way, forming what is called the gray market for slots—gray in the sense that such transactions do not form part of the formal secondary market in slot swaps.[28] This position is incongruous with the general approach in the EU where greater reliance on market mechanisms to allocate scarce airport resources is encouraged to improve economic efficiency. The continental EU prefers and adheres to administrative-based rules in slot administration and allocation.

Several aspects of the EU gray market could be corrected through legalization. The slots are traded mostly among the members of each alliance of air carriers, and as alliances expand, it becomes easier to extend the gray market.

---

27. Note that in contrast to the FAA definition, which refers only to runway use, the EU definition as amended in 2004 does not limit a slot to the use of the runway space but also considers the infrastructure needed to complete an arrival or a takeoff at an airport and the exchange of passengers.

28. This differs from the United Kingdom, where secondary trading is encouraged and there is a relatively active albeit thin market.

The lack of a public notice for each intended sale or purchase means many potential buyers and sellers are excluded from the trading table. Therefore greater transparency is needed. The uncertainty that accompanies the events in the gray market, especially among foreign air carriers, has led to acquisitions of the entire business of airlines in order to gain access to some slot-constrained markets.

The continental EU's adherence to administrative rules for slot administration leads to a less efficient use of available slots as well as to a lower total numbers of slots; both of these outcomes result in economic losses. It seems clear that the airports, airlines, and slot coordinators prefer the administrative route to protect incumbents. The European Commission, which is much more consumer oriented, is pushing for the greater use of market forces and for allowing and encouraging secondary trading in slots.

In response to the fear expressed by policymakers over legalization of the gray market, the EU Competition Authority argues that existing competition law is sufficient to correct or prevent anticompetitive behavior such as intra-alliance transactions and slot hoarding. These sanctions under the Competition Authority would have a far greater chance of being correctly applied if slot transactions were open and transparent to ensure an active secondary slot market.

There are two recurrent themes among scholars and regulators with respect to the grandfather rule criterion.[29] The first contends that grandfather rights stifle competition and nurture inefficiency in the airline industry. Because air carriers must give up a slot that is not used at least 80 percent of the time, the carriers have an incentive to meet the 80 percent requirement even when it is unprofitable to do so. This practice, known as slot hoarding, cripples the ability of new entrants to gain access to specific markets.[30] The consequence of relying on slot allocations based principally on grandfather rights is that there are no signals to either allocate scarce airport capacity or to indicate how much and what type of investment in new capacity should be undertaken.

An alternative view maintains that the regularly observed slot abuses result not from anticompetitive behavior but rather from "the business environment in which airlines are required to operate."[31] Some of these inefficiencies that are generally cited as airline misconduct include "late handbacks" and "no-shows." Late handbacks occur when airlines argue they are compelled to hold on to the slots that they have not fully used, sometimes past the return

---

29. See DotEcon (2001); Nera (2004); Task Force (2005); and Madas and Zografos (2005).
30. Matthews (2003).
31. Bauer (2008).

deadline, while they wait for confirmation for landing rights at other airports. No-shows—airlines that do not operate flights at their scheduled slot times—could occur either out of negligence or intentional wrongdoing, and both are punishable under the slot allocation regulation. However, both late handbacks and no-shows amount to an insignificant 0.5 percent of total capacity, and a solution to eliminate this behavior would not greatly improve capacity utilization.[32]

Summary and Conclusions

This paper has examined three key areas in airport management and policy in the European Union: privatization, regulation, and slot allocation and management. It analyzes the major trends of economic and institutional change over the last two decades. These changes raise two fundamental policy questions. First, will the goal of fair and efficient pricing be achieved given the current trends of aviation liberalization, privatization, and competition? If so, the major policy reforms of European aviation would be deemed to be successful. However, if current trends do not move in the direction of achieving the goals, major policy reforms will be necessary to increase the efficiency of the system. This leads to a second question: What are the options for policy reforms regarding slot allocation and economic regulation of airport charges? These questions are summarized in table 3-4, which shows the trends and tendencies of the changing governance on cost efficiency, efficient use of airport capacity, and optimal investment.

The EU has been one of the leaders in moving to greater privatization with complementary regulatory changes. The underlying forces for this shift in governance include the integration of aviation policy into general EU transport policy and the movement of transport policy toward reliance on market forces rather than government ownership to discipline the behavior of firms. There is also a growing recognition that financing and pricing new infrastructure to handle the increasing air traffic congestion may well require more private sector ownership and management. The numerous airports in the EU, spread across member states, also provide a sense of comfort, rightly or wrongly, that major airports will not be able to exploit their market power; that the sheer number and proximity of airports provide effective competition. This will of course depend on whether large markets are getting larger or if there are more markets being created as carriers join more city pairs. Evidence suggests that it is the latter and that the recent EU-U.S. open-skies

32. Bauer (2008).

Table 3-4. *Options for Policies Regarding Slot Allocation and Economic Regulation of Airport Charges*

Category	Cost efficiency	Efficient rationing	Optimal investment
Commercialization of public airports	Some incentives to reduce X-inefficiency	Some efforts for efficient pricing, but also for use of market power	Overinvestment
Partial privatization	Mild cost-cutting	Mild efforts for efficient pricing but also for use of market power	Tendency to overinvest
Full privatization	Tendency to cut costs	Use of market power limited by nonaviation complementarity	Careful investments across airport facilities
No slot reform	No incentives. High switching costs. Slot rent captured by incumbent	Inefficient and low utilization of capacity	Price does not signal investment
Slot reform	Increases airport competition	Efficient rationing of existing capacities	Price does signal investment
Dependent regulator with cost-based regulation	Gold-plating and high transaction costs	No peak pricing, inefficient price structure	Overinvestment
Independent regulator with incentive regulation for monopolistic bottleneck (dual till)	Incentive to reduce X-inefficiency and to develop nonaviation	Incentives for price differentiation and peak pricing	Less overinvestment if regulator is committed

agreement will lead to more direct flights rather than to flights that are routed through the traditional megahubs.

Public airports in the continental EU are showing a strong tendency toward commercialization but a slower tendency toward privatization. Overall, commercialization has given airport management incentives to achieve efficient pricing, but these incentives are rather weak and could be strengthened with full privatization. Commercialization sets some incentives to reduce X-inefficiencies, but the managers of partially privatized airports face strong pressure from owners to reduce costs, especially where the public owner is in the minority. Efficient rationing of demand could be achieved by efficient airport charges, but thus far neither commercialization nor privatization has resulted in peak and congestion pricing. Privatization also sets strong incentives to raise charges as management objectives shift from ensuring service and access to maximizing shareholder returns, albeit with regulatory constraints in most cases.

In our view the key elements of policy reform in the EU involve economic regulation of airports and slot reform. EU policy could leave regulation as it is or demand substantial changes. We examined both dependent and independent regulators and found that systems with dependent regulators and cost-based regulation result in X-inefficiency and gold-plating, inefficient price structures with no peak pricing, and overinvestment. The prevailing system of European airport regulation is not only setting the incentives too low but also pointing them in the wrong direction. Airport pricing does not reflect the relative scarcity of airport and airway resources, which distorts airline competition and lessens the welfare gains of liberalization.

In contrast, we found that systems with independent regulators, incentive-based regulation, and dual tills have incentives to reduce X-inefficiency and to develop complementary nonaviation business revenue. There are incentives for price differentiation to increase traffic and to manage demand through peak pricing. Underinvestment could occur, but that can be prevented by a committed regulator.

The current debate on reform of charges and slots is a sign of intensified conflict between airlines and airports.[33] Slot allocation will not go away even with airport expansion; there will always be a need to have some basis of allocation. Issues of equity, efficiency, and competition are all intertwined in such methods of allocation. The continental EU clearly favors administrative rules and, despite a growing gray market, argues slot trading is not appropriate for improving the system. Even though the IATA process protects the status quo, entrenches incumbents, is anticompetitive, and is generally blocking effective entry, the EU slot coordinators have stated they feel the current system is working and the issue is more one of fine-tuning and adding capacity than a wholesale change in the IATA approach—despite the growing evidence from the U.K. active secondary slot trading market. However, the director general of the EU Competition Authority has indicated that the agency favors a shift toward market mechanisms. Under such mechanisms, the grandfather rule

33. IATA (2005); ACI (2006).

could be replaced by a system, such as a slot auction, that would make the initial allocation of slots through an ongoing and anonymous primary market.

References

Airports Council International. 2006. *Understanding Airport Business* (www.aci-europe.org).

Bauer, J. 2008. "Do Airlines Use Slots Efficiently?" In *Airport Slots: International Experiences and Options for Reform,* edited by Achim I. Czerny and others. Aldershot, U.K.: Ashgate.

Civil Aviation Authority. 2001. *Heathrow, Gatwick, Stansted and Manchester Airports Price Caps - 2003–2008: CAA Preliminary Proposals—Consultation Paper.* London (www.caa.co.uk).

———. 2002. "Competition Commission Current Thinking on Dual Till. CAA Statement on Process." Press release, August 13, London (www.caa.co.uk).

Commission of the European Communities, Commission Staff Working Document. 2004. "Commercial Slot Allocation Mechanisms in the Context of a Further Revision of Council Regulation (EEC) 95/93 on Common Rules for the Allocation of Slots at Community Airports." September 17, Brussels.

Council of the European Communities. 1993. Council Regulation (EEC) No. 95/93 on Common Rules for the Allocation of Slots at Community Airports, January 18 (europa.eu.int/eur-lex/lex/LexUriServ/LexUriServ.do?uri=CELEX:31993R0095:EN:HTML).

———. 2004. Regulation (EC) No. 793/2004 of the European Parliament and of the Council, Official Journal of the European Union. April 21 (europa.eu.int/eur-lex/pri/en/oj/dat/2004/l_138/l_13820040430en00500060.pdf).

Cranfield University. 2002. *Study on Competition between Airports and the Application of State Rules.* Report prepared for the European Commission, Bedfordshire, U.K.

Davy European Transport and Leisure. 2004. *Late Arrival: A Competition Policy for Europe's Airports.* Davy Research Department, Dublin.

DotEcon. 2001. *Auctioning Airport Slots.* A Report for HM Treasury and the Department of the Environment, Transport and the Regions, London.

Erste Bank. 2006. *Flughafen Wien.* Company report, April 11 (www.erstebank.at).

European Commission. 2006. *Guide to Community Legislation in the Field of Aviation.* Report issued for Director General, Energy and Transport, May (http://europa.eu.int).

———. 2007. *Activities of the European Union: Summaries of Legislation* (http://europa.eu.int/scadplus/leg/en/lvb/l24085.htm).

European Commission, Transport Directorate. 1995. *Towards Fair and Efficient Pricing in Transportation, Policy Options for Internalizing The External Costs of Transport in the European Union.* Brussels.

Eurostat. 2005. (http://epp.eurostat.ec.europa.eu/portal/page?_pageid=1090, 30070682,1090_33076576&_dad=portal&_schema=PORTAL).

Federal Aviation Administration. 2005. "Reservation System for Unscheduled Arrivals at Chicago's O'Hare International Airport." *Federal Register* 70, no. 130 [July 8, 2005].

Forsyth, P., and H.-M. Niemeier. 2003. "Price Regulation and the Choice of Price Structures at Busy Airports." Paper given at the Air Transport Research Society Conference, Toulouse, France.

Frerich, J., and G. Müller. 2004a. *Europäische Verkehrspolitik – Von den Anfängen bis zur Osterweiterung der Europäischen Union*, Band 1: *Politisch-ökonomische Rahmenbedingungen – Verkehrsinfrastrukturpolitik.* München: Oldenbourg.

———. 2004b. *Europäische Verkehrspolitik – Von den Anfängen bis zur Osterweiterung der Europäischen Union*, Band 2: *Landverkehrspolitik (Straßenverkehr, Binnenschifffahrt, Eisenbahnverkehr).* München: Oldenbourg.

———. 2006. *Europäische Verkehrspolitik – Von den Anfängen bis zur Osterweiterung der Europäischen Union*, Band 3: *Seeverkehrs- und Seehafenpolitik - Luftverkehrs- und Flughafenpolitik - Telekommunikations-, Medien- und Postpolitik.* München: Oldenbourg.

Graham, A. 2004. *Managing Airports: An International Perspective.* 2d ed. Amsterdam: Elsevier.

IATA. 2005a. *Airport Privatisation* (www.iata.org).

———. 2005b. *Worldwide Scheduling Guidelines.* 12th ed. December (www.iata.org/NR/ContentConnector/CS2000/SiteInterface/sites/whatwedo/scheduling/file/fdc/WSG-12thEd.pdf).

Immelmann, T. 2004. "Regulation in Times of Crisis: Experiences with a Public-Private Price Cap Contract at Hamburg Airport." In *The Economic Regulation of Airports: Recent Developments in Australasia, North America and Europe*, edited by Peter Forsyth and others. Aldershot, U.K.: Ashgate.

Klenk, M. 2004. "New Approaches to Airline/Airport Relations: The Charges Framework for Frankfurt Airport." In *The Economic Regulation of Airports*, edited by P. Forsyth and others. Aldershot, U.K.: Ashgate.

Madas, M., and K. Zografos. 2005. "Practical Implementation of Airport Demand Management: From Instruments to Strategies." Paper presented at the 84th Transportation Research Board Annual Conference, Session on Management and Analysis of Airport Demand and Delay. Washington, January 10.

Matthews, B. 2003. "Airport Capacity: The Problem of Slot Allocation." Paper given at the GARS workshop "How to Make Slot Markets Work." University of Applied Sciences, Bremen, November 7–8 (http://www.garsonline.de/).

Morgan Stanley. 2006. "Aeroports de Paris Attractive Catalysts… But in 2010." London (July 31).

Morrell, P. 2006. "Airport Competition and Network Access? A European Perspective." Cranfield University.

Nash, C. 2000. "Transport and the Environment." In *Environmental Policy,* edited by D. Helm, pp. 241–59. Oxford University Press.

NERA (National Economic Research Associates). 2004. *Study to Assess the Effects of Different Slot Allocation Schemes: A Final Report for the European Commission*, January (http://europa.eu.int/comm/transport/air/rules/doc/2004_01_24_nera_slot_study.pdf).

Niemeier, H.-M. 2002. "Regulation of Airports: The Case of Hamburg Airport—A View from the Perspective of Regional Policy." *Journal of Air Transport Management* 8: 37–48.

Rothengatter, W. 2003. "How Good Is First Best? Marginal Cost and Other Pricing Principles for User Charges in Transport." *Transport Policy* 10: 121–30.

Schneider, F. 2004. "Privatization in Austria: Some Theoretical Reasons and First Results about the Privatization Proceeds in General and of Vienna Airport." In *The Economic Regulation of Airports*, edited by P. Forsyth and others. Aldershot, U.K.: Ashgate.

Sherman, R. 1989. *The Regulation of Monopoly*. Cambridge University Press.

Task Force, European Civil Aviation Conference. 2005. *Outcome of Study on Slot Allocation Procedures, European Civil Aviation Conference*, DGCA/124-DP/6. Paris (December).

TRL (Transport Research Laboratory). 2005. *Review of Airport Charges.* Wokingham, U.K.

Williams, G. 2005. "A Comparison of Airports in the EU." Research Paper. Cranfield University, Department of Air Transport.

Appendix Table 3A-1. *Current Type of Airport Regulation in EU Member Countries*

Country	Airport	Independent regulator	Type of regulation	Till type
Austria	Vienna	Yes, since 2001	Price cap with sliding scale	Single till
Belgium	Brussels	No	Rate of return with yardstick elements	Single till, gradually introducing dual till
Czech Republic	Prague	No	Charges set by airport	Not defined
Estonia	Tallinn Ulemiste	No	Cost regulated	Not defined
Denmark	Copenhagen	No	Price cap	Dual till
Finland	Helsinki	No	No regulation, charges based on cost recovery	n.a.
France	Paris	No	Hybrid average revenue based price cap	Single till
Germany	International airports	No	Price cap with sliding scale (HAM), revenue sharing (FRA,DUS)	Dual till in HAM and FRA
			All other airports are cost plus regulated	All other single till
Greece	Athens	No	Airport sets own charges	Dual till
Hungary	Budapest, Ferihegy	No	Price cap	Dual till
Ireland	Dublin	Yes	Price cap revenue based	Single till

Country	Airport	Regulated	Charge setting	Till
Italy	Rome	No	Airports set own charges	Dual till
Latvia	Riga	No	Set by government	Not defined
Lithuania	Vilnius	No	Set by government	Not defined
Malta	Malta International	No	Price cap	Dual till
Netherlands	Amsterdam	Yes	Rate of return with weighted average cost of capital as asset base	Dual till
Norway	Oslo	No	Cost based	Single till
Poland	International airports	No	Set by government	Not defined
Portugal	ANA	Yes	Cost based	Single till
Slovak Republic	Bratislava	No	Set by government	Not defined
Slovenia	Ljubljana	No	Set by government	Not defined
Spain	AENA	No	Cost based	Single till
Sweden	Stockholm	No	Cost based	Single till
Switzerland	Zürich, Geneva	No	Not regulated	n.a.
United Kingdom	BAA	Yes	Price cap	Single till

Sources: Davy (2004); European Commission (2006); Graham (2004); Cranfield (2002); IATA (2005); TRL (2005).
n.a. = Not applicable.

PART TWO

Australia, New Zealand, the United Kingdom, and Canada

PETER FORSYTH

4

Airport Policy in Australia and New Zealand: Privatization, Light-Handed Regulation, and Performance

Australia and New Zealand moved to private ownership of their major airports between 1996 and 1998. After a period of formal price-cap regulation that ran from 1997 to 2002, Australia adopted New Zealand's use of a light-handed form of regulation. Currently in both countries prices are not explicitly regulated, but regulation could be imposed if performance is considered to be poor. Such a regulatory environment for airports is rare around the world—most regulation is much more prescriptive. Together Australia and New Zealand constitute a useful case study of how light-handed regulation works with airports.

Under government ownership, a number of airport policy issues were resolved by the government acting without input from others. These matters included determining the extent of cost recovery, assessing major investment proposals, and resolving conflicts with environmental objectives. In the private, regulated environment, the solution to these issues depends on the firm's objectives, the regulatory structure, and the pressures from competition. Governments still have a role in resolving issues, particularly those that concern environmental aspects, such as whether a new runway can be built in a sensitive area. Governments also still seek to influence decisions, perhaps working through a regulator to encourage major investments. Since privatization, however, it is private owners, operating within the regulatory framework, who determine airport prices, operating efficiency, and the investments airports in

I am grateful to Hans-Martin Niemeier for valuable comments on an earlier draft and to Nathalie McCaughey and Neelu Seetaram for helpful research assistance.

Australia and New Zealand make. Thus, this chapter focuses primarily on airport ownership and regulation and their effects on pricing, efficiency, and investment.

The motivations for privatization were several, and efficiency objectives were important. During the 1990s governments in Australia and New Zealand were privatizing many public enterprises, especially those in the transport sector, as part of a general push to improve microeconomic performance. While airport performance was not regarded as poor, policymakers considered that privatization would sharpen incentives for efficiency and induce the airports to pursue commercial opportunities, particularly from the non-aeronautical side of the business such as retail stores in terminals. There was little political opposition to privatization of airports. Air traffic control was not privatized, but the air traffic control authority was corporatized and subjected to a form of price monitoring. Some governments also saw privatization as a means of improving their budgetary position. While maximizing revenue from sale was not a main consideration with the earlier privatizations, it became a more important factor over time. By the time Sydney airport was privatized in 2002, the government had taken actions, such as almost doubling the aeronautical charges at the airport and promising a lighter form of regulation, which had the effect of raising the sale price.

Granted that ownership and regulation are critical to performance, it is important to ask what the regulation seeks to achieve. Regulation could be about promoting economic efficiency, in the manner in which the incentive regulation literature stresses. Governments may have other objectives for regulation, however. In reality governments and regulators often stress minimizing profits and keeping prices close to cost. That may be an objective in itself, even though achieving it is very likely to impose a cost in terms of efficiency. Regulation that in reality is effectively cost-plus regulation is often clothed in the rhetoric of incentive regulation. Thus in Australia and New Zealand, while the regulation imposed on airports is light-handed, one can argue that it is oriented toward keeping prices at cost rather than promoting efficiency. Light-handed regulation is about process, not content—it is possible to have light-handed, cost-plus regulation.

This chapter's overall assessment of the Australian and New Zealand approaches to airport regulation is that they work quite well in most but not all aspects.

—Privatization has resulted in airports that are more oriented toward profit, although the presence of shareholders with objectives other than profit influences their behavior.

—While prices are somewhat high at some airports, they are well below monopoly levels, and there are no major efficiency losses from this pricing.

—The system is consistent with good incentives for productive efficiency, and most airports perform well in terms of productivity.

—Price caps as previously implemented in Australia had advantages and disadvantages. In particular they created pressure for cost reduction and required explicit scrutiny of investments, but they imposed significant financial risks on the airports.

—The weak link in the regulatory environment, especially in Australia, concerns investment incentives. Many airports are under pressure from regional interests to make excessive investments, and the airports can recover the costs of these investments by passing them on to users.

—The way all regulatory systems work, light-handed or otherwise, depends on the guidelines or principles that are set for them—these can either emphasize efficiency incentives or seek to keep prices close to cost. The guidelines for both countries' frameworks are decidedly vague but emphasize a cost-plus approach, although they have been implemented in a more flexible manner. Unless these guidelines are clarified and improved, there is a danger that the framework may degenerate into light-handed, cost-plus regulation with adverse implications for efficiency.

In the light of this assessment, two policy priorities emerge:

—First, a more rigorous system for assessing investment must be developed.

—Second, clear guidelines, consistent with strong incentives for efficiency, need to be set for the operation of light-handed regulation.

To examine how ownership and regulation affect the performance of the airports, this chapter begins with some background on airports of the two countries and their performance. It then explores the issues of ownership, competition, and the pressures on airports from owners and governments to pursue nonprofit objectives. The next section consists of a detailed examination of how regulation works and its impacts on performance. Finally, some conclusions are drawn from the Australian and New Zealand experience.

Overview: Airports in Australia and New Zealand

Australia is a highly urbanized society with a few large cities spread over a wide area. Five cities, separated from one another by at least 700 kilometers, each have a population of over 1 million inhabitants. In addition, several industrial cities such as Newcastle and resort cities such as Cairns have populations between 100,000 to 400,000. New Zealand, a long, thin country, is much

Table 4-1. *Traffic: Australian and New Zealand Airports, Fiscal Year 2004–05*

Airport	Passengers (thousands)	Aircraft movements (thousands)	International passengers (percent)
Australia			
Adelaide	5,361	69	6
Brisbane	15,358	137	21
Canberra	2,477	37	0
Darwin	1,211	16	8
Melbourne	20,274	170	20
Perth	6,525	56	29
Sydney	27,936	252	33
Cairns	3,551	45	28
Gold Coast	3,142	28	5
Hobart	1,523	15	0
Launceston	826	10	0
Townsville	1,049	18	0
New Zealand			
Auckland	11,120	154	55
Christchurch	5,136	90	33
Wellington	4,602	100	13

Sources: Department of Transport and Regional Services (2006a); ATRS (2006).

smaller in area, but it too has a low population density. Its largest city, Auckland, has a population of over 1 million; two other major cities, Christchurch and Wellington, each have less than 500,000. The nations' airports reflect this distribution. Australia has five moderately large airports (Sydney, Melbourne, Brisbane, Perth, and Adelaide), some medium-size airports, and a large fringe of small airports, while New Zealand has one large airport (Auckland), as well as a range of smaller ones (table 4-1).

Australian and New Zealand airports tend to be far apart from each other. Most airports that can handle Boeing 737–type aircraft are more than a three- or four-hour drive from another airport with the same capabilities. Thus, the low-cost carriers (LCCs) that rely on this type of aircraft cannot make much use of secondary airports and must use the major city airports. Some airports, such as those at Adelaide, Sydney, and Wellington, are located close to the city center. These airports tend to have relatively constrained sites, which can make expansion costly. Furthermore, their location means that noise and other environmental problems are significant and can impose limits, such as night curfews, on their operation. Airports located farther from the city center, such as those at Brisbane and Melbourne, tend to face fewer environmental constraints.

Governments have two main direct policy roles regarding airports: monitoring their environmental impacts and setting the regulatory framework. Governments are closely involved when new airports or major investments such as new runways are proposed; the environmental implications of these will be scrutinized before approvals are granted. Airports are subject to environmental regulation—Sydney is subject to night curfews, for example, along with a specific noise standard designed to encourage airlines to use less noisy aircraft.

Financial and Economic Performance

The financial performance of the airports has been changing, especially in Australia. The changes are summarized for the five largest Australian airports in table 4-2. At the end of the price-regulation period, in 2000–01 (the last full fiscal year of regulation), profitability was poor, especially when measured by operating profit relative to total assets. Since then revenues have increased significantly at most of these airports. Costs also rose at most airports but not at the same pace as revenues, and the outcome was a sharp increase in operating profits at all the airports—a near doubling in most cases. The pattern for profits after interest and taxes is less clear, largely because of change in financial structures and much higher interest payments. Total assets have increased, as a result of investments (in the case of Adelaide, for example) and asset revaluations (in the case of Sydney, for example). Profitability at the New Zealand airports has also increased over the past five years, sharply at Wellington.

Lack of data and a paucity of analytical studies make any assessment of economic efficiency more problematic. One core aspect of efficiency is productivity, or the extent to which costs are minimized. For this aspect of efficiency, the indicators are mixed. The Air Transport Research Society (ATRS) measures of productivity are reported for 2001 (the most recent year for which comparable measures are available) in table 4-3. The measure of residual total factor productivity attempts to correct for factors (such as scale and traffic mix) that might influence measured productivity. The New Zealand airports and Sydney perform well relative to the mean for regions such as Europe and North America. Later ATRS studies suggest that other Australian and New Zealand airports have productivity comparable to that of Sydney and higher productivity on average than major Asian region airports.[1] Thus it

1. ATRS (2005).

Table 4-2. *Financial Data, Australian Airports, 2000–01 and 2004–05*
In $A thousands

Airport/ fiscal year	Total revenue	Non-aeronautical revenue	Total expenditure	Operating profit	Profit after interest and taxes	Net assets
Adelaide[a]						
1999–2000	49	39	24	26	–7	476
2004–05	65	35	35	30	–6	686
Brisbane						
2000–01	136	90	67	69	–11	1,548
2004–05	229	142	102	127	21	1,697
Melbourne						
2000–01	191	128	87	104	–32	1,374
2004–05	315	178	130	185	71	1,412
Perth						
2000–01	77	56	42	35	–20	666
2004–05	140	90	80	60	0	891
Sydney						
2000–01	378	221	247	131	52	3,241
2004–05	638	324	232	406	–257	4,757

Source: ACCC (2005, 2006a).
a. Adelaide figures are for 1999–2000.

might be concluded that the Australian and New Zealand airports are relatively productively efficient.

Little assessment has been made of changes in productivity performance over time. Productivity growth for two airports, Sydney and Brisbane, is reported in table 4-4. These data show little change in total factor productivity. Rapid growth in revenues has occurred at the Sydney airport since privatization in 2002; Brisbane experienced rapid growth in productivity after privatization but while prices were still regulated; since then, however, productivity has fallen. The periods of productivity reduction at both airports might be explained by heavy investments.

Any assessments of productive efficiency must therefore be qualified. The airports of Australia and New Zealand may be about average or somewhat better—they do not seem to be systematically worse than average. There may be scope for them to catch up with the more efficient of the North American airports; thus promoting productive efficiency would seem to be a key objec-

Table 4-3. *Productivity Comparisons: Australian and New Zealand Airports and Rest of World, 2001*[a]

Vancouver airport = 1.0

Airport	Gross total factor productivity	Residual total factor productivity	Residual variable factor productivity
Auckland	1.213	1.251	0.797
Christchurch	0.660	0.872	0.739
Sydney	1.109	0.906	0.715
Europe mean	0.790	0.580	0.289
North America mean	0.775	0.670	0.553
Asia Pacific mean	0.865	0.774	0.393

Source: ATRS (2003).

a. Gross total factor productivity is an unadjusted measure of TFP, whereas the residual measures of productivity indicate productivity after allowance has been made for the effects of uncontrollable factors, such as scale, on productivity. Variable factor productivity is a measure based on variable factors alone.

tive of any regulatory system. This is an important issue that needs more analysis before it can be resolved definitively.

Another aspect of efficiency concerns the provision of capacity: with capital-intensive industries such as airports, capacity issues are particularly important. Is the amount of capacity being provided inadequate, excessive, or about right? There is evidence that investment in airports in the two countries may have been excessive rather than inadequate. If investment in capacity were about right, allowing for the presence of indivisibilities, one would expect that some airports would have too much capacity, while others would not have enough and need to ration demand through delays, slot allocation, or pricing. In fact, no airport in either country has a capacity rationing problem.

Table 4-4. *Productivity, Unit Revenue, and Unit Cost Growth, Sydney and Brisbane Airports, 1992–93 to 2003–04*

	Sydney			Brisbane		
Year	Total factor productivity	Unit cost	Unit revenue	Total factor productivity	Unit cost	Unit revenue
1992–93	100.0	100.0	100.0	100.0	100.0	100.0
1996–97	102.6	108.8	108.1	79.4	140.6	104.9
2001–02	96.9	139.3	154.0	94.5	110.9	107.0
2003–04	109.0	127.3	163.6	87.5	123.2	125.3

Source: Author's calculations, based on Federal Airports Corporation, annual reports, various years, Sydney, and ACCC, *Airport Monitoring and Financial Reporting*, various years, Canberra. Brisbane airport was privatized in 1996–97 and Sydney airport was privatized in 2002.

The one exception may be Sydney, which has had a peak rationing problem in the past and because of traffic growth is about to enter such a phase again.

Investments in airports in Australia and New Zealand are highly politicized. Residents may object to expansion because of noise pollution, but there are strong regional pressures to ensure that airport facilities are of a high standard and do not constrain growth of air traffic. Significantly, the government did not conduct a cost-benefit analysis of a third runway added to Sydney airport in the early 1990s, although a lobby group opposed to the runway commissioned one.[2] This poses a question: What mechanisms are in place to ensure that investment is not excessive? Under public ownership these mechanisms probably did not exist, although during the price-cap period in Australia, the regulator reviewed investments. Under the light-handed regulation now operating in both countries, no government mechanism exists for assessing whether major investments are worthwhile. This issue is explored further later.

The Institutional Framework: Privatization, Ownership, and Objectives

Since the mid-1990s most of the major airports in Australia and New Zealand have been privatized. Until their privatization, the large airports were owned by the national governments. In Australia they were operated by a government department, but in the 1980s they were corporatized; the Federal Airports Corporation (FAC) was established to own and operate major airports around the country.[3] Under corporatization, airports had a more commercial focus—they were expected to achieve cost recovery as a group (although there were cross-subsidies from large to smaller airports), and their accounts were made publicly available. Smaller airports were either owned by the federal or local governments, and in the 1980s the federal government transferred its ownership of smaller airports to local governments. The three main New Zealand airports were corporatized in the late 1980s.

In Australia privatization was a staged process. The first phase, during 1996 and 1997, involved the sale of three major airports other than Sydney—Brisbane, Melbourne, and Perth.[4] About a year later the remaining airports owned by the federal government were privatized. Privatization took the form of trade sales to consortia formed to bid for the specific airports. No airports in

---

2. Airport Co-Ordinating Task Force (1990).
3. Prices Surveillance Authority (1993).
4. Airport Sales Task Force (1995); Forsyth (2002); Department of Transport and Regional Services (2006b).

Australia are publicly listed, although the main shareholder in Sydney, Macquarie Airports, which also has stakes in airports in Europe, is listed on stock exchanges. Privatization in New Zealand was more gradual. Although corporatized, the three largest airports had government owners. In the late 1990s, government shareholdings in Auckland and Wellington were sold down, and the airports now have majority private ownership, with Auckland being publicly listed. Christchurch remains majority government owned.

Privatization of the Sydney airport was delayed until 2002 while several public policy issues were resolved. The construction of a third runway led to great public outcry about airport noise, but those complaints had died down by the time of privatization.[5] In contrast to earlier sales, when the government had imposed tight price regulation, the government sought to maximize the revenues it received from the sale of the Sydney airport by nearly doubling the airport's aeronautical charges before the sale. In addition, the light-handed monitoring regime was announced just before final bids were put in. The sale price for Sydney was $A4.6 billion—Melbourne airport, which is about two-thirds of the size of Sydney and has a similar traffic mix, sold for $A1.3 billion in 1997.

Ownership Patterns and Financial Structures

As a broad generalization, in both countries most of the medium and large airports are privately owned, and most of the smaller airports are owned by local governments (table 4-5). Most of the major airports in Australia have three to five main shareholders; in some cases one of these shareholders is a foreign airport operator (London-based BAA for Melbourne; Schiphol in the Netherlands for Brisbane). Financial institutions, such as banks, pension funds, and infrastructure investment trusts, are on most airports' share registers. In some cases, construction or property companies have a shareholding. State or local governments can have significant shareholdings directly or indirectly. For example, the Brisbane Port Corporation, a state-owned enterprise, owns more than a third of Brisbane airport. Christchurch airport is majority owned, and Wellington airport partly owned, by local government. With one exception, the larger airports in Australia do not have majority owners.

As in other respects, Sydney airport is different. While several companies have shareholdings, Macquarie Airports has a majority holding and is the effective manager of the airport. Macquarie Airports is linked to Australian-based Macquarie Bank, which has developed a model of setting up infrastructure investment trusts, which serve as vehicles for investment by individuals or

---

5. Fitzgerald (1998).

Table 4-5. *Ownership Patterns, Australian and New Zealand Airports, 2006*

Airport	Local/regional government share?	Airport operator share?	Majority owner?	Listed?
Adelaide	No	No	No	No
Brisbane	Yes	Schiphol Amsterdam	No	No
Melbourne	No	BAA	No	No
Perth	No	BAA	No	No
Sydney	No	Macquarie	Macquarie	No
Cairns	Yes	No	Local government	No
Auckland	Yes	No	No	Yes
Christchurch	Yes	No	Local government	No
Wellington	Yes	Infratil	Infratil	No

Source: Compiled from airport annual reports and websites.

funds. However, since 2002 Macquarie Airports has developed as a specialist airport operator, with stakes in several airports overseas, including Copenhagen and Brussels. It prefers to own and control its airports, rather than be a passive investor, has been developing expertise in airport management, and is more focused than many airport investors on the bottom line.

Australian terminals are not necessarily owned and operated by the airport. The historical pattern was for airports to own the international terminals, which were common-user terminals, and for the domestic airlines to own (strictly speaking, they held very long leases) the domestic terminals. When the second-largest domestic airline, Ansett, collapsed in 2001, most of its terminals were bought by the airports for use as common-user terminals. Currently Qantas is vertically integrated with its own terminals, but other domestic airlines, such as Virgin Blue, rely on the airports' terminals.

In New Zealand each of the three largest airports has a different ownership pattern. Auckland airport is a listed public company, although the local government holds a substantial minority stake. The airport was subjected to takeover bids in 2007. Christchurch airport remains owned by local government (a majority) and the central government. Wellington is an example of the emerging form of ownership, with a specialist airport operator, Infratil, holding a majority stake and being the effective manager. The local government also has a stake in this airport.

The ownership patterns of airports can have implications for their behavior. An owner such as Macquarie Airports is carefully monitored by the stock market and has a strong focus on financial performance. The owners of airports other than Sydney may have other objectives. A majority of the stock of the privatized Brisbane airport is in fact owned by government corporations (counting Schiphol Airport and Port of Brisbane Corporation as government enterprises). Government enterprises may be commercially focused, but they need not be pure profit maximizers. They may be expected to pursue the objectives of their government owners—for example, to stimulate state development. The focus on profit and on cost minimization differs according to ownership patterns. Airports that are majority privately owned (Sydney) or publicly listed (Auckland) are likely to have the strongest focus on profit. Airports that are owned by consortia (Melbourne) are still focused on profit although different owners will have different priorities. Airports that are part government-owned (Brisbane) face pressure from these owners to pursue objectives other than profit.

In general, at the time of privatization, the airports opted for high debt-to-equity ratios, reflecting a view that the airports represented a low risk and in Australia that they were considered regulated utilities. The high debt-to-equity ratios posed severe problems for several of the airports during the price-regulation period.

Competition between Airports

The low population density and geography of Australia and New Zealand mean that airports have little scope for competition. Most major airports are quite distant from each other, although a few are closer together. For example, Gold Coast airport is about sixty kilometers from Brisbane airport, in a residential region of about 250,000 inhabitants. The same LCCs operate from both of these airports. Avalon airport is about forty kilometers further from Melbourne's central business district than Melbourne airport and is close to an industrial city with a quarter of a million inhabitants. The Qantas-owned LCC, Jetstar, operates some of its flights (ones that might compete directly with Qantas services if operated from Melbourne) from Avalon. Avalon and Melbourne are more complements than competitors, and Gold Coast and Brisbane are competitive only across a limited range of services. New entry by airports in the major cities would be very difficult. Environmental issues would rule out many sites, and city fringe sites for airports, if available, would suffer considerable locational disadvantages compared with the incumbent airports.

There is little scope for competition between airports to be the main hub. Sydney is located in the largest and busiest region and is unlikely to be supplanted as the main international or domestic hub. Brisbane, Melbourne, and Perth are the main regional hubs. To a limited extent they compete with Sydney for direct services to international destinations. Airports can compete with one another for airline operational bases. Most terminals are owned by the airports or by Qantas; while competition in terminal services is feasible in principle, in practice it is limited because much of the traffic has little choice about what terminal to use.

The lack of actual or potential competition between airports means that airlines have very limited countervailing power to negotiate their charges with airports. To have countervailing power, a buyer must have a feasible alternative source of supply to which it can credibly threaten to shift its business. An airline may be large and powerful, and it may represent a high proportion of an airport's aeronautical revenue, but this does not mean that it possesses countervailing power, because it may be locked into using that airport (at best an airline with political influence may pressure the government to use regulation to control airport charges, but that is not the use of countervailing power in the normal sense). If an airline wishes to fly in and out of Sydney, it must use the Sydney airport—there is no viable alternative airport within 150 kilometers. The Australian Productivity Commission considered that the major airports possessed significant market power, but it was less concerned about the smaller airports.[6] If they could use countervailing power, airlines such as Virgin Blue would not enter expensive litigation with airports in an attempt to get them to lower their charges. Airlines would like some airports to reduce their charges, but they have not been able to force them to do so.

Regional Development and Airport Strategies

Airports are seen as gateways to regions and as catalysts in regional economic development.[7] Airport strategies can influence regional economic development, a situation that gives rise to potential conflict between profit and regional development objectives.

Given the involvement of private shareholders and regional governments in ownership of the airports, conflicts between objectives can arise. These tend to occur at the level of the capital city airports, such as those of Adelaide, Brisbane, and Melbourne. As private firms these airports might be expected to maximize profits. However, regional governments want the airports to stimulate economic activity—states such as Victoria (Melbourne), Queens-

6. Productivity Commission (2002).
7. For a good airport economic impact study, see Melbourne Airport (2003).

land (Brisbane), and South Australia (Adelaide) are active in attracting business. They have an interest in having direct flights to major destinations, rather than indirect flights through Sydney, and they have an interest in the airports' setting moderate aeronautical charges, rather than making the most effective use of their market power.

There is evidence that community preferences are affecting the major airports' strategies and that airports are becoming lobbyists for the regions on aviation issues. Even though home carriers like Qantas prefer to use Sydney as the hub for international flights, other airports have become articulate advocates of international air transport liberalization so as to enable direct flights from their facilities; Brisbane and Melbourne, for example, would like to have more direct flights to Asia and the Middle East.[8] But having more direct international flights is likely to mean that these airports lose connecting traffic; the main beneficiaries will be the regions and passengers, not the airports themselves. Community pressure may also be a factor in explaining the airports' moderation in the use of market power in aeronautical charges. Regional influences are evident in other ways. Some governments have been prepared to pressure airports to make investments that might not be warranted, because the airports are seen as gateways to the state. For example, the South Australian government induced Adelaide airport to make (possibly excessive) investments in a terminal, the costs of which it passed on to the airlines, and ultimately, passengers.

Thus many of the Australian and New Zealand airports act as if encouraging regional economic activity is one of their key objectives. Up to a point, they are trading regional development off against profit.

Regulation and Its Reform:
The Light-Handed Regulation Experiments

The core airports policy issue in Australia and New Zealand is how these facilities should be regulated. The regulatory experience of the two countries is the most interesting feature of their handling of airports. Australia had a system of incentive regulation that encountered problems and was replaced with a loosely specified monitoring system. New Zealand has operated without explicit regulation but with the threat of regulation should performance be unsatisfactory. This threat almost became reality for Auckland airport after a review.

---

8. This viewpoint is evident from their submissions on international aviation policy and on competition policy. See Melbourne Airport and TRL (2006) and Wellington Airport/LECG (2006).

This section briefly considers the rationale for airport regulation, an understanding of which is essential if the shifts in policy are to be understood. It then looks at Australia's price-cap period, the problems encountered, and the move to monitoring. The monitoring approach is then evaluated and options for reform are considered. Then the New Zealand experience is discussed.

Regulation and Efficiency in Airports

A starting point for a discussion of regulation is the observation that airports possess considerable market power and that regulation is necessary to restrain the use of this power to keep prices at a (possibly second-best) efficient level. Modern regulatory theory analyzes how to set regulation to maximize efficiency, possibly allowing for some distributional preferences.[9] Thus it is often assumed that the sole or dominant purpose of regulation of monopolies is to achieve maximum economic efficiency. In reality, however, regulation may be about more than this—a key role of regulation as actually practiced may be that it keeps prices close to average costs, possibly at the expense of efficiency.

Several aspects of efficiency might be considered regarding airports. The most important of these are

—Setting prices at the efficient level and ensuring the efficient allocation of capacity when it is scarce

—Achieving productive efficiency, by keeping costs to a minimum

—Ensuring that investment is neither inadequate nor excessive

—Taking advantage of opportunities for commercial development

The cost and demand conditions under which airports operate have particular implications for the pursuit of allocative efficiency. Airports typically represent large sunk costs, and investment encounters significant indivisibilities. Once the airport is built, the marginal costs of runway use may be low (though not necessarily trivial).[10] Variable costs of terminal use are related to passenger throughput and may be significant. Demand overall is very inelastic, but some users, such as flights employing large aircraft, will be more inelastic than others. Some users may have moderately elastic demands—such users could include LCCs and regional airlines that use small aircraft. With some airports, demand could be lower than capacity, and there will be no capacity-rationing problem. This is currently the case for all Australian and New Zealand airports. Demand may press against capacity, in which case the issue is how to avoid delays and how to allocate the scarce capacity, either at

---

9. For background, see Armstrong, Cowan, and Vickers (1994).
10. Hogan and Starkie (2004).

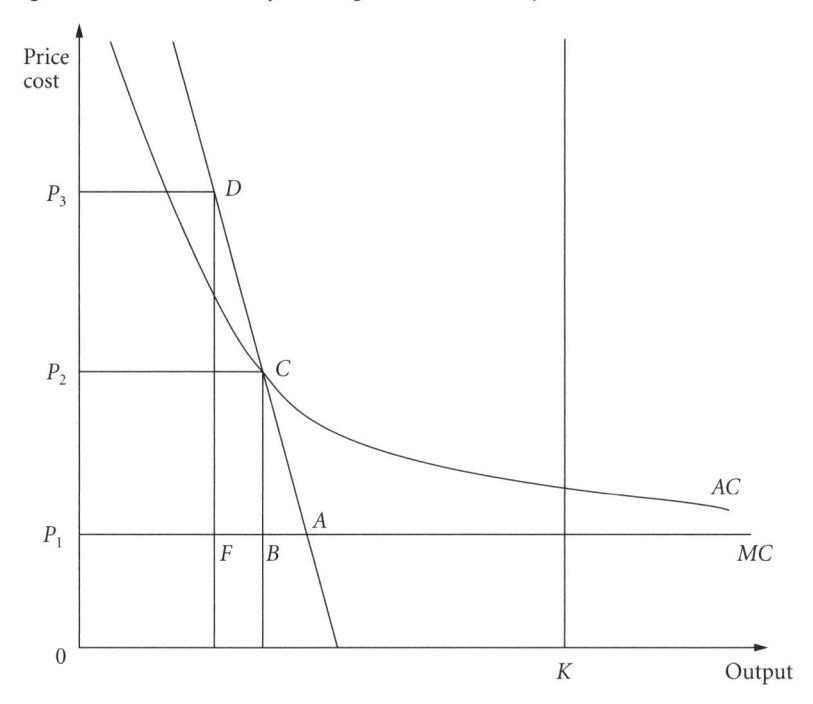

Figure 4-1. *Illustration of the Airport Cost Recovery Problem*

Source: Author's depiction. See text for description.

the peaks or through the whole day. A peak problem will probably develop at Sydney airport over the next few years. This discussion, however, focuses on regulation of airports with ample capacity, since that is the predominant situation at the region's airports.

These airports are likely to experience cost recovery problems. Figure 4-1 illustrates the problem. Assume that marginal costs of runway use are low but that marginal costs of terminal use are significant. In the diagram, *AC* represents average costs, *MC* is marginal cost, and maximum capacity of the airport is shown as *K*. Setting prices at P_1, equal to marginal cost, will lead to losses. A price set at P_2 would cover costs and is the second-best single-price solution. A deadweight loss, *ABC*, is associated with this price, but with low demand elasticity, this loss will be small. Even if prices are set somewhat above average cost, at P_3, the efficiency cost will be small. The deadweight loss rises by the amount *BCDF*. The deadweight loss of cost recovery, or of setting prices above marginal cost, can be further reduced by setting higher prices for the inelastic users and lower prices for the relatively elastic users. This rough

Ramsey pricing could be achieved by relating prices to aircraft weights or, as is now being used in Australia, to passenger loads.[11]

This suggests that the relationship of the overall level of prices to cost, be it average or marginal cost, is not a major issue for efficiency. Prices could be, say, 50 percent above average cost without there being a large deadweight loss. Clearly monopolistic, profit-maximizing prices, which would be a significant multiple of average cost, could be quite inefficient, but actual prices are likely to be well below this level. Thus, for efficiency purposes with airports that have spare capacity, it is not important to ensure that prices are close or equal to costs or that cost recovery is achieved with the minimum feasible prices—that is something that need not be true for other regulated industries. If achieving optimality in this respect were costless, it should be done; however, there are costs in doing so.

The second aspect of efficiency, productive efficiency, is given explicit recognition in the incentive regulation literature.[12] Cost-based regulation, such as traditional rate-of-return regulation, leads to higher costs, because the regulated firm can easily pass on higher costs to its customers and thus has no strong incentive to keep costs down. Incentive regulation seeks to get around this problem by setting allowable prices with little or no reference to the firm's own costs. This gain in efficiency is not costless, because the stronger incentives come with greater risks for the firm. The firm might earn very high profits if conditions turn out well, or it might incur losses—there is a cost in this situation because the firm will be, at least to some extent, risk averse. If the efficiency cost of having prices somewhat above costs is small, as has been argued to be the case with airports with adequate capacity, an efficient solution could be to have a price cap that is fairly generous to the firm and that embodies little likelihood of its incurring a loss. Alternatively, no explicit price regulation would be consistent with good incentives for productive efficiency. These options would result in higher prices to users, however.

The third aspect of efficiency concerns getting investment right. Given that airports are very capital-intensive operations, this aspect can be very important. As the Averch and Johnson effect illustrates, cost-based regulation leads to excessive investment and in turn to unnecessarily high costs.[13] Excessive investment can increase the firm's profit by expanding the firm's rate base, and its costs can be passed on to its customers. In contrast, incentive regulation can lead to underinvestment—for example, a firm might not undertake investment to improve the quality of service because it cannot

---

11. Morrison (1982).
12. Armstrong, Cowan, and Vickers (1994).
13. Armstrong, Cowan, and Vickers (1994), pp. 85–91.

recoup the cost.[14] This problem is recognized by regulators, who devise mechanisms to reward investment—for example, by allowing a higher price if certain investments are undertaken. This mechanism means that efficient investments will be made, but it gives the regulator large discretion over the investment program of the airport. In addition it can lead to regulatory gaming: the airport can threaten to not make an investment that the community sees as necessary unless it is offered a higher return. This has become a particular issue in Australia, with complaints about inadequate infrastructure and firms claiming that regulators are stifling their investments.[15]

The fourth aspect of efficiency concerns whether the airport is making the most of its commercial opportunities. If the price the airport is allowed to charge for aeronautical services is directly linked to revenues it earns from commercial activities (the greater the commercial revenues, the lower the price the airport may charge for aeronautical services), it may not seek to develop commercial activities as a source of revenue. This is a problem with that single-till regulatory system, which sets the prices an airport may charge based on revenues from both airport and nonairport activities. A dual-till system avoids this problem, because the airport is able to keep the fruits of its efforts. A dual-till system may have other deficiencies, however.

The situation of ample capacity also has less obvious implications for regulation. In Australia, if airport charges are increased, it is the passengers who pay most of the increased cost. Since all airlines are similarly situated, they would be able to pass on most cost increases in much the same way that they have passed on fuel cost increases (on most routes, airlines face only limited competition from surface transport). Thus the airlines have a relatively limited incentive to keep airport charges low. By contrast, major airports in Europe are often slot constrained, with the airlines possessing the slots. When airport charges go up, it is the airlines that suffer: their slot rents decrease because they are unable to pass on the increase in costs, because air fares into the slot-constrained airports are set at market-clearing levels. Airlines, and especially the International Air Transport Association (IATA), are much more critical of airport price levels in Europe than they are in Australia and New Zealand. If regulators do wish to keep fares to passengers low, they cannot rely on the airlines to negotiate with airports on passengers' behalf, because they only have a limited interest in keeping airport prices low.

Regulation can be designed to promote efficiency. Such regulation would pay less attention to the exact relationship of price to cost and more to setting

---

14. Helm and Thompson (1991).
15. Export Infrastructure Taskforce (2005).

prices with little reference to the airport's actual cost and more reference to efficient benchmarks. A price cap that allows the airport to be quite profitable most of the time could well be a good approach on efficiency grounds. However, in reality, there are often strong pressures to keep prices close to cost and profits at a "reasonable" level. Governments frequently do not wish to see airports using their monopoly power, while users and regional communities want low prices. Thus there is strong pressure for regulation to be effectively cost based even though such regulation weakens incentives for minimizing costs and encourages inefficient investment. This is the dilemma that underlies airport regulation policy in Australia and New Zealand (and elsewhere).

The Price-Cap Period in Australia, 1997–2002

When the large and midsize Australian airports (except Sydney) were privatized, they were subjected to a price cap of the *CPI-X* form, under which prices are set so as to allow for increases in the consumer price index less a percentage X. These caps were to hold for five years, at which time the price-cap system would be reviewed.[16] At the time, it was expected that price caps would be continued. The caps were administered by the Australian Competition and Consumer Commission (ACCC), a general regulator, as well as a competition policy authority, with responsibilities in telecommunications, energy, and other industries—the ACCC regulates telecommunications with a *CPI-X* cap. From the start, regulation was on a dual-till basis. This meant that aeronautical and nonaeronautical services had to be defined. A tariff-basket approach to measuring actual prices was adopted, that is, a revenue-weighted index of the prices for the different services was calculated and compared with the allowable price.[17] Caps were set without close attention to the airports' costs, and the system could be regarded as strong incentive regulation.

The level of the price cap was based on existing charges, which had been adjusted upward by about 12 percent for the major airports just before privatization. The airports were regulated separately, and different X factors were set for the different airports. Perth airport, with strong growth prospects, was set an X of 5.5 percent, while Canberra was set an X of only 1 percent. Most Xs were set at around 3–4 percent. In retrospect, these caps were quite demanding, requiring a real reduction in charges over the five-year period of some 20–25 percent.

An interesting feature of the regulatory arrangement was its specific provision for investment—the necessary new investment, or NNI, provisions.

---

16. Productivity Commission (2002); Forsyth (2002).
17. ACCC (1997).

An airport that was making a new investment—extending a runway, for example—could apply to the ACCC to increase prices to cover additional costs associated with the investment.[18] The ACCC would assess how much investment was needed and determine an appropriate cost of capital to be applied to it. The ACCC would take various factors into account, as set out in the legislation, including whether the investment had the support of the users. In making its assessment, the ACCC sometimes needed to determine how much of an investment (say, in a terminal) was required by the provision of aeronautical services and how much was required by the provision of nonaeronautical services; only the aeronautical component could count toward a price increase in aeronautical services. In this fashion, the regulatory system addressed the concern that price caps would lead to underinvestment.

Airports were also subject to regulation of access to essential facilities, partly through the Airports Act (this section has now been repealed) and partly through the general competition policy act, the Trade Practices Act. Part IIIA of that act defines a general access regime that allows firms to seek to have access "declared" where it will promote competition in a related market (for example, granting a competitor access to the local loop of a telecommunications firm will enable the competitor to compete with the firm in offering broadband services). Once access is declared, access disputes (typically about price) can be appealed to the ACCC for arbitration. Thus an airport with cargo handling operations might be required to grant facilities to a competitor at an arbitrated price so that it too can operate cargo handling at the airport, thus promoting competition in the cargo handling market. Several facilities around airports have been declared for access under the law, and disputes have been arbitrated and prices set by the ACCC. The Part IIIA provisions continue to be applied to airports, but their application is controversial (see below).

During this period, the government retained ownership of Sydney airport, although it intended to privatize the airport when the time was appropriate. The airport was not subject to *CPI-X* regulation, but it was required to submit any proposals for price increases to the ACCC, which would evaluate the proposal and recommend a specific price increase to the government. It was not clear what would happen if the airport increased prices by more than the ACCC recommendation. In the late 1990s the airport sought an increase of more than 100 percent in aeronautical charges to cover the costs of preparing its facilities to deal with the traffic expected during the 2000 Olympic Games in Sydney. The ACCC approved an increase of about 100 percent, and the airport was privatized shortly afterward.

18. ACCC (2000).

The Workings of Price-Cap Regulation

As it turned out, the price caps were set very tightly. By 1999–2000 nearly all of the airports were incurring losses after interest and taxation, and for some such as Brisbane, the losses were large. To some extent, growth in demand had not been as great as anticipated, partly because of the Asian financial crisis. High debt-to-equity ratios also meant that interest expenses were high. However, it does seem that annual real price reductions of 4–5 percent are a demanding target for airports, especially those that were moderately productively efficient at the beginning of the period.[19] Airports improved their productivity to some extent but not enough to ensure profitability (table 4-4).

The investment provisions worked, in that the ACCC approved or was prepared to approve both major and smaller investments. For example, a runway extension was built at Adelaide airport using ACCC-approved price increases, and the agency was prepared to grant a significant price increase to cover the costs of a proposed new terminal in Adelaide. There were several quite small investments that needed to be assessed and approved by the ACCC; for example, Canberra airport was permitted to raise charges by $A0.10765 per passenger when it built a new walkway.[20] But concerns were raised about the costs of compliance and lengthy delays while the ACCC reviewed investment proposals. Had regulation continued, these problems might have been eliminated through streamlining of the procedures.

Overall, the outcomes were those that might have been expected of strong incentive regulation: good pressure for cost reductions along with sharp volatility of profits. The rigidity of the price cap meant that unexpected factors led to profitability problems for the airports. It is possible that the airport pricing had been too highly geared in light of the risks that such regulation poses; in other words, airports may have been overly regarded as "safe utilities."

The End of Price Regulation

Two unrelated factors brought price capping of airports to an end. The first was a revenue crisis sparked by the collapse of Ansett, Australia's second-largest airline, in September 2001. The second was a recommendation by the Productivity Commission, the government's main microeconomic adviser, that the government move away from direct price regulation.

19. Forsyth (2003).
20. ACCC (2001).

The financial performance of the airports was already poor when Ansett's collapse caused an immediate reduction in traffic at most airports—by as much as 40 percent in some cases. Many airports sought a relaxation of the price caps or their total removal. In October the government temporarily lifted regulation on most airports and allowed Brisbane, Melbourne, and Perth to raise their charges by 6–7 percent.[21] Most of the airports took advantage of their new pricing freedom and increased charges significantly. Sydney airport was unaffected by these changes.

A month before Ansett collapsed, the Productivity Commission had released a draft report recommending that price regulation be replaced by monitoring. This recommendation reflected the commission's view that actual price regulation weakens incentives for cost reduction, and some pricing above cost under a more liberal environment would create less efficiency loss than would result from costs being higher than they need be in a regulated system. The government released the commission's final report in May 2002 and announced that it was replacing regulation with monitoring for seven major capital city airports and would neither regulate nor monitor other airports.[22]

The Monitoring System

The monitoring system, in effect since 2002, combines oversight with review and holds out the threat of sanction for poor performance. The ACCC monitors prices, costs, and profits, along with quality. Except for a price cap on regional flights coming in and out of Sydney airport, prices are not regulated. The information from the monitoring would be used in a review to be completed before the end of the first five years under the new monitoring environment. This review could determine if explicit price regulation should be reintroduced. This provision was intended to discourage airports from using their market power excessively. The airlines and airports would have the freedom to negotiate commercial agreements involving charges, investments, and other matters. Regulation of access to essential facilities through Part IIIA was to continue.[23]

The government issued guidelines for determining good or bad performance. A critical guideline states that airports "should generate expected revenue that is not significantly above the long-run costs of efficiently providing aeronautical services. . . ." The guidelines also allow for the possibility that

---

21. Forsyth (2003).
22. Productivity Commission (2002).
23. Forsyth (2004).

prices at capacity-constrained airports could generate revenues in excess of costs but stipulated that "any additional funding that is generated should be applied to the creation of additional capacity or undertaking necessary infrastructure improvements."[24]

These guidelines are poorly thought out and are likely to lead to problems in implementation. Requiring that revenues not significantly exceed "efficient" costs presupposes that the problem that has bedeviled regulators for more than a century—that of determining what such costs are in the presence of regulation that affects incentives—has somehow been solved. The second guideline mentioned here requires that scarcity rents be used for investment whether or not it is efficient to do so.

Performance under Monitoring

In 2006 the government asked the Productivity Commission to investigate whether airports had performed within the terms of the guidelines. The commission issued its report in December 2006, recommending continuation of the current system with some modifications.[25]

Since direct regulation was removed, aeronautical revenues per passenger have increased significantly at most of the seven monitored airports. The increase was highest at Adelaide, rising 162 percent between 2000–01 and 2005–06.[26] The lowest increase was at Sydney (21 percent), although Sydney had sharply increased its charges just before privatization in 2002. Prices rose 59 percent at Brisbane airport, 25 percent at Canberra, 78 percent at Darwin, 39 percent at Melbourne, and 73 percent at Perth. These price hikes might appear to be sharp, but they came on a low base, and most airports were incurring losses at the beginning of the period. There are also measurement problems in that airports supply more terminal facilities than before as the result of taking over former Ansett terminals. Some price increases, such as those at Adelaide, have been introduced to cover the costs of new investments. Airports also have revalued their assets, especially land; this revaluation has not caused the price rises, but it better reflects opportunity costs and results in prices' being seen as closer to measured costs. The new environment has thus given the airports considerable pricing flexibility. Price increases do not appear to have deterred demand perceptibly. The airports clearly have a strong hand in negotiating with airlines, which have had to accept what the airports have offered. Qantas complains that the only acceptable medium-term con-

---

24. Productivity Commission (2006a, p. 4).
25. Productivity Commission (2006b).
26. ACCC (2007).

tract it has been able to negotiate is with Cairns, a publicly owned airport.[27] The airlines have been especially critical of Sydney airport (even though it has had the smallest increase in charges since monitoring was introduced); the complaints arise partly because it has had the highest charges and partly because it has changed its charging structures.

While charges have increased, it is clear that they are well below monopoly levels. That could be because of the threat of reregulation in the event of poor performance, which is regarded as a serious sanction, granted the difficulties the airports experienced under price regulation. Concerns about the possibility of Part IIIA's being used as a backdoor method of regulation might also have induced airports to keep their pricing levels within bounds. In addition, with the exception of Sydney, most airports have strong local representation on their boards (Brisbane is majority owned by government-owned enterprises), which may keep them from behaving as typical profit maximizers. While prices may be somewhat above cost, it would be very difficult to argue that they are set at inefficiently high levels.[28]

Elsewhere in this chapter, it has been noted that regulators are often under pressure to keep prices close to cost and to eliminate any monopoly profits. In the current Australian (and New Zealand) context, such pressure seems muted. Governments have preferred light-handed regulation, and they have not been very concerned about exact price-cost relationships. Airlines would prefer that airport prices be at a minimum consistent with cost recovery, and they have been very critical of the airports' prices. However, their opposition has been tempered by the realization that they can pass most of these charges on to passengers, and they have preferred to use their lobbying capital with governments to influence them on other policy issues. Consumer and tourism lobby groups have not taken a strong stand on airport charging (although the ACCC seeks to promote consumer interests).

It is noteworthy that most of the relevant parties—airlines, airports, and the ACCC—see the performance of the system more or less solely in terms of how high prices are in relation to costs. This viewpoint is evident in the submissions to the Productivity Commission inquiry (see table 4-6, which summarizes the positions taken by interested parties), and also the position taken by the Productivity Commission in its report. For example, the ACCC does not examine how efficient the outcomes have been, but instead concludes that prices are too high because they are above costs, and it recommends tighter regulation to correct this problem.

27. Qantas (2006).
28. Productivity Commission (2006b).

Table 4-6. Views of Interested Parties and the Productivity Commission on Price Monitoring and Alternative Options

Party	Current system effective?	Advocate relaxation of controls?	Advocate introduction of dispute mechanism?	Use Part IIIA?	Reintroduce price regulation?	Approach to land valuation?
ACCC	No	No	Yes (ACCC)	Yes	No	Historical
National Competition Council	n.a.	n.a.	n.a.	No	n.a.	n.a.
Sydney airport	Yes	Yes	No	No	No	Surrounding land value
Brisbane airport	Yes	Yes	No	No	No	Surrounding land value
Melbourne airport	Yes	Yes	Yes (not ACCC)	No	No	Surrounding land value
Adelaide airport	Yes	Yes	No	No	No	Surrounding land value
Qantas	No	No	Yes	Yes	No	Historical
Virgin Blue	No	No	Yes (ACCC)	No	No	Historical
Board of Airline Representatives Australia	No	No	Yes	No	No	Historical
Regional airlines	No	No	n.a.	No	Yes	n.a.
IATA	No	No	n.a.	No	Yes	Historical
Productivity Commission	Yes	Minor relaxation	No	No	No	Permit no further revaluations

Source: Compiled from submissions to Productivity Commission (2006a, 2006b).
n.a. = Not applicable.

There has been little analysis of the productivity performance of the airports since privatization. The Productivity Commission did not undertake new productivity studies for its review but instead referred to already completed studies. According to these studies, Sydney airport has increased total factor productivity since 2002 (see table 4-4). Brisbane airport improved productivity during the price-cap period but has fallen back somewhat since, although its performance is still well above the performance before privatization. International comparisons indicate that the productivity performance of Australian airports is above that of Asian and European airports but below that of North American airports. Price comparisons suggest that aeronautical charges are average compared with others around the world, or a little less. Additional analysis is needed to be definitive about productivity performance in the regulation and monitoring periods. It is possible that prices are above the costs of "efficiently providing services" because actual costs are above those that could be achieved if the airports were as productively efficient as feasible.

Thus it is too early to be conclusive on how light-handed approaches have performed in stimulating productive efficiency, relative to the alternatives. Most likely, it will take a longer time period to establish patterns, and even then, the choice of counterfactual will be controversial. It could be that effective incentive regulation would achieve the same results; however, it is unlikely that regulation will remain strongly incentive based. More likely, actual regulation would become, over time, more cost based, which weakens incentives for cost reduction. It should also be remembered that both the Australian and New Zealand systems of light-handed regulation pay considerable attention to the relationship of prices to costs as a measure of performance, and in this respect, their incentive properties are weakened. A tentative conclusion would be that the monitoring system has worked moderately well in terms of productive efficiency.

There are concerns with how well monitoring has worked in delivering efficient levels of investment. The airports are happy with the investment mechanism, since they can simply raise prices to cover the costs of the investments they make. However, nothing guarantees that the investments they make are warranted. Thus Adelaide airport has just completed construction of a large, high-standard terminal (strongly advocated by local politicians). It also now has the highest charges of any major airport other than Sydney.[29] Was this terminal investment excessive? Ideally the Productivity Commission would examine not only whether the price increases covered the costs of investments

---

29. Melbourne Airport and TRL (2006).

but also whether the investments were warranted. However, such a review would require a large amount of information gathering and analysis, and the commission review did not undertake such a cost-benefit analysis. In short, there is a considerable danger that if airports can always pass through the costs of their investments by raising prices, there will be no check on investment programs, which could lead to a de facto Averch and Johnson world where airports make excessive investments to increase their profitability. As noted before, Australian and New Zealand airports are relatively well endowed with capacity.

The airports have been keen to increase their nonaeronautical revenues since privatization—they have pursued new opportunities such as non-aviation-related retail and have also increased charges for services such as car parking (see table 4-2). Thus they seem to be making the most of their commercial opportunities.

The monitoring period has also been one of litigation. One long-running case was initiated in 2002, when Virgin Blue sought to use Part IIIA (intended to promote access to essential services) as a means of achieving ACCC arbitration of the level and structure of Sydney airport charges. While there are doubts as to whether this is the appropriate avenue to address issues of the use of market power and the overall price levels charged by airports, it is certainly a cumbersome avenue, given the delays and, no doubt, cost to the litigants (as Virgin Blue now argues).[30] The most recent court decision was in favor of Virgin Blue, and the airport and airline negotiated new charges, under the threat of arbitration by the ACCC, in mid-2007. This decision poses a problem for airport policy—airlines that do not like an airport's prices could seek ACCC arbitration, using this backdoor method to have regulation reinstated and jeopardizing the objectives of light-handed monitoring. The ACCC has historically taken a relatively cost-based approach to Part IIIA arbitrations. The policy problem was considered by the Productivity Commission (see below) and the government responded.

Overall, if efficiency is the objective, the current system has performed fairly well in some aspects (productive efficiency) and more questionably in others (investment), though time and more rigorous assessment is needed to make a more conclusive assessment. This could be a task for a review. The purpose of the Productivity Commission is not to assess efficiency, however, but to determine whether airports have met the guidelines, which emphasize keeping revenues close to costs (in theory, close to efficient levels of costs, but

---

30. For a discussion on use of Part IIIA to force arbitration of airport charges, see National Competition Council (2006) and ACCC (2006c). For Virgin Blue's perspective on the litigation, see Virgin Blue (2006).

in practice, probably close to actual costs). The Productivity Commission report concluded that there is no evidence that prices have been raised significantly above the costs of efficiently delivering the services; in other words, pricing behavior has been consistent with the guidelines.

To a significant extent, the Productivity Commission was asked to answer the wrong question. It could conclude that the monitoring and review system had performed very well in terms of the main aspects of economic efficiency. However, it could also conclude that revenues had been significantly above the costs of efficiently providing the services—this may be the price that has to be paid if strong incentives for cost reduction are to be present. To this end, the commission could conclude that performance had been "poor" and warranted the sanction of reintroduction of regulation. Reregulation might lead to less efficient performance, and even if that did not happen, it would promote a cost-plus approach to airport pricing, which would lead to weakened incentives and performance in the long term.

Reforming the System

Although the Productivity Commission's review of the monitoring system was intended primarily to assess performance and decide whether the sanction of regulation should be reintroduced, it was also an opportunity to consider reforms of the system. The review called for submissions from interested parties, and many of these stated the expected—airports are happy with the system, while airlines would prefer tighter regulation (see table 4-6)—but there was not much support for a return to full regulation. A number of possible reforms were raised, however.

In particular, several airlines and the ACCC criticized the effectiveness of the review-sanction approach, contending that it was not strong enough to limit the use of market power.[31] These parties suggested establishing a dispute-resolution mechanism, under which disputes over the level of charges (and other matters) would be arbitrated by a third party, possibly the ACCC. This negotiate-arbitrate approach is used in access regulation under Part IIIA. In such a system, many disputes are resolved before arbitration, although the principles that the arbitrator uses, and the ways in which they are interpreted, are crucial to the outcome. The ACCC takes a rather cost-based approach to Part IIIA disputes and could be expected to take a similar approach with airports. Such a dispute mechanism would replace reliance on Part IIIA as an indirect means of limiting the use of market power, something that is not its intended function.

31. ACCC (2006b).

Issues would be resolved more quickly under a dispute-resolution system than in a review-sanction system, although regulatory intervention is likely to be more frequent. The outcomes in terms of prices and efficiency would depend on the principles adhered to and their implementation, which would depend critically on who the arbitrator is. Clearly many participants (including the ACCC) believe that with the ACCC as arbitrator, airport prices would be lower. If the same principles were to be implemented for a dispute-resolution system as for a review-sanction system, there is no reason why this system would require any less information than the review-sanction system. The parties showed very little interest in investment issues, other than the compliance aspects. However, as indicated above, excessive investment could be a significant source of inefficiency if investment proposals are not scrutinized carefully. A move to a dispute-resolution mechanism could result in better ex ante scrutiny of investment. Costly investments would necessitate price rises, and airlines would take these to arbitration if they felt they were excessive. In those cases the arbitrator would submit investment proposals to more scrutiny than currently takes place. It is probably easier to discourage excessive investment before it is made than to punish it after it has been undertaken, which is what happens under the current review-sanction approach.

In its final report, the Productivity Commission recommended continuation of the monitoring regime for another six years, with two important changes that the government accepted.[32] First, it urged a change in Part IIIA so that it could not be used as a form of price regulation of airports. Second, the commission decided against a dispute-resolution mechanism, but instead recommended a "show-cause" mechanism. Under this mechanism, which was intended to strengthen the threat of reregulation, an airport could be asked to show cause why its conduct should not be investigated further and the relevant minister could choose to implement a pricing inquiry.

Removing Part IIIA as a device for regulating airports will strengthen the review-sanction system. While the show-cause mechanism will make the reregulation threat more effective, it does give considerable discretion to the minister. Pricing inquiries are likely to happen when airport pricing becomes a politically sensitive issue, and the conduct of such inquiries need not stimulate efficiency. Much depends on what criteria are used to determine whether the need for an inquiry is established and whether conduct has been acceptable.

The guidelines and principles set out for performance reviews and for price inquiries are critical determinants of how the system works. Essentially they

32. Department of Transport and Regional Services (2007).

specify whether light-handed regulation is intended to promote incentives for efficiency, or maintain prices close to actual costs. The current principles are severely flawed. While they do not actively promote inefficiency, they try to be both cost-plus and incentive regulation at the same time. The government has announced that it plans to revise the principles, mainly to address such issues as asset valuation. However, the revision offers an opportunity for a much-needed clarification of the objectives of the regulatory system and for finding a balance between keeping prices down and promoting efficiency that can be implemented. In particular, guidelines need to be set for the ways in which a review panel or a price inquiry is to determine whether airports are efficient, be this through benchmarking, detailed analysis of costs, or cost-benefit analysis of investments. Without such guidelines there is a distinct likelihood that the system will degenerate into a light-handed form of cost-plus regulation, with adverse consequences for the efficiency of the airports.

The New Zealand Experience

New Zealand took a different approach to light-handed regulation. Instead of an explicit review-sanction mechanism, the New Zealand approach involved a general provision in the relevant legislation to enable the relevant minister to undertake at any time a review of pricing in industries such as airports. Thus reviews might take place periodically, or never. In 1998 the minister initiated a review of pricing at Auckland, Christchurch, and Wellington airports. The Commerce Commission, which undertook the review, recommended price regulation of Auckland airport, but the minister rejected the recommendation in 2003, and the airports continue unregulated.[33]

The criteria for whether imposition of regulation was warranted are even vaguer in New Zealand than in Australia. The Commerce Commission stated as a key principle that prices should cover efficient operating costs and earn a normal rate of return. The commission took a distinctly cost-plus approach to testing whether this was the case at the airports and made detailed estimates of the asset base and the allowable weighted average cost of capital. It assumed that productive inefficiency at Auckland airport was equal to 1–3 percent of operating costs (and found similar amounts of productive inefficiency at the other airports) and also assumed the presence of some dynamic inefficiency (which it interpreted as inefficient use of assets). It did not assess investment, assuming implicitly that the efficient provision of capacity was the same as the actual capacity. The commission concluded that the efficient cost per passenger at

33. New Zealand Commerce Commission (2002); McKenzie-Williams (2004).

Auckland was below the actual cost. Prices were not above efficient levels at Christchurch and Wellington. On the basis of these estimates, it recommended price regulation of Auckland airport, though not of the price-cap form.

This review showed little cognizance of the problems recognized in the incentive regulation literature. Basically, it took actual costs as the measure of the efficient level of costs. The commission does not appear to have tested this assumption, for example, by using benchmarking studies. Indeed, benchmarking studies indicate that costs at New Zealand airports are not at a minimum. Instead, the commission undertook a simple cost-benefit analysis of price regulation, and in doing so, it assumed that such regulation would achieve both productive and dynamic efficiency. In effect, it presumed that price regulation that had no cost in terms of efficiency would be feasible—a heroic assumption.

The significance of the review lies in the signals that it gives. While the recommendation to regulate was ultimately rejected, the process indicated that there was a real threat that regulation might be introduced. A similar review next time around might have a different outcome. Thus there is some threat of sanction if behavior is poor. The worrying aspect, however, is that the review saw adequacy of performance very much tied to the relationship of prices to actual costs, suggesting that airports can safely have prices well above efficient levels of costs as long as prices are close to actual costs. In short, this is signaling a light-handed form of cost-plus regulation. Airlines have been very critical of airport pricing, and the New Zealand government has recently announced that it may move to more explicit mechanisms to impose regulation if considered necessary.

Conclusions

Australia and New Zealand have both privatized their major airports and subjected them to light-handed regulation. Ownership of these airports may be spread over several different entities, with conflicting objectives, and local or regional governments may have substantial shareholdings. Thus the airports need not behave as traditional profit-maximizing firms. However, as with overseas airports, there is something of an emerging trend toward specialist airport operators with a strong focus on profit; such operators are more likely to operate like traditional firms.

The economic performance of the airports depends on the institutional framework within which they operate, especially the ownership and regulation aspects. One aspect of efficiency performance, very important in North

America and Europe, concerns the efficient use of scarce capacity. This has not been a problem in Australia and New Zealand because capacity has been ample. It will become an issue at Sydney in the near future, however. The indicators on airport productivity are conflicting, suggesting scope for improvement to match the better-performing airports around the world. Finally, while it is not possible to be definitive, some evidence suggests that investment in capacity has been excessive. This all indicates that the design of regulation is important, and that there is scope for a better framework to stimulate economic efficiency.

It is in their approach to regulation that Australia and New Zealand have differed from other countries. Both have moved away from direct regulation of airports and implemented a review-sanction model to moderate the use of market power. The stated objectives have been those of achieving light-handed regulation and ostensibly the promotion of economic efficiency, although keeping prices close to cost emerges as the dominant actual objective in both countries. The experience suggests some tentative lessons, given the limited time span of the experiments.

Airports in the two countries do possess market power, and the use of countervailing power by airlines or commercial negotiations is not strong enough to eliminate this market power. Competition between airports is not strong, because airports are too far apart from each other, and new entry is not likely to change this. Thus airports do have the scope to set prices above cost and to make investments that are not cost effective.

The Australian and New Zealand experience with light-handed regulation of airports suggests several observations:

—Technically "private" airports need not be profit-maximizing airports, and ownership of private airports in Australia and New Zealand is consistent with some emphasis on nonprofit objectives. There seems, however, to be a developing trend (as in Europe) toward more purely private airports with a stronger focus on profit and shareholder value.

—Under light-handed regulation, prices have been somewhat above what they might have been under tighter regulation, but they are well below monopoly levels. The threat of sanctions such as reimposition of regulation, along with pressure from owners with regional development objectives, is likely to moderate pricing behavior. In Australia the threat of access regulation might also have helped moderate prices.

—The Australian price-cap experience provides a good illustration of the advantages and disadvantages of price caps. It suggests that tight price caps, which risk losses for the regulated airports, are very difficult to maintain, even if they are useful in pressuring non-profit-maximizing airports to minimize costs. It provided close scrutiny of investment, but it gave the regulator large discretion over investment projects.

Tentative assessments of productivity performance suggest that light-handed regulation as practiced so far in Australia and New Zealand is consistent with good incentives for cost minimization.

—The least satisfactory aspect of current regulatory frameworks concerns investment incentives—there are no incentives to get investment right. Airports face strong pressure from regional governments to make excessive investments; these costs are passed on to users (initially the airlines, but ultimately the passengers).

—Light-handed regulation is about process, or the flexibility with which regulation is exercised, rather than about content. It can be cost based or incentive based. As practiced so far in Australia and New Zealand, it has been more incentive based than cost based. However, the principles on which this light-handed regulation rests are vague and predominantly cost based. Thus there is a risk that the systems could revert to much more of a cost-plus form of regulation with adverse consequences for incentives for efficiency.

The Australian and New Zealand systems generally perform well in promoting efficiency, although problems do exist that suggest priorities for policy reform. These concern how investment is handled and the guidelines for light-handed regulation.

Within the current light-handed regulatory environments, some disincentives for excessive investment need to be adopted in both countries. An explicit external assessment of investment could exist within a review-sanction approach, where the review undertakes an ex post assessment of major investments and is prepared to implement sanctions if excessive investment has taken place. Alternatively, if a dispute-resolution mechanism or show-cause–price-inquiry mechanism is in place, the arbitrator, when assessing proposals for price increases based on the costs of new investments, could assess whether such investments were excessive according to set criteria. Alternatively the price inquiry could evaluate the need for investments that have led to price increases.

Second, the guidelines under which a light-handed system of regulation operates are critical: these could be the guidelines for a review and the imposition of sanctions, or if a show-cause mechanism and possible inquiry were to be implemented, the guidelines for an inquiry. Cost-based guidelines will result in inefficient cost-plus regulation. To promote efficiency, it is necessary to develop guidelines that mandate incentives for efficiency. Governments need to determine the purpose of regulation—is it to promote efficiency, or is it to ensure that prices are kept close to costs and that profits are "reasonable"? As the modern theory of regulation stresses, these are conflicting objectives that cannot be resolved by careful use of ambiguous terminology, and the balance between them needs to be explicitly determined in a manner capable of practical implementation. As yet, the frameworks that guide light-handed regulation of Australian and New Zealand airports have not directly addressed this issue. Airport pricing remains a controversial issue, and governments in both countries have indicated recently that they may move to make their approaches to regulation less light handed.

References

ACCC (Australian Competition and Consumer Commission). 1997. *Administration of Airport Price Cap Arrangements.* Melbourne (January).

———. 2000. "New Investment Cost Pass-Through." Position Paper. Melbourne.

———. 2001. "ACCC Draft Decision on New Walkway at Canberra Airport." Media release. Melbourne (February).

———. 2005. *Airport Monitoring and Financial Reporting 2003–04.* Canberra.

———. 2006a. *Airport Monitoring and Financial Reporting 2004–05.* Canberra.

———. 2006b. *Submission to the Productivity Commission's Inquiry into Price Regulation of Airport Services.* Melbourne (July).

———. 2006c. *Supplementary Submission to the Productivity Commission's Inquiry into Price Regulation of Airport Services.* Melbourne (August).

———. 2007. *Airports Price Monitoring and Financial Reporting, 2005–06. ACCC Monitoring Report.* Melbourne (February).

Airport Co-Ordinating Taskforce (Australia). 1990. *Sydney Airport Third Runway Cost/Benefit Analysis, Final Report.* Sydney: Coopers & Lybrand Consultants (December).

Airport Sales Task Force, Commonwealth of Australia. 1995. *Sale of Federal Airports, Phase 1.* Department of Finance, Canberra (October).

Armstrong, M., S. Cowan, and J. Vickers. 1994. *Regulatory Reform: Economic Analysis and British Experience.* MIT Press.

ATRS (Air Transport Research Society). 2003. *Airport Benchmarking Report, 2003.* Vancouver.

———. 2005. *2005 Airport Benchmarking Report: Global Standards for Airport Excellence.* Vancouver.

———. 2006. *Airport Benchmarking Report, 2006 Summary.* Vancouver.

Department of Transport and Regional Services, Australian Government. 2006a. *Aviation Statistics: Airport Traffic Data, 1994–95 to 2004–05.* Canberra.

———. 2006b. *Submission to the Productivity Commission Review, Price Regulation of Airport Services.* Canberra.

———. 2007. *Government Response to the Productivity Commission Inquiry—Review of Price Regulation of Airport Services.* Canberra (April).

Export Infrastructure Taskforce, Australia. 2005. *Report to the Prime Minister by the Export Infrastructure Taskforce.* Canberra (May).

Fitzgerald, P. 1998. *The Sydney Airport Fiasco: The Politics of an Environmental Nightmare.* Sydney: Hale and Iremonger.

Forsyth, P. 2002. "Privatisation and Regulation of Australian and New Zealand Airports." *Journal of Air Transport Management* 8: 19–28.

———. 2003. "Regulation under Stress: Developments in Australian Airport Policy." *Journal of Air Transport Management* 9: 25–35.

———. 2004. "Replacing Regulation: Airport Price Monitoring in Australia." In *The Economic Regulation of Airports: Recent Developments in Australasia, North America and Europe,* edited by P. Forsyth and others, pp. 3–22. Aldershot, U.K.: Ashgate.

Helm, D., and D. Thompson. 1991. "Privatised Transport Infrastructure and Incentives to Invest." *Journal of Transport Economics and Policy* (September): 213–46.

Hogan, O., and D. Starkie. 2004. "Calculating the Short-Run Marginal Infrastructure Costs of Runway Use: An Application to Dublin Airport." In *The Economic Regulation of Airports,* edited by P. Forsyth and others, pp. 75–82. Aldershot, U.K.: Ashgate.

McKenzie-Williams, P. 2004. "A Shift towards Regulation? The Case of New Zealand." In *The Economic Regulation of Airports,* edited by P. Forsyth and others, pp. 23–44. Aldershot, U.K.: Ashgate.

Melbourne Airport. 2003. *Melbourne Airport Economic Impact Study, Public Report* (March).

———. 2006. *Authorisation of the Qantas Airways and Air New Zealand Tasman Networks Agreement. Submission to the ACCC Authorisation Application* (May).

Melbourne Airport and TRL. 2006. *Benchmarking International Airport Performance, Final Report* (June). Appendix 1 of Melbourne Airport, Productivity Commission Inquiry, Price Regulation of Airport Services, 2006 submission.

Morrison, S. 1982. "The Structure of Landing Fees at Uncongested Airports: An Application of Ramsey Pricing." *Journal of Transport Economics and Policy* 16, no. 2: 151–59.

National Competition Council (Australia). 2006. *Price Regulation of Airport Services: Submission to the Productivity Commission Inquiry.* Canberra (July).

New Zealand Commerce Commission. 2002. *Final Report. Part IV Inquiry into Airfield Services at Auckland, Wellington and Christchurch International Airports.* Wellington (August).

Prices Surveillance Authority (Australia). 1993. *Inquiry into the Aeronautical and Non-Aeronautical Charges of the Federal Airports Corporation.* Melbourne (August).

Productivity Commission (Australia). 2002. *Price Regulation of Airport Services.* Report 19. Canberra: AusInfo.

———. 2006a. *Price Regulation of Airport Services.* Issues paper. Canberra (May).

———. 2006b. *Review of Price Regulation of Airport Services.* Report 40. Canberra.

Qantas Airways Limited. 2006. *Submission to the Productivity Commission Inquiry into Current Arrangements for the Price Regulation of Airport Services.* Sydney (July).

Virgin Blue Airlines. 2006. *Price Regulation of Airport Services: Submission to the Productivity Commission.* Brisbane (July).

Wellington Airport/LECG. 2006. *Benefits and Costs to the Public of the Proposed Air NZ and Qantas Code Share: Trans-Tasman Services to Wellington.* Report prepared for Wellington Airport by LECG Limited, Wellington (July).

ANNE GRAHAM

5

Airport Planning and Regulation in the United Kingdom

This chapter investigates the effectiveness of the airport planning and regulatory system in the United Kingdom and assesses the appropriateness of the current ownership structure. The airport industry has shifted from public to private sector ownership over the last twenty years as a result of new policy directions initiated by the desire of the 1980s conservative government to privatize public utilities. At the same time, air traffic growth has been strong, encouraged by a more liberal environment and in particular by the emergence of low-cost carriers (LCCs). Moreover, throughout this period there have been pressures on capacity at airports in London and the southeast of England, especially at Heathrow, and these pressures have had a major impact on the development of the U.K. airport industry.

Today the U.K. government has very limited influence over the air transport sector through ownership—the airline industry is entirely private and the airport industry is now mainly private. The only remaining limited control lies with en route air traffic control, which is provided by a mixed public-private organization that took over from a public agency in 2001. Therefore the main ways in which the government can influence the U.K. airport industry are through the planning system and regulation. Three other sets of policies that affect the airport industry are not considered directly in this chapter. The first set is the U.K., European, and international policy measures designed to mitigate the environmental impacts of aviation, such as local regulations regarding air quality and noise, and possible wider controls related to climate change and emissions. These policies clearly have a major impact on the planning process and are likely to have an increasing influence over future traffic volumes and costs of the industry. The second set of policies affects the use of existing capacity, such as the current slot allocation system and the lack of a transparent secondary market. Third are the bilateral restrictions on U.K. airlines for services outside of Europe.

As background, this chapter begins by considering the nature and traffic characteristics of the airport industry in the United Kingdom. It then reviews the U.K. airport policy and planning framework and discusses the ownership structure and regulatory regime of the airports. This leads to an assessment of the effectiveness of the planning, regulatory, and ownership system, and to the implications of making changes to this system. The paper concludes that the planning process is too long and needs to be shortened and that the regulatory regime has produced economic distortions that need to be corrected. The chapter is also critical of the structure of the BAA airport group, formerly the British Airports Authority, which was set up when privatization occurred and economic regulation was introduced. In short, it is argued that the regulatory and industry structure that was established twenty years ago is now outdated and in need of a full-scale, coordinated review.

The U.K. Airport Industry

Geography (a large number of towns with significant population volumes and an island characteristic) and a relatively high per capita income help explain the extensive number of international regional airports in the United Kingdom. In 2006 twenty airports in the United Kingdom each served more than 1 million passengers, ranging from London Heathrow with over 67 million passengers to Cardiff in Wales with just under 2 million passengers. The distribution of traffic is clearly uneven, with London currently handling 58 percent of the traffic (table 5-1). Bilateral air service agreements and traffic distribution rules have meant that Heathrow has traditionally been the main international airport in the United Kingdom, handling much business and connecting traffic; in 2006 its share of the U.K. market alone was 29 percent. London Gatwick and Stansted have more leisure traffic and low-cost carriers, as has the smaller airport of London Luton. Stansted, in particular, has experienced very high growth rates in the last ten years because of the LCC sector. The BAA-owned airports of Heathrow, Gatwick, and Stansted have 91 percent of all air traffic in and out of London—although this share has decreased slightly over the years (96 percent in 1990), primarily because of the development of Luton and London City airports.

The regional airports have grown in a less coordinated manner. Most were owned by local governments for many years, which often meant that they were expanded more for local regional pride or broader economic reasons

Table 5-1. *Number of Passengers at U.K. Airports, 1990–2006*
Millions

Airport	1990	2000	2005	2006	Percent growth 1990–2006	Percent market share in 1990	Percent market share in 2006
Heathrow	42.6	64.3	67.7	67.3	58	42	29
Gatwick	21.0	31.9	32.7	34.1	62	21	15
Stansted	1.2	11.9	22.0	23.7	1,875	1	10
All London	67.5	115.8	133.5	136.9	103	66	58
Manchester	10.1	18.4	22.1	22.1	119	10	9
All regions[a]	34.9	64.2	94.7	98.2	181	34	42
All airports	102.4	180.0	228.2	235.1	130	100	100

Source: CAA.
a. "All regions" refers to all airports outside of London, including Manchester.

rather than to meet any specific demand criteria. Often little consideration was given to their commercial viability or to other airport developments in neighboring local authority areas. This can be illustrated by a comparison of average operating margins (that is, operating profit as a share of total revenues). In 1989–90 the main regional airports (excluding Manchester) had an average operating margin of 5.4 percent, compared with values of 30.4 and 37.7 percent respectively at Gatwick and Heathrow airports. As a result some areas had more capacity than was needed—although in recent years that excess capacity has provided the opportunity for the development of substantial LCC operations. In particular a number of "airport pairs" emerged that were very close to each other and had overlapping catchment areas, such as Cardiff-Bristol, Birmingham-Nottingham East Midlands, and Liverpool-Manchester.[1] More recently a few former military regional airports, most notably Doncaster Finningley and Manston, have also been developed to take commercial services. Manchester airport, which is the largest of the regional airports, has an overall market share of 9–10 percent and handles around two-thirds of all passengers across the north of England. BAA owns three major Scottish airports, namely, Glasgow, Edinburgh, and Aberdeen, which together have a market share of 86 percent of all the Scottish airports.[2]

In the last ten years or so, a more commercial and proactive approach by many of the regional airports, combined with the rapid expansion of the LCC

1. Humphreys (1999).
2. OFT (2006b).

sector, has led to the development of a much more extensive network of scheduled services in the regions. Growth at these airports has been much stronger than at the congested airports of Heathrow and, to a lesser extent, Gatwick, and the market share of the London airports has decreased as a result. This regional airport growth has been encouraged not only by incentives related to airport charges and other marketing support being offered by the airports, but also by route development funds (RDFs) that have been provided to a few Scottish and Northern Irish airports by regional development bodies to support new services deemed beneficial to a region's overall economic development.[3]

Since 1990 traffic at U.K. airports has increased by 130 percent. Between 2000 and 2006 it increased by 27 percent, which resulted from a 305 percent increase in LCC traffic offset by declines of 5 percent and 8 percent in traditional scheduled and charter traffic respectively.[4] Passenger numbers are generally predicted to grow substantially at U.K. airports in the future, with the latest official government forecasts for unconstrained demand predicting 490 million passengers in 2030 nationally, with 300 million passengers in London and southeast England.[5] This is more than double the current figures. However, forecasting the actual airports that passengers will be using is becoming a more difficult task because of the much more competitive, diverse, and cost-conscious airline market. Growth at Heathrow (which will be particularly stimulated by the introduction of the EU-U.S. open skies agreement in 2008) seems likely to continue to be capacity constrained as it has been in the past, while the exact rate of growth at the other airports is more uncertain and depends very much on factors such as the nature of the traffic handled, additional investment considerations, and the extent of competition from other airports.[6]

The Airport Policy Framework in the United Kingdom

The key development in airport policy in recent years came in the mid-1980s, when the conservative government under Prime Minister Margaret Thatcher moved to commercialize and privatize the nation's airports and to set up a regulatory system to accommodate privatization. The new policy was part of the

---

3. Graham and Dennis (2007).
4. OFT (2006c).
5. Department for Transport (2006).
6. The open skies agreement liberalizes the rules for aviation markets on the North Atlantic and, starting in 2008, will allow any European or U.S. airline to fly any route between any city in the European Union and any city in the United States.

Thatcher government's drive to privatize nationalized industries, such as utilities and communications, to lessen the burden on the state, and to increase share ownership among the U.K. population. The key elements of the new policy were outlined in a white paper on airport policy issued in 1985 and the Airports Act passed in 1986. On the same day as it published the white paper, the government also approved the development of capacity at Stansted airport to 15 million passengers; Stansted was considered the most suitable option in the short term for increasing the much needed capacity in the London area. At the same time, planning permission for Heathrow Terminal 5 was refused, primarily because it would have required the relocation of a sewage farm, which would have taken a considerable amount of time (although permission for the relocation was subsequently granted in 2001). This 1985 decision had major implications for the provision of airport infrastructure in southeast England and followed a long public inquiry that had considered proposals for the development of both of these airports.

The next main statement on government policy came in 2003, with the publication of a white paper on "The Future of Air Transport," which brought together both airport and aviation policy. It looked some thirty years ahead with the aim of addressing the previous lack of strategic planning for the overall air transport industry. On the development of new airport capacity, the white paper drew upon seven lengthy consultations that had taken place for different U.K. areas. For London and southeast England, it concluded that two new runways would be needed in the next thirty years. It proposed construction of a second runway at Stansted as soon as possible (around 2011–12) and of a third runway at Heathrow in 2015–20 provided stringent environmental conditions could be met (the most difficult were related to air quality limits set by the European Union that will apply after 2010). If the Heathrow option was not feasible, then the paper recommended that a second runway be built at Gatwick but not until after 2019 because of a planning agreement between BAA and the local government preventing earlier development. The paper also offered expansion proposals for the other U.K. regions.

The white paper provides a strategic framework for future development, which the government believes would be in the national interest provided all local impacts are addressed, but it does not grant final approval. Any airport development in the United Kingdom is still required to go through the formal planning process before any final decision for expansion is given. Also the exact timing and nature of airport development remain commercial decisions for the relevant airport operator. In May 2006 BAA published its capital investment plans, indicating that it was planning to build a second runway at Stansted that was not likely to be operational until 2015–16 (with the earliest possible opening in late 2013). The plans assumed an actual annual forecast growth rate of 3 percent to 2015–16, compared with a potential 4 percent rise for unconstrained demand (the difference being 19 million "lost" passengers) because of growth restrictions caused by capacity constraints and the planning process.[7]

Airport Ownership

The most significant change in the pattern of airport ownership resulted from the 1986 Airports Act, which incorporated the government's policy objectives outlined in the 1985 white paper. That paper called for the commercialization and privatization of the nation's airport system, by encouraging "enterprise and efficiency in the operation of major airports by providing for the introduction of private capital." It also stated that "air transport facilities should not in general be subsidized by the taxpayer or the ratepayer. Airports, whoever their owners, should normally operate as commercial undertakings."[8]

In 1986 nearly all the U.K. commercial airports were controlled by local governments or the British Airports Authority. The exceptions were Southampton airport, which was privately run, and a collection of eight small airports in the Scottish Islands and Highlands that remained under central government ownership to preserve essential social links. The first part of the 1986 act provided for the British Airports Authority to become a private company, BAA, through a 100 percent share flotation in 1997. This very much reflected the overall aim of the conservative Thatcher government to privatize nationalized industries. The seven airports within the BAA group were set up as limited companies that were subsidiaries of BAA plc. The U.K. government retained a special preference, or "golden," share that gave it the right of veto over undesirable takeovers deemed to be against national interest; the government also capped the amount of shares that any one shareholder could hold at 15 percent. However, the European Court of Justice declared this type of shareholding to be illegal in 2003 because it prevented capital movements within the EU. This ruling was quite significant because it meant that BAA could be bought outright. That happened in 2006, when BAA was bought by a consortium led by Ferrovial, the Spanish construction, infrastructure, and services group.

The second part of the 1986 law required all other airports with a turnover of more than £1 million in two of the previous three years to be corporatized. At the time sixteen airports were affected, ranging from Manchester airport, which had 9 million passengers a year, to Southend airport on England's east

---

7. BAA (2006b).
8. Department of Transport (1985, paragraphs 3.1, 3.2).

coast, handling just over 100,000 passengers. The shareholders at these airport companies were initially the local government owners, but the shares could then be sold off, partially or totally, to private investors if desired by the public sector owners. Again this was the ultimate aim of the proprivatization conservative government.

While BAA was transferred to private ownership after the Airports Act of 1986, the U.K. airports that were required to corporatize remained under public sector ownership—at least for a few years. By the early 1990s, however, the regional airports were finding it increasingly difficult to borrow funds because of restrictive borrowing limits on the public sector. Then in 1993 the government announced that there would be no further public sector spending allocation for airports. In effect this meant that any airport that wished to invest in capital improvements had no real option but to privatize its operations, and various airport privatizations occurred (table 5-2). In 1999 legislative changes freed the larger profitable airports, which were still in local government hands, from public sector restrictions and allowed them to borrow money from the commercial markets. But the trend toward privatization has continued, with only Manchester airport remaining in total public ownership.

Most of the privatizations have involved a trade sale to a strategic partner or consortium. The exception is Luton, where a thirty-year concession to run the airport was granted in 1998, because the local authority did not want to relinquish total control of this publicly owned asset to private hands. Other airports, including Birmingham and Newcastle, have only been partially privatized so that some local public influence is retained. Most of the regional airports are now owned by airport companies that have interests in more than one airport, such as the private companies BAA, TBI (acquired by the ACDL—Airport Concessions and Development Ltd.—consortium led by Abertis in 2005), Peel Airports, Macquarie Airports, and the publicly owned Manchester airport. The latest major development regarding airport ownership has been the £10 billion acquisition of BAA by the Airport Development and Investment Limited (ADI) consortium led by Ferrovial. This acquisition was completed in 2006 following a fierce takeover battle against a rival consortium led by Goldman Sachs, the U.S. investment bank. London City airport was also sold in 2006 to a consortium of financial investors, and in 2007 Leeds Bradford airport was acquired by the European private equity firm Bridgepoint.

Airport Regulation

Many aspects of aviation regulation, such as traffic regulation and air service agreements, aviation security, and environmental protection, come under the direct control of the U.K. government. However, some others—namely, safety

Table 5-2. *Ownership Patterns at Main Airports in the United Kingdom, 2007*

Airport	Current ownership[a]	Private interest (percent)	Privatization date
Aberdeen	ADI (BAA)	100	1987
Belfast City	Ferrovial	100	n.a.
Belfast International	ACDL (TBI)	100	1994
Birmingham	Local authorities, employees, Ontario Teachers' Pension Plan, Victorian Funds Management Corporation	51	1997
Bristol	Macquarie Airports	100	1997
Cardiff	ACDL (TBI)	100	1995
Edinburgh	ADI (BAA)	100	1987
Glasgow	ADI (BAA)	100	1987
Leeds Bradford	Bridgepoint	100	2007
Liverpool	Peel Holdings	100	1990
London City	AIG/GE/Credit Suisse	100	n.a.
London Gatwick	ADI (BAA)	100	1987
London Heathrow	ADI (BAA)	100	1987
London Luton[b]	ACDL (TBI)	100	1998
London Stansted	ADI (BAA)	100	1987
Manchester	Local authorities	0	n.a.
Newcastle	Copenhagen airport	49	2001
Nottingham East Midlands	Manchester airport	0	1993
Prestwick	Infratil Ltd.	100	1987
Southampton	ADI (BAA)	100	1961

Source: Compiled by author from various sources for all airports in the United Kingdom with more than one million passengers in 2005.
n.a. = Not applicable.
a. The table shows the most recent owner, not necessarily the first private sector owner.
b. The private investors have a thirty-year concession contract. Ownership remains with the local authorities.

regulation, economic regulation, airspace policy, and consumer protection—come under the responsibility of the Civil Aviation Authority (CAA), which is the main U.K. regulatory agency for air transport.[9] All airports that exceed the £1 million turnover threshold have to seek permission from the CAA to

9. The 1986 Airports Act gave the CAA the role of airport economic regulator. Economic regulation of the British airports comes under Part IV of the act and, in Northern Ireland, the Airports (Northern Ireland) Order 1994.

levy airport charges, and they have to meet certain conditions in the presentation of their accounts that must be annually submitted to the CAA.

The CAA has four duties as regulator:

—To further the reasonable interests of users of U.K. airports

—To promote the efficient, economic, and profitable operation of those airports

—To encourage timely investment in new airport facilities to satisfy anticipated demand

—To impose the minimum restrictions necessary consistent with the CAA's performance of its duties.[10]

However, the law gives no guidance as to how the CAA should weigh these various statutory duties, particularly if the minimum restrictions imposed by the agency conflict with its other duties. These duties mean that the CAA can investigate and impose remedial conditions on airports if they are found to be unreasonably discriminating between users or to be exploiting their bargaining position or engaging in predatory pricing. Since 1987 the CAA has received eleven major complaints concerning such practices and conducted formal investigations. In four instances the CAA concluded that the airport had not been discriminatory or exploited its position; in other cases, however, the CAA required the airport to remedy a certain situation by permitting greater competition, for example, or by putting certain services up for tender.[11]

The secretary of state for transport also designates airports for price regulation, and since 1986 four airports—London Heathrow, London Gatwick, London Stansted, and Manchester—have been so designated. No statutory criteria for such designation were laid down by the Airports Act, although the general reasons for designating airports were detailed in the Airports Policy white paper:

> It will be necessary to ensure not only that overall charges are not excessive, but that charges are cost-related and that smaller operations are not priced out of congested airports contrary to the Government's civil aviation policy. Safeguards will also be necessary against distortion of the air travel market through predatory pricing by an airport authority—i.e. abuse of an airport authority's monopoly power in order to attract traffic from elsewhere regardless of the cost. However effective control of prices also requires some safeguard against lax cost control and inefficiency.[12]

10. Airports Act (1986, Paragraph 39.2).
11. CAA (2006c).
12. Department of Transport (1985, paragraph 10.9).

Consequently the government identified four criteria for designation when it reviewed the airport regulatory regime in 1995.[13] These were the market position (including the extent of competition from other airports and other modes of transport); evidence of excessive profitability or abuse of monopoly position; the scale and timing of investment and implications for profitability; and the efficiency and quality of service. No criteria were defined for the de-designation of airports.

The designated airports are subject to a price cap known as *RPI +/– X* with *RPI* being the retail price index and *X* the percentage increase or decrease in revenues in real terms. The price caps are applied to aeronautical-revenue-per-passenger figures and the aeronautical revenue obtained from landing charges, passenger charges, and aircraft parking charges. The formula also contains a security component that allows airports to pass through and exclude from price regulation additional security costs that are largely beyond the airport's control. Total revenue subject to price regulation is calculated by defining a regulated asset base (RAB), valuing it at the beginning of the price control period, and then subsequently enlarging the base to take account of projected capital expenditure. A cost of capital allowance and depreciation allowance based on this RAB is then added to the projected level of operating expenditure (which will have taken account of any feasible improvements in efficiency) to arrive at the total revenue requirement. The RAB valuation and the cost-of-capital assumptions are therefore key in determining the maximum level of prices that are allowed.

This price cap is set every five years; table 5-3 shows the *X* values since 1987. Most of the time the *X* factor has been negative, resulting in lower real prices. The high positive *X* factor at Heathrow of 6.5 percent (enabling a real price increase) for the fourth quinquennium (Q4), between 2003 and 2008, primarily reflected the large future investment needs at this airport, particularly for Terminal 5. In Q4 a service-quality condition was included for the first time that makes rebates available to users if certain service-quality standards are not achieved. Since then, in most cases, the standards have been achieved, with the main exceptions of pier service in Heathrow Terminal 4 and Gatwick North Terminal and in security queuing. In general BAA's performance improved with the introduction of these incentives in 2003. Recently, however, there has been growing and unprecedented criticism from airlines and passengers about the quality of BAA's service (largely related to major security and weather events in 2006). In response, the CAA has proposed that the service-quality incentives should cover more specific areas and that the scale

---

13. Department of Transport (1995).

Table 5-3. *The X Value Used for U.K. Airport Price Caps*
Percent

Airport			X value			
London area	1987–91	1992–93	1994	1995–96	1997–2002	2003–08
Heathrow	−1	−8	−4	−1	−3	+6.5
Gatwick	−1	−8	−4	−1	−3	0
Stansted	−1	−8	−4	−1	+1	0
Manchester	1988–92	1993–94	1995	1996–97	1998–2002	2003–09
	−1	−3	−3	−3	−5	−5

Source: CAA.

of rebates should be more substantial.[14] Another new feature in 2003 was the designation of six "trigger" points (five at Heathrow; one at Gatwick) related to failure to achieve particular capital milestones on time; under these trigger points, which had not been applied as of this writing, BAA can be subject to penalties through the price-cap formula.

The airport charges are calculated using a single-till approach, whereby nonaeronautical or commercial revenue is included alongside aeronautical revenues, as opposed to the dual till, which treats the aeronautical and non-aeronautical areas as separate financial entities. Hence under this single-till approach, the RAB includes all airport assets regardless of their function. The current regulatory policy uses a "stand-alone" approach, which means that the charges for each airport are regulated individually on the basis of its individual costs, revenues, and market conditions, and the costs at each airport must be entirely covered by the airport's own revenues. In 2003 this approach replaced the "system funding" approach, which had allowed for cross-subsidization between the London airports in the system when investment was being considered.

Before setting the price caps, the CAA carefully reviews the designated airports and then makes an automatic reference to the Competition Commission, which is the general trading regulator in the United Kingdom. The Competition Commission consequently undertakes an extensive assessment of the airport's operations, financial performance, and future plans and also decides whether the airport operator has been acting against the public interest in relation to its charges, the operational activities it provides, and the way it grants rights for activities to be undertaken at the airport. The commission then makes recommendations to the CAA concerning the most appropriate

14. CAA (2007a).

level of price control. The CAA is not obliged to follow these recommendations, although it must provide a valid justification if it does not. The CAA also has to impose new conditions if the commission finds that the airport has been acting against the public interest. This regulatory system is thus different from other regulated industries in the United Kingdom, where the Competition Commission becomes involved only if it receives specific references from the other regulators. This means that the other regulated industries have an appeals process (the Competition Commission) that is not available under the airport regulatory system; under that system, the only appeal available is through a judicial review on technical grounds.

Air Traffic Control

Although a detailed consideration of U.K. air traffic control operations is beyond the scope of this chapter, it is important to note that the government has sought to privatize this part of the aviation industry as well. The main air navigation service provider in the United Kingdom is NATS (formerly National Air Traffic Services Ltd.). It became part of the CAA in 1972, and by 1992 privatization had been discussed (although it did not happen then). In 1996 NATS was reorganized as a wholly owned subsidiary of the CAA in order to separate the CAA's roles as the provider and regulator of air traffic control. In 2001 NATS became a partially private company when 51 percent of its ownership was transferred to the private sector. Currently 42 percent belongs to the major U.K. airlines, 4 percent to BAA, and 5 percent to NATS employees.

NATS is the sole provider of en route air traffic control, operating under license from the CAA. This part of the business is also price regulated by the CAA, because it is a monopoly, in a way similar to the airport industry. In addition NATS has been chosen by fifteen major airport operators, including all the London airports, to provide local air traffic control at the actual airports, but this activity is not price regulated. At other U.K. airports, air traffic control services are provided directly by the airport operator or other privately owned service companies. Thus the influence of the public sector on air traffic control operations, as with airport operations, has become far less significant in recent years.

Key Policy Issues

This paper now addresses some key policy issues, related to both the planning and regulatory system, which are considered likely to have major implications for the future growth and development of the U.K. airport industry.

The Planning Process

One of the dominant issues that has preoccupied many of those involved with the U.K. airport industry over the years is the provision of adequate airport capacity for London and southeast England. Demand has exceeded supply for many years, particularly at Heathrow, which is clearly demonstrated by the congestion patterns and the large amounts of money that airlines are prepared to pay for runway slots in the secondary, "gray" slot market. BA provided a recent example, paying £7 million to Malev and £13 million to United, each time for two pairs of slots at Heathrow airport.[15]

In the United Kingdom, it is the airport operators that decide whether particular projects are economically viable and whether they should be built. For any proposed infrastructure development, planning approval must be sought from the local government. However, if the project is large or controversial and considered to have implications of more than local significance (which is very often the case with airports), the planning application may be "called in" by the secretary of state, who orders a public planning inquiry. Thus this planning system is a way in which both national and local government can influence airport development. At the end of this inquiry, the secretary of state considers the inquiry inspector's report and decides whether and on what terms the planning approval should be given. Approval under this planning process creates an entitlement for the developer to build but does not impose an obligation or requirement to do so.

One of the key issues related to the planning process is the length of time and huge expense involved for all parties when a public inquiry is held. The Terminal 5 inquiry at Heathrow airport was exceptionally lengthy, becoming the longest public inquiry ever held in the United Kingdom. BAA submitted its planning application in February 1993 and the secretary of state called in the application in July. The public inquiry began in May 1995 and was completed in March 1999, with the inspector's report being submitted to the government in December 2000. Costs of the planning process were estimated at £80 million. Just the public inquiry took 524 days and involved 724 witnesses, 5,900 documents, 27,500 written representations, and around 100 site visits.[16] This lengthy procedure leads to much uncertainty; it also may have detrimental effects on regional and national economies and be uncompetitive compared with other airport developments in Europe.

15. K. Done, "UAL Drops London to New York Flights," *Financial Times*, July 28, 2006.
16. Heathrow T5 Inquiry Secretariat (1999).

In 2001 the government proposed a package of measures for streamlining and speeding up the planning procedure for major infrastructure projects.[17] This proposal included the requirement to have up-to-date statements of government policy before the projects are considered in the planning process, to help reduce the time spent on debating the policy and to help concentrate on the detailed local issues related to the proposed development. It also proposed that Parliament be given the opportunity to debate and approve a project in principle before the detailed public inquiry; this proposal too was designed to reduce the amount of time spent addressing the "need" for the project. It was argued that such a procedure would not reduce the public involvement in the planning process because the parliamentary stage would follow the development of the national policy statement that would normally require public consultation. In addition people would have the right to make their views known before the Parliament debate, and there would still be the public inquiry where public views could be expressed.

However, the proposal raised strong opposition, primarily on the grounds that Parliament was not designed for this purpose, that public opinion would still be weakened in such a process, and that environmental concerns might be ignored in order to push through nationally important projects. In the end the proposal was dropped, but the package contained other measures to streamline the actual inquiry procedures. Introduced in 2002 (and amended in 2005), these measures aim to enforce a more rigid timetable and encourage parties to agree on common ground so that a greater focus can be placed on areas of disagreement. Concurrent sessions with different inquiry inspectors reporting to a lead inspector are now also allowed for the first time.[18]

In a recent development, a newly published white paper entitled "Planning for a Sustainable Future" makes suggestions for substantial changes to the planning process.[19] For major infrastructure projects, such as airports, the government is proposing to streamline certain procedures and to have an independent planning commission that will make decisions within the framework of already established national policy statements produced by the government after public consultation. This approach would produce a much clearer separation between policy and decisionmaking and would lead to a more timely and efficient planning process. At the current time, these are just proposals, but concerns have already been voiced that such

---

17. Department of Transport, Local Government and the Regions (2001).
18. Office of the Deputy Prime Minister (2005).
19. Department of Communities and Local Government (2007).

changes will reduce public accountability and limit local involvement in decisionmaking.

Airport Efficiency and Price-Cap Regulation

Turning now to regulation, clearly a very important issue to consider is the extent to which the U.K. airport industry is operating in an economically efficient manner, particularly given the statutory role of the CAA "to promote the efficient, economic and profitable operations" of airports.

Consider productive efficiency first. In theory the incentive properties of the *RPI +/– X* mechanism should mean that the price-regulated airports can benefit from any unforeseen reductions in costs during the price-control period, until the control is reset after the end of the period. A review of unit operating costs since 1990 shows that in real terms these costs fell quite considerably between 1990 and 2000 for Heathrow, Gatwick, and Manchester (table 5-4). At Stansted costs went up after the new terminal was opened in 1991 but have subsequently fallen quite substantially, in part because of the dramatic increase in passenger numbers over this period. BAA argues that the increase in costs in the most recent years at Heathrow and Gatwick results primarily from additional security measures that could not have been avoided.[20] More focused independent research related specifically to efficiency is somewhat limited and rather inconclusive. For example, Parker used data envelopment analysis (DEA) to calculate the overall productive efficiency of BAA airports and found no significant efficiency gains since privatization and price regulation, while Yokomi employed DEA and the Malmquist index and found consistent efficiency improvements after privatization.[21]

Table 5-4 shows that BAA and other airports that are not price regulated have also benefited from reductions in unit costs. These decreases are likely to have been driven mainly by relatively high growth patterns, economies of scale from larger operations, airport privatization trends, and the development of the more competitive and cost-conscious aviation environment. Their labor productivity has also improved at a faster rate than that of the regulated airports (figure 5-1). Moreover, overall operational profitability (as measured by the operating margin) at the non-price-regulated airports has also increased significantly since 1990 and is now fairly comparable to the price-regulated airports. Overall these measures of performance indicate a relatively healthy financial situation for U.K. airports, although clearly they present only a very general and aggregate picture. Note, too, that Stansted

20. BAA (2006c).
21. Parker (1999); Yokomi (2005).

Table 5-4. *Financial Performance of U.K. Airports for Selected Fiscal Years*
In pounds

Airport	1989–90	1994–95	1999–2000	2004–05	2005–06
Operating costs per WLU[a]					
Gatwick	13.12	10.37	7.08	7.43	7.98
Heathrow	13.83	8.72	7.77	8.82	9.59
Stansted	12.68	18.02	7.28	5.18	5.24
BAA London	13.21	12.37	7.38	7.14	7.60
Other BAA[b]	13.84	9.98	9.06	6.60	6.54
Manchester	18.07	13.58	12.51	8.94	7.52
Other U.K.[c]	18.50	14.68	9.77	7.19	6.87
Regulated[d]	14.42	12.67	8.66	7.59	7.58
Unregulated	17.42	13.20	9.55	7.01	6.77
Operating margin (percent)					
Gatwick	30.4	24.9	35.3	29.1	22.3
Heathrow	37.7	40.4	38.9	36.7	34.7
Stansted	–42.0	–32.3	22.1	27.4	26.1
BAA London	8.7	11.0	32.1	31.1	27.7
Other BAA[b]	27.0	28.2	31.0	35.4	36.0
Manchester	31.3	21.5	19.5	29.4	24.7
Other U.K.[c]	5.4	5.7	24.3	27.7	31.4
Regulated[d]	14.4	13.6	29.0	30.6	27.0
Unregulated	10.4	12.2	26.2	29.9	32.7

Source: Centre for the Regulated Industries.

a. WLU = One passenger or 100 kilograms freight; in real 2005 terms.

b. Excludes Southampton for 1989–90.

c. All airports with more than one million annual passengers in 2005 except Belfast City and Prestwick, where data were not available.

d. Gatwick, Heathrow, Stansted, and Manchester.

airport did not move into a profit-making situation until the late 1990s (a profit was first actually recorded in 1997–98).

Another efficiency issue to consider is whether regulation has improved the allocative efficiency of the airports by making better use of scarce resources. This question needs to be related to the single-till approach used at the designated U.K. airports. The various merits of the single- and dual-till approaches were debated for years, and a major examination was undertaken during the review for the setting of the 2003–08, or Q4, price cap. Some key players, such as the CAA and BAA, favored a move to the dual till. In essence the key rationale for the dual till is that regulators should intervene only where there is evidence of considerable market dominance and thus should regulate only

Figure 5-1. *WLUs per Employee at U.K. Airports*[a]

Thousands

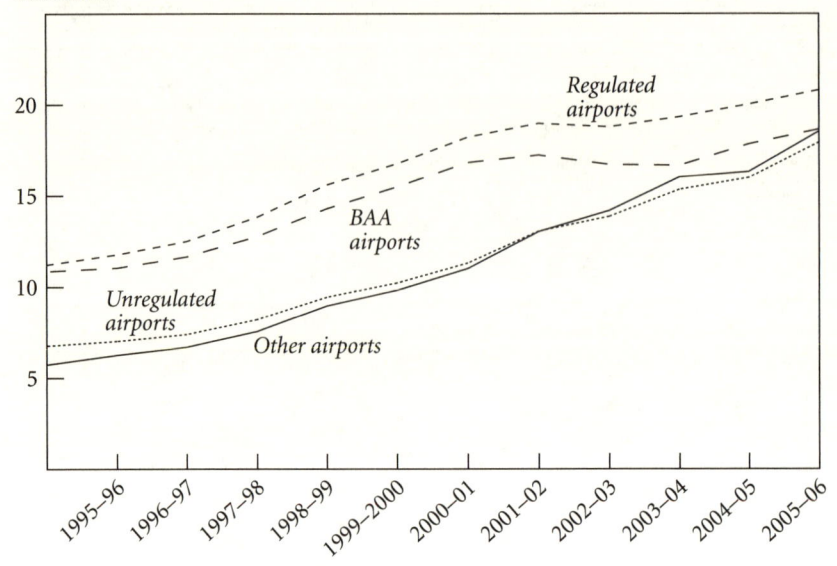

[Line chart showing WLUs per employee from 1995–96 to 2005–06 for Regulated airports, BAA airports, Unregulated airports, and Other airports]

Source: Centre for the Regulated Industries.
a. One WLU equals one passenger or 100 kilograms of freight.

revenues generated by the aeronautical activities at airports and not those generated from commercial activities. Conversely, the logical argument for the single till is that without the aeronautical activities, there would be no market for the commercial operations and hence it is appropriate to offset the level of airport charges with profits earned from nonaeronautical facilities.[22]

From the perspective of allocative efficiency, an important aspect of this debate for congested airports is the problem associated with the economically inefficient prices that the single till produces. These prices do not reflect the economic value of using the airports (nor the environmental impacts), and so they do not encourage efficient resource allocation and may potentially distort related investment decisions. This is a particular issue at Heathrow, where commercial success and a negative price cap over the years have meant that the relative level of charges has come down as the level of congestion and delays have gone up. Indeed despite the high congestion levels at Heathrow, the airport at its cheapest time in 2002 (before being allowed a 6.5 percent real

---

22. The detailed arguments for each approach have been well documented; for examples, see CAA (2000b).

increase in 2003) ranked thirty-fifth out of fifty major international airports in the Transport Research Laboratory's global study of airport charges. It moved up slightly to twenty-seventh position by 2005 but was still ranked very favorably compared with Paris (seventh), Frankfurt (ninth), and Amsterdam (twelfth).[23] Another argument in favor of the dual till is that it can provide better incentives for aeronautical investment. This is mainly because in addition to earning the allowed rate of return on the cost of aeronautical investment, the airport can also benefit from increased unregulated commercial revenues that will have been generated because of the additional passenger volumes from the aeronautical investment.

During the Q4 BAA review, the CAA in its recommendation to the Competition Commission argued that the dual till should be used to promote a better use of capacity as well as providing better incentives for investment, which in turn would limit the scope of regulation to instances where monopoly power existed.[24] However, the Competition Commission responded by stating that it had found no evidence of underinvestment and that it did not agree that the dual till would bring better aeronautical investment—indeed it might be worse, the commission said, with commercial investment being favored over aeronautical investment. Moreover the commission contended that improvements in utilization would probably be only marginal because of the already significant excess demand at Heathrow. Moreover, separating aeronautical from commercial activities was difficult, particularly when one looks at capital expenditure, space, and management overheads, the commission said, and the benefits from commercial revenues should be shared by the airlines that bring the passengers.[25] In the end, the CAA, in the face of strong opposition to the dual till from the airlines as well as from the Competition Commission, decided to retain the single till.[26] The CAA itself has also indicated that it will not reopen the debate during the current review process for the 2008–13, or Q5, period. Hence a major weakness of the regulatory process, namely, the single-till approach and the perverse pricing signals that it produces, still remains, primarily because of strong opposition from the airlines for any change.

No discussion of current capacity allocation would be complete without mentioning the slot allocation system. The current "grandfather" system set by EU rules clearly prevents the best use of scarce slot capacity and does not allocate the capacity to the airlines that would value it the most. Hence this rule further exacerbates the problem of inefficient resource utilization. Other

23. TRL (2006).
24. CAA (2002).
25. Competition Commission (2002).
26. CAA (2003).

allocation mechanisms, particularly secondary slot trading, could potentially encourage a more efficient use of scarce capacity. The theoretical arguments related to this have been well documented, and so any further discussion related to this issue was considered beyond the scope of this chapter.[27]

Investment Incentives

Another important issue regarding the U.K. airport industry is whether investment at the airports has been appropriate and timely. To some extent, this issue is linked to the planning system, but the regulator's role must also be considered here, particularly in view of the CAA's statutory duty "to encourage investment in new facilities at airports in time to satisfy anticipated demands by the users of such airports."

One of the criticisms of the *RPI +/– X* regulatory mechanism is that it tends to focus on short-term operational efficiencies and hence gives inadequate incentives to invest. Another problem is the lumpiness and long lead time of investments and the relatively short, five-year span for each price-control period. That means consideration of a price increase related to investment might be put off to a future regulatory review, thus introducing uncertainty about whether the increase will be allowed and perhaps negatively affecting incentives to invest. Moreover, users could face a huge rise in prices. Lengthening the period of price controls could be one solution, or there could be some form of price profiling or revenue advancement as was used for Heathrow Terminal 5 in 2003–08. This prefunding, however, was not popular with all the users and continues to be a subject of much debate for the Q5 review.

At the same time, it could also be argued that the increasing emphasis that is placed on calculating the RAB and the cost of capital during the regulatory process for the designated airports means that in practice the regulation is converging toward rate-of-return regulation. This type of regulation can encourage higher-than-necessary levels of investment in capacity, or costly gold-plated investment, to increase the value of the RAB. To overcome these problems, the regulator ideally needs to scrutinize any proposed capacity expenditure program in great detail. To date, however, the CAA has tended to accept the capital expenditure information provided by the airports without detailed examination (although, as discussed later, a somewhat different approach is now being tested).

The expansion of Stansted airport is inevitably a key issue whenever airport investment in London is being considered. It could be argued that the invest-

---

27. For a review of the theoretical arguments on slot allocation mechanisms, see, for example, NERA (2004).

ment incentives for BAA were adequate in that a major new terminal was built in the late 1980s and early 1990s (opening in 1991) even though there was no overwhelming evidence of strong demand specifically for this airport. This expansion took place when the "system funding" regulatory approach was used, meaning that the cumulative asset base of all three regulated London airports was used to calculate the allowed rate of return. Then it was up to BAA to decide how it would recoup the return through charges at the individual London airports (even though the airports were subject to separate price caps). This system approach meant that revenues from charging Heathrow and Gatwick users were set high enough to ensure that the development at Stansted was remunerated at the allowed rate of return even though the expansion by itself was not economically viable and was not driven by market forces.

As a result, average charges at Stansted airport have remained low, affecting neighboring airports, particularly Luton, which in the early 1990s saw the transfer of much of its Ryanair traffic to Stansted. Luton airport complained to the CAA in 1993, and although the CAA agreed that the pricing levels were harmful, it concluded that the problem was caused by the excess capacity that existed at Stansted, which made the low prices unavoidable.[28] As table 5-4 shows, Stansted airport continued to make an operating loss for many years and in fact is not expected to earn a return above its cost of capital until 2008. Stansted has never charged up to its price cap and, for example, its average charges per person (net of discounts) in 2004–05 were just £2.61, compared with £4.42 at Gatwick and £7.05 at Heathrow.[29] Thus it appears that the regulatory system has encouraged inappropriate and too early investment rather than simply ensuring adequate incentives to invest. The steep rise in unit costs at Stansted airport after the new terminal was built, in contrast to the continually declining unit costs at Manchester airport (see table 5-4) despite the addition of a second runway and new terminal, also adds weight to the argument that the investment at Stansted was excessive.

The stand-alone approach to regulation introduced for the Q4 period has changed the risk profile of the airports. The arguments for system versus stand-alone regulation were fiercely debated. The CAA argued that stand-alone regulation gives the correct incentives for the individual airports to invest where demand is strongest and new capacity is needed and when the expansion will be commercially viable. Thus price caps based on a stand-alone approach will prevent any cross-subsidized investment that is premature or gold plated and will be more suited to the unique demand and capacity

28. Starkie (2004).
29. CAA (2005).

conditions at the airports. Any interdependence of demand at the London airports is irrelevant here as the demand should be strong enough in its own right to pay for new investment. Furthermore, the CAA argued, such an approach is likely to avoid any unfair competitive advantage that system funding could give to BAA airports over non-BAA-owned airports, particularly in the case of Stansted over Luton, and generally put the BAA airports on a more equal playing field with other airports.[30] Most airlines at Heathrow and Gatwick supported the CAA views, primarily for fear that with a system approach they would be subsidizing development at other airports.

In contrast, supporters of the system approach, such as BAA, argued that the growth of Stansted could benefit users in the airport system because demand at the London airports was interdependent and an expansion at one London airport would relieve demand pressures at others, particularly Heathrow. The Competition Commission favored the system funding approach because it also saw the airports, to a certain extent, serving the same market and thought it would be inappropriate to have higher prices at Stansted, which had the most spare capacity. Moreover, the commission contended that a stand-alone approach could result in BAA's return for all airports falling short of the overall cost of capital, a situation that could jeopardize BAA's ability to finance future investment.[31] However, in the end the CAA was not convinced by the Competition Commission's arguments and opted for stand-alone pricing for Q4 on the grounds that it would improve the transparency of regulation, would provide a more level playing field with nondesignated airports, and would remove a potential distortion whereby investment takes place at Stansted even though users do not value the investment sufficiently to pay for its costs. The CAA did state that it was prepared to review this decision in the future if there were compelling evidence that it should do so.[32]

The CAA decision was made before the publication of the 2003 white paper that favored the development of a new runway at Stansted. There has subsequently been considerable debate as to whether the airport could generate a sufficient return on this expansion of runway capacity with the stand-alone approach. The white paper argued that the expansion at Stansted would promote the growth of air travel, ensure wider economic benefits, and minimize environmental damage, even though there has been no discussion as to how environmentally acceptable an airport might be if potentially it cannot even cover its own investment costs.

30. CAA (2002).
31. Competition Commission (2002).
32. CAA (2003).

In response to the consultation for the white paper, BAA argued that airport charges at Stansted would have to go up by around 120 percent to £5.10 per person in 2003–04 prices if a new runway were built and stand-alone regulation were retained, compared with an increase of £1.50, or 35 percent, if system regulation were reintroduced.[33] To support system pricing, BAA argued that there were public interest benefits related to the provision of capacity in the southeast, namely, in the relief of congestion and in increasing competition. In essence BAA argued that Stansted would relieve congestion elsewhere in the system by charging lower prices that would attract airlines that otherwise would have used the other airports. Moreover even if the pricing differentials did not actually shift traffic between airports, BAA said, low charges and spare capacity at Stansted would increase competition in air services overall by lowering air fares at other airports. However, others were not persuaded by these arguments, noting, for example, that there had been lower fares and spare capacity at Stansted for some time and many airlines at Heathrow had shown no inclination to transfer to Stansted.[34] Switching from Gatwick to Stansted was more likely, but the impact would be less favorable since the congestion levels at Gatwick were currently not that acute. Others noted that greater fare competition at competing airports was no longer such a relevant issue because of the well-established, competitive LCC sector, and that further cross-subsidy of airport expansion at Stansted could have a detrimental effect on competition and the investment plans of nearby airports at Luton, Norwich, and the Midlands.

During its current review for Q5, the CAA has once more confirmed its support for stand-alone pricing and has disputed BAA's arguments that a system approach that allows more flexibility in funding arrangements would produce user benefits throughout the southeast in terms of competition, choice, and lower airfares; BAA sees the system approach as being more consistent with the CAA's statutory duties of furthering the interests of users and encouraging timely investment.[35] Given the identified weaknesses in BAA's arguments, this stand-alone approach is clearly a better option to follow.

However, the low-cost carriers at Stansted believe that they should not bear the full costs of adding extra airport capacity in the southeast, and hence they too are in favor of a system approach. Moreover, there is considerable disagreement regarding the size, nature, timing, and costs of any second runway, arguments that circle back to the gold-plating investment issue related to the regulatory regime. The scale of investment required to add a second runway

33. Department for Transport (2003a).
34. Starkie (2004).
35. CAA (2006a, 2006b); BAA (2006c).

at Stansted is very large compared with the current RAB and can potentially have a major impact on investment incentives for BAA. For this reason the airlines are claiming the proposed investment (for the new runway) is far too costly—four times the cost of one of their own proposals.[36]

Finally, these funding issues need to be considered within the context of the recent takeover of BAA by the Ferrovial consortium. The takeover has resulted in a significant increase in the indebtedness of the company, which could potentially put pressure on the company to raise prices or to defer investment. However, to date the company has not announced any major changes, and it has stated that it will be putting in a planning application for a second runway at Stansted as planned in 2007 after reviewing the current plans and costs.[37]

The Regulatory Review Process: Roles of the Airport Operator and Its Users

To use the *RPI +/– X* price control effectively to provide an incentive for efficiency, the CAA needs to have realistic values of projected operating and investment costs as well as traffic forecasts and knowledge of the scope for future efficiency savings. The past reviews have shown that obtaining this information can be very time-consuming and costly. For example, the last review of BAA took thirty-two months, BAA alone submitted almost 800 papers, and the review cost the CAA and Competition Commission £3.2 million.[38] BAA has estimated that the level of paperwork involved in this process has increased by roughly 50 percent at each quinquennium.[39] Moreover it can be argued that a more effective way forward is for the airlines and airports to work together commercially as they would in normal markets and agree as much as possible between themselves. This could replace the more defensive approach that emerges through the formal regulation process and could reduce the need for the CAA to undertake its own detailed and costly analysis. A lighter regulatory approach would entail less regulatory risk as the airports and the airlines should be better placed than the regulator to understand user needs. In fact in 2001 the Government's Better Regulation Task Force recommended that the government consider lifting price controls on BAA airports entirely to encourage direct negotiation with airlines; under that approach, the government would retain reserve, or "shadow," regulatory powers. Such an approach has

36. OFT (2006c).
37. BAA (2006a).
38. CAA (2004).
39. Nelson (2006).

been adopted in some other countries such as Australia, but was unpopular with the airlines in the United Kingdom and was not implemented.

Instead in the Q5 BAA review, the CAA has introduced "constructive engagement," whereby it has encouraged the airports and airlines at an early stage to discuss, and if possible agree on, generally less controversial matters such as traffic projections, capacity requirements and investment, nonregulated aeronautical revenues, and service quality. The area of capital investment is particularly important because of the problems associated with price-cap regulation and determining appropriate levels of investment. Constructive engagement is not, however, without its problems. In particular, the views of LCCs may differ from the full-service carriers in terms of their requirements for facilities and service standards. For this very reason when the CAA made its initial proposals in December 2006, BAA and the airlines at Heathrow and Gatwick had made generally good progress, but constructive engagement had not worked at Stansted.[40] Moreover airports tend to be much more concerned with longer-term planning horizons than airlines, and they are usually in a more favorable position than airlines to offer adequate resources and expertise to develop detailed capital expenditure programs.[41] Nevertheless, these shortcomings with this new process are outweighed by the potential benefits of getting more informed outcomes and in reducing the role of the regulators.

Roles of the Regulators

The other key issue related to the regulatory review process is the role of the two regulators, namely, the CAA and the Competition Commission. The initial reasoning for this unique regulatory situation was that the CAA had the detailed knowledge of the aviation industry while the Competition Commission had regulatory expertise on technical issues such as the cost of capital. So it was thought that their roles would be complementary. However, in practice the distinct role and responsibilities of the two regulators have been less than clear, leading to an ever longer review process and a considerable amount of uncertainty. As a result more and more issues are being considered in greater detail by both organizations, which sometimes leads to disagreement and conflict, particularly as the two have different statutory objectives. The differences in opinions about the single- versus dual-till and stand-alone pricing for the BAA Q4 review have already been discussed, but there are numerous

40. CAA (2006a).
41. Starkie (2005).

other examples of divergences of views, particularly regarding assumptions about the cost of capital.[42]

The review process has also become progressively longer, largely as the result of having these two regulators. The BAA Q2 review took fourteen months, the Q3 review took twenty-one months, and the Q4 review, as already noted, took thirty-two months. This later review involved the CAA's consulting interested parties and making suggestions to the Competition Commission between July 2000 and February 2002. The Competition Commission review and recommendations to the CAA took place between February and October, and then after another period of consultation the CAA confirmed the final price determination at the end of February 2003. This drawn-out process contrasts to that experienced by the U.K. utilities, which deal with a specific industry regulator that determines the price; the Competition Commission is involved only if an appeal is made concerning the regulator's decision. In 1998 the government proposed that airport regulation should be brought into line with this more coherent and transparent U.K. utility model.[43] However, that proposal was never acted upon, and what appears to have been an ideal opportunity to improve the regulatory process was lost.

Changes to the Airport Ownership and Regulatory System

The discussion so far has concentrated on identifying some of the drawbacks of the current planning and regulatory system related to the U.K. airport industry. This section discusses more fundamental changes that could possibly be made to the industry in the future.

Designation of Airports

Since the initial designation of the four U.K. airports in 1987, two subsequent separate attempts have been made to extend the list of airports subject to price-cap regulation. The first attempt, in 1994, involved the BAA Scottish airports, which had been somewhat surprised that they had not been designated initially given that they enjoyed regional dominance similar to that of BAA's London airports. BAA forestalled the move in 1994 by suggesting a voluntary package of price cuts and other measures. Then in 2000 easyJet called for Luton airport to be designated for price caps. The CAA investigated this case and considered the four key criteria (market position, excessive profitability, investment situation, and efficiency/service). The CAA argued against desig-

42. Toms (2003).
43. Department for Trade and Industry (1998).

nation, primarily on the grounds that the airport suffered from direct competition from Stansted and was not very profitable.[44] The government accepted this argument. While it could still be possible to designate additional airports, de-designation seems more appropriate in today's competitive aviation environment. De-designation would reduce the regulatory burden and increase reliance on market forces, and it would not require any primary legislation but merely a decision by the secretary of state. The most suitable airports for de-designation would be Manchester and Stansted.

One might ask whether price-cap regulation is even suitable for the publicly owned Manchester airport. The airport is less likely to engage in monopolistic behavior because it is under less pressure than a private company to pay dividends and because it has broad public sector objectives, such as job creation and regional economic development. Moreover, even though its market share has remained constant at about 10 percent, Manchester airport is now facing much more effective competition from other airports than it did when it was initially designated. A number of the airports neighboring Manchester such as Liverpool and Leeds Bradford have increased in relative size, and Manchester also now faces fresh competition from Doncaster Finningley airport, the old military airport. During its Q3 review, Manchester airport asked, unsuccessfully, that it be de-designated, arguing that regulation was burdensome given the more competitive environment the airport was now operating in; it also claimed its charges were set in relation to market conditions and that the price cap had no impact. More than ten years later, Manchester's case for de-designation appears even stronger. Airport competition is even stronger than it was, and Manchester's prices are still set below the cap. Moreover, figure 5-2 shows that charges at Manchester have mirrored very closely the charges at the unregulated airports, indicating the importance of market conditions in pricing.

The case for keeping Stansted a designated airport also seems weak. When it was designated in 1987, it had only half a million passengers and no market power. Even though its traffic has increased rapidly in recent years, it also does not price up to its notional set price cap and has low charges compared with other airports (see figure 5-2). Its market power generally remains weak, particularly because of its reliance on the price-elastic market segments, and it is in a very competitive situation with Luton airport, which has a very similar passenger profile. Furthermore since Stansted is now regulated through a standalone rather than systemwide approach, the actual process of de-designation would be much easier to achieve. However applying the designation criteria to

---

44. CAA (2000a).

Figure 5-2. *Real Aeronautical Revenue per Passenger at U.K. Airports*

2005 pounds

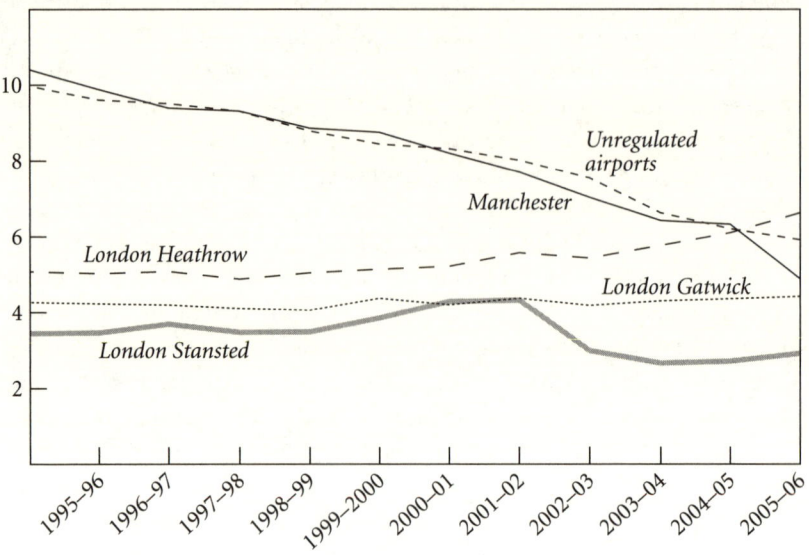

[Chart showing real aeronautical revenue per passenger at U.K. airports from 1995–96 to 2005–06, with lines for Unregulated airports, Manchester, London Heathrow, London Gatwick, and London Stansted]

Source: Centre for the Regulated Industries.

Stansted, and indeed to Manchester, is difficult because the criteria are a mixture of a test (that is, market position) and evidence to support the test (that is, profit, investment, and efficiency/service levels). Since the airports are already price controlled, the test in the case cannot be valid. Instead, some criteria for de-designation are needed to enable designated airports to be removed from price controls. Even in the absence of such criteria, however, the relative weak market power of these airports is a very strong reason for them to be de-designated.

Moreover, the formal designation criteria do not consider the costs and distortions associated with regulation. This omission is particularly relevant to Stansted airport, where the airlines fear that the gold-plating effect caused by price controls is giving the airport operator incentives to invest in a new runway but not necessarily in the most timely, efficient, and cost-effective manner. Hence if Stansted were de-designated, the investment plans could be very different. Both the CAA and the Office of Fair Trading (OFT) recently called for the government to consider the costs as well as the benefits of regulation, and to consider criteria for de-designation, when assessing the whole airport designation issue.[45]

45. CAA (2006a); OFT (2006c).

Consequently in 2007 the government adopted the following new designation criteria after a consultation process:

Designation of an airport is appropriate if, in the view of the Secretary of State:
    1. The airport, either alone or together with any other airport(s) in common ownership or control, has or is likely to have substantial market power; and
    2. Domestic and EC competition law may not be sufficient to address the risk that, absent regulation, the airport would increase and sustain prices profitably above the competitive level or restrict output or quality below the competitive level; and
    3. Designation . . . would, taking account of the magnitude of the risk identified in (2) and its detrimental effects were it to materialise, deliver additional benefits (i.e. over and above competition law) which exceed the costs and potential adverse effects of such designation (i.e. the incremental benefits are positive)

De-designation is appropriate if, in the view of the Secretary of State any of these factors would cease to apply were the airport to be de-designated.[46]

Since 2006 a number of organizations, including the CAA, the OFT, Manchester airport, and the Transport Select Committee, have argued for the de-designation of Stansted, Manchester, or both. The CAA has now advised the government that from its analysis neither Stansted nor Manchester airport now meets the revised criteria for designation.[47] The final government decision has yet to be made and will follow a stakeholder consultation.

Clearly the more extreme case would be to de-designate all four airports, eliminating all price regulation and instead relying on normal competition law. Heathrow clearly has strong market power because of its location, its role as a hub, and its extensive mix of short- and long-haul services; Gatwick enjoys some market power as well. However, it can be argued that airports with market power need not necessarily be expected to abuse this position, hence making regulation unnecessary.[48] Under this reasoning, an operator would have a strong incentive not to raise airport charges because of the detrimental impact a price increase could have on demand and consequently on nonaeronautical revenues. If the BAA airport group remains as it is currently structured, however, it seems unlikely that full deregulation would happen in

46. Department for Transport (2007, pp. 7–8).
47. CAA (2007b).
48. For example, see Starkie (2001).

the near future, given the amount of opposition that would likely be raised, particularly from the airlines.

BAA Common Ownership

A more radical change than merely de-designating some of the current designated airports could be the splitting up of the common ownership of the BAA airports. Such a split would also strengthen the arguments for de-designation or lighter regulation, as market power would be reduced.

At the time of the BAA privatization, the arguments in favor of the retention of a single entity, unsurprisingly supported by BAA management, included the existence of very limited competitive pressures because of product diversity at the airports and the dominance of Heathrow, the small effect of airport charges on airline costs, economies of scale in airport operations, less uncertainty and a higher share price, and less risk of underinvestment with an overall investment strategy.[49] Moreover, it was claimed that group ownership was needed to enforce the government's traffic distribution rules. These rules had originally been set up in 1977 at Heathrow when it was decided to redirect traffic from this congested airport to a nearby airport that had spare capacity. A final argument was that group ownership was needed for the proposed development of Stansted, which was being cross-subsidized at the time by airport charges at Heathrow and Gatwick. These arguments were disputed by those who contended that competition between airports was an essential element in the case for privatization.[50] Moreover, it was claimed that Gatwick and Stansted could compete for charter traffic and that Gatwick was developing into a credible alternative airport to Heathrow.

In the end the government opted for single ownership, in line with the other U.K. privatizations, such as British Telecommunications and British Gas, which had occurred without restructuring, and before privatization's role in facilitating competition became widely accepted.[51] Thus this airport privatization transferred public assets into private ownership but did not increase any airport competition. Hence as a substitute for a more competitive privatization, price regulation was introduced to prevent BAA's abuse of its dominant market position under this single-entity privatization.

In the early 1990s the government decided to relax its traffic distribution rules, which undermined the rationalization that common ownership would both facilitate the administration of such rules and minimize their commercial impact on any individual airport. Moreover, growing airline liberalization

49. Foster (1984).
50. Starkie and Thompson (1985); Barrett (1984).
51. Starkie (2004).

at this time meant that the government's control over route licensing was weakening. Hence the arguments in favor of group ownership to help facilitate government airline policies became much weaker and a more liberal environment became a reality.

Over the years various reviews have investigated whether BAA should be split up, but these have generally concluded that the scope for more competition would be limited, particularly with Heathrow's dominant position, and would be more than offset by a loss of economies of scale, the fragmentation of financial strength, and the dispersion of expertise.[52] The link between this issue and the provision of adequate capacity in London was key when a breakup was rejected in an investigation led by the deputy prime minister in 1999:

> The conclusion was that the scope for such competition was currently constrained by the lack of unused capacity and by the planning regime, which means that decisions on whether there should be substantial new airport infrastructure in South East will in practice be a matter for government. If the BAA airports were in separate ownership it is unlikely that they would be able to compete more vigorously for new traffic than they already do. The Government has therefore decided that for the time being it will not pursue further the possibility of breaking up BAA.[53]

Interestingly, just as the government had stated that it was not in favor of a breakup "for the time being," the Competition Commission argued in its subsequent BAA Q4 review, that although it could not find significant evidence to justify a split then, the debate might have to be reopened after the publication of the 2003 white paper.[54]

In 2006 the Office of Fair Trading investigated the U.K. airports market. The timing of this inquiry was significant, coming soon after the 2003 white paper and at a time when passengers were experiencing much greater competition between airlines. BAA had just been taken over by new ownership and was coming under increasing criticism from certain airline groups, in particular the LCCs at Stansted, who complained that the company was unresponsive to customers' needs. Moreover on August 10, 2006, the government imposed an unprecedented "critical" level of security, which meant that there had to be a 100 percent hand search of all passengers and all cabin baggage had to be reprocessed as hold baggage. These heightened security requirements created great disruption and delays at BAA airports. BAA recruited more security staff,

52. Toms (2004).
53. Department of Environment, Transport and the Regions (2000, paragraph 220).
54. Competition Commission (2002).

but it took some time for these new staff to be trained and ready for the job—and many passengers and airlines still claimed that the number was insufficient. This negative passenger experience led to criticism of BAA's management and raised additional questions about the ability of a large multiairport group to serve its customers satisfactorily in such circumstances.

The OFT inquiry concluded that the BAA group should be referred to the Competition Commission for more detailed investigation, which could ultimately lead to a demand for BAA to divest one or more of its airports:

> We believe that the current market structure does not deliver best value for air travellers in the UK and that greater competition within the industry could bring significant benefits for passengers. There is evidence of poor quality and high charges—BAA's investment plans, which are of great importance to the UK, have raised significant concerns among its customers. There are signs of a market not working well for consumers and we believe that a full inquiry into BAA's structure is justified.[55]

The OFT was critical of the BAA joint ownership of the southeast and Scottish airports and identified this joint ownership as a key factor (together with development constraints and the regulatory regime) that could be preventing, restricting, or distorting competition. The Competition Commission is expected to reach its own conclusions in late 2008. In the meantime criticisms of the quality of BAA's service continue to grow, with a number of high-profile politicians, such as the mayor of London and the City of London minister, publicly making negative comments about the service provided at Heathrow.[56]

Clearly the more competitive airline industry and the criticism that BAA has received from its customers weaken the arguments for common ownership. Moreover individual, rather than group, ownership could erode some of the market power that the airports have. In the short term, even if the capacity constraints in the southeast hinder full competition, separate ownership could allow the airports to be more responsive to customer needs and provide satisfactory levels of service. More important in the longer term, it could allow the airports to make decisions on investment that are not influenced by any potential impact on other airports in the group and that allow greater competition to occur between airports once there is additional capacity. In short

---

55. OFT (2006a).
56. D. Robertson, "Airlines Urge End of BAA's Heathrow Grip," *The Times*, August 1, 2007.

in today's mature aviation environment, the argument for keeping common ownership, which BAA has claimed is needed primarily because a more fragmented ownership would undermine vitally needed investment, seems unconvincing when compared with the competition benefits that could be gained from splitting up the group.

Conclusions

The move toward private ownership of U.K. airports, together with the liberalization of airline markets, means that the planning and regulation systems are now the only two remaining policy levers that the government has to exert influence over the U.K. airport industry. These two policy areas, in addition to the joint ownership of BAA airports, are the key factors that will determine the future of the industry. The government has a role to play in improving the planning system, particularly by dwelling less on the "need" for a particular development while still taking full account of the impacts that any development will cause. It remains to be seen whether the government's latest proposals for independent planning commissions, if and when they are introduced, will actually achieve this.

Generally the U.K. airport industry appears to be in a relatively healthy financial position, with evidence showing that improvements have been made over the years. However, the regulatory process that exists for designated airports has produced economic distortions, particularly at the London airports where the single-till price cap has prevented the best use of scarce capacity and has distorted investment signals. The lack of an economically efficient slot allocation process has further exacerbated the problem of scarce capacity. The regulatory shortcomings have existed for several years and have been debated at length in the search for a better balance between imperfect competition and economic regulation. This chapter has suggested three possible improvements, namely, adopting the dual- rather than single-till approach, changing the role of the regulators, and increasing the direct dialogue between the airports and the airlines.

Given that the CAA itself has indicated that it will not reopen the single- versus dual-till debate during the review process for the Q5 period, it is unlikely that changes can be made in this area until at least the next review, when they will still be subject to much opposition from the airlines, primarily because of the resultant increases in airport charges. The changed role of the regulators seems a simpler case, as the government already has made proposals that would bring regulation of the airport industry more into line with other regulated industries.[57] Finally there are signs that increasing the airport-airline dialogue could be further developed, at least for Heathrow and Gatwick airports, and should be encouraged. Eventually such dialogue could be a route to lighter or even shadow regulation.

I have given little consideration here to the U.K. regional airports, other than Manchester and the BAA Scotland airports, as there does not appear to be much evidence to suggest that these airports are facing problems that are hindering the development of air services and the provision of appropriate infrastructure. Overall their financial situation seems to be improving, a development that is in part attributable to the shift to private sector ownership. However, although privatization has erased most direct local and regional involvement with these airports, these governments are likely to want to remain involved in airport development issues so that they can gain access to the wider benefits of economic development. While any more direct government intervention appears unnecessary in this situation, perhaps initiatives similar to the route development funds may play a limited role here so long as they comply with EU guidelines. This form of subsidization has not been without criticism, however, particularly in Northern Ireland, where the funding was described as being awarded in an "ad-hoc and disorganised way," which threatened the realization of "the full potential benefits for Northern Ireland. . . ."[58] It is essential, therefore, that any such scheme is appropriately designed and executed so that it encourages regional development.

There may also be a need to ensure that competition from these regional airports is not restricted with changing ownership patterns. Two examples of this have already occurred. In the mid-1990s, TBI, the owner of Belfast International, was prevented from buying neighboring Belfast City airport after the Competition Commission concluded the purchase would create a monopoly in the provision of airport services in Northern Ireland. More recently in 2005 the owners of Bristol airport (Ferrovial/Macquarie) were selected as preferred bidders for the nearby Exeter airport but pulled out when the OFT said that the pending purchase would be investigated by the Competition Commission to ensure that it did not have a negative impact on competition in the region. General competition law should mean that any further acquisitions do not restrict competition.

These regional airport cases are somewhat inconsistent with the approach adopted toward BAA common ownership over the years, which is yet another

---

57. The House of Commons Transport Select Committee made such a recommendation in 2006; see Transport Committee (2006).

58. Northern Ireland Affairs Committee (2005, paragraph 47).

reason why the BAA group structure, together with airport designation, are critical issues for future U.K. airport policy. The arguments for continuing to regulate Stansted and Manchester or for maintaining the BAA group structure do not now seem convincing in today's air transport environment. A number of organizations such as the CAA and OFT have reached such conclusions and these issues are being further explored. The airport industry today is very different from the one that existed in 1986 when the original regulatory regime was set up and BAA was privatized. The basic regulatory approach has changed very little in the last twenty years with no lessening of the burden of regulation as the competitive forces have become stronger. Now seems an opportune time to make some major changes to the regulatory process and structure of the industry to better meet the future needs of the U.K. aviation industry.

References

BAA. 2006a. "ADI Confirms Commitment to Stansted Second Runway." Press release, July 6 (www.baa.com).

———. 2006b. "BAA Committed to Developing Its Airports to Support Growing Airline and Passenger Demand." Press release, May 3 (www.baa.com).

———. 2006c. "BAA Response to CAA Policy Issues." Consultation Paper (www.caa.co.uk).

Barrett, S. 1984. *Airports for Sale: The Case for Competition.* London: Adam Smith Institute.

CAA (Civil Aviation Authority). 2000a. "Advice to the Secretary of State for the Environment, Transport and the Regions on the Application of easyJet to Designate Luton Airport" (www.caa.co.uk).

———. 2000b. "The Single Till and the Dual Till Approach to the Price Regulation of Airports." Consultation Paper (www.caa.co.uk).

———. 2002. "Heathrow, Gatwick and Stansted Price Caps 2003–2008, CAA Recommendations to the Competition Commission" (www.caa.co.uk).

———. 2003. "Economic Regulation of BAA London Airports 2003–2008" (www.caa.co.uk).

———. 2004. "Airport Regulation: Looking to the Future—Learning from the Past" (www.caa.co.uk).

———. 2005. "Airports Review—Policy Issues." Consultation Paper (www.caa.co.uk).

———. 2006a. "Airports Price Control Review—Initial Proposals for Heathrow, Gatwick and Stansted" (www.caa.co.uk).

———. 2006b. "Airports Review—Policy Update" (www.caa.co.uk).

———. 2006c. "The CAA's Use of Section 41 of the Airports Act 1986: A Consultation Document" (www.caa.co.uk).

———. 2007a. "Airport Price Control Review—CAA Recommendations to the Competition Commission for Heathrow and Gatwick Airports" (www.caa.co.uk).

———. 2007b. "De-designation of Manchester and Stansted Airports for Price Control Regulation: The CAA's Advice to the Secretary of State" (www.caa.co.uk).
Competition Commission. 2002. *BAA plc: A Report on the Economic Regulation of the London Airports Companies.* London: Stationery Office.
Department of Communities and Local Government. 2007. *Planning for a Sustainable Future White Paper* (www.communities.gov.uk).
Department of Environment, Transport and the Regions. 2000. "The Future of Aviation: The Government's Consultation Document on Air Transport Policy" (www.dft.gov.uk).
Department of Trade and Industry. 1998. *A Fair Deal for Consumers: Modernising the Framework for Utility Regulation—The Response to Consultation.*
Department of Transport. 1985. *Airports Policy White Paper.* Cmnd 9542.
———. 1995. *Review of the Framework for the Economic Regulation of Airports.*
———. 2003a. *Funding the First Runway Development at an Airport in the South East of England* (www.dft.gov.uk).
———. 2003b. *The Future of Air Transport White Paper* (www.dft.gov.uk).
———. 2006. *The Future of Air Transport Progess Report* (www.dft.gov.uk).
———. 2007. "Decision on Proposed Designation and De-designation Criteria for Airports" (www.dft.gov.uk).
Department of Transport, Local Government and the Regions. 2001. *Major Infrastructure Projects: Delivering a Fundamental Change.*
Foster, C. 1984. "Privatising British Airports: What's to Be Gained?" *Public Money* (March): 19–23.
Graham, A., and N. Dennis. 2007. "Airport Traffic and Financial Performance: A UK and Ireland Case Study." *Journal of Transport Geography* 15, no. 3: 161–71.
Heathrow T5 Inquiry Secretariat. 1999. *Heathrow Terminal 5 Inquiry: Administration and Procedure* (www.dft.gov.uk).
Humphreys, I. 1999. "Privatisation and Commercialisation: Changes in the UK Airport Ownership Patterns." *Journal of Transport Geography* 7, no. 2: 121–34.
Nelson, Stephen. 2006. Speech by BAA chief executive officer to Global Airport Development Conference, Rome (November).
NERA. 2004. "Study to Assess the Effects of Different Slot Allocation Schemes." Brussels.
Northern Ireland Affairs Committee. 2005. *Air Transport Services in Northern Ireland—Eighth Report of Session 2004–05* (www.parliament.uk).
Office of the Deputy Prime Minister. 2005. "Planning Inquiries into Major Infrastructure Projects: Procedures." Circular 07/2005 (www.communities.gov.uk).
OFT (Office of Fair Trading). 2006a. "OFT Proposes to Refer BAA Airports to the Competition Commission." Press release, December 12.
———. 2006b. *UK Airports* (www.oft.gov.uk).
———. 2006c. *UK Airports: Report on the Market Study and Proposed Decision to Make a Market Investigation Reference* (www.oft.gov.uk).
Parker, D. 1999. "The Performance of BAA before and after Privatization: A DEA Study." *Journal of Transport Economics and Policy* 33, no. 2: 133–46.

Starkie, D. 2001. "Reforming UK Airport Regulation." *Journal of Transport Economics and Policy* 35, part 1 (January): 119–35.

———. 2004. "Testing the Regulatory Model: The Expansion of Stansted Airport." *Fiscal Studies* 25, no. 4: 389–413.

———. 2005. "Airports Regulation." *CRI Regulatory Review 2004/5*. Bath: Centre for the Regulated Industries.

Starkie, D., and D. Thompson. 1984. *Privatising London Airports*. London: Institute for Fiscal Studies.

Toms, M. 2003. "Is Airport Regulation Fit for Purpose?" In *Air Transport and Infrastructure: The Challenges Ahead*, edited by D. Helms and D. Holt. Oxford, U.K.: Oxera.

———. 2004. "UK Regulation from the Perspective of BAA plc." In *The Economic Regulation of Airports*, edited by P. Forsyth and others. Aldershot, U.K.: Ashgate.

Transport Committee. 2006. *The Work of the Civil Aviation Authority—Thirteenth Report of Session 2005–2006* (www.parliament.uk).

TRL (Transport Research Laboratory). 2006. *Review of Airport Charges 2005*. Wokingham, U.K.

Yokomi, M. 2006. "Measurement of Malmquist Index of Privatized BAA plc." Paper presented at the Air Transport Research Society Conference, Rio de Janeiro (July).

6

MICHAEL W. TRETHEWAY *and* ROBERT ANDRIULAITIS

Airport Policy in Canada: Limitations of the Not-for-Profit Governance Model

This paper examines the development of airport investment policy in Canada. Canadian airports were operated as a single system by a federal department that found itself unable to finance needed rates of capacity expansion and renewal. The government decided to quasi-privatize the airport system by transferring individual airports to locally based airport authorities.[1] These authorities were created as private sector companies but with no equity capital. That is, they are not-for-profit corporations. This governance model achieved the government's aim of increasing investment. (Correspondingly, at the key airports of Toronto and Vancouver, the increased investment resulted in decreased congestion.) To generate needed equity capital, however, the not-for-profit corporations were forced to charge fees on current users for the benefit of future users, raising intergenerational issues. In addition, concerns about the perceived accountability of the private, not-for-profit corporations has resulted in proposed legislation. That legislation, however, is overly detailed and does not involve any price or access regulation.

This paper examines the development of the policy toward the operation and financing of the Canadian airports. It reviews the development of the policy, comments on the financing paradox in the governance model, and points out that this paradox requires the absence of any price regulation. The paper concludes that the not-for-profit governance model has achieved its objective of increased investment (and decreased congestion), but that the model is

---

1. While the airports were the first to be quasi-privatized (transferred to not-for-profit authorities), the policy was eventually applied to air navigation, ports, and the Canadian portion of the management of the St. Lawrence Seaway. Canada's national passenger rail service continues to be operated by the federal government.

paradoxical, in that the only way it can achieve the government's policy objectives is by generating significant annual net surpluses of revenue over expenses. That requires removal of pricing controls, which in turn has led to accountability and overpricing concerns. Proposed legislation adopts a detailed, almost intrusive approach to corporate governance and transparency that avoids dealing with the fundamental paradox of the governance model. It will not address the pricing concerns of users.

Development of the Not-for-Profit Airport Governance Model

Between 1920 and the early 1980s, the federal government became financially involved with Canadian airports.[2] In the last half of the 1900s, the government provided direct financial support for the development and operation of Canada's airport system, which required considerable and continuous investment. By the early 1970s, virtually all of Canada's airports were operated by Transport Canada, the department that administers the mandate of the minister of transport. In 1985 the government began a reexamination of its policy of operation and subsidy by a federal department, largely in response to increasing pressure to reduce the federal deficit. At the time, the federal government was subsidizing the airport system at roughly $250 million a year, plus amounts for operation of the air traffic control system. A tax on airline tickets generated revenues equal to roughly half of the combined deficit, although eventually the government attributed the tax to costs of the air navigation system and not to airport operation and investment. Even at a net subsidy of up to $500 million a year, needed investments in systems (air traffic control) and at individual airports were being deferred. Congestion emerged as a major problem at the two largest airports, Toronto and Vancouver. Communities across the country complained about inadequate infrastructure.

An extensive review of policy options by Transport Canada resulted in a recommendation in 1987 to transfer operation of airports from the department to not-for-profit authorities. At the time, there was limited experience anywhere in the world with operation of airports by for-profit private sector companies (Britain did not privatize the British Airports Authority until 1987), and it would be some years before the record of private sector operation became clear. The policy review rejected the U.S. approach, which involves operation of airports by local government or airport authorities that were often elected and had taxation and other government powers. This model was rejected for many reasons, but the main one may have been the

2. McGrath (1990).

view that near universal use in the United States of revenue bonds to finance airport infrastructure was resulting in negative consequences for airline policy. The bond guarantees provided by airlines came with constraints on airport investment that seemed to have worked to the detriment of airline competition in a number of cases. As a result, the Canadian government opted for a not-for-profit governance model for airports. This model freed the airports from the financial constraints of federal operation, avoided the competition problems in the U.S. approach, and avoided the perceived risk and thin record of pure private sector operation. The implementation of the new Canadian airport policy has taken place in four phases, thus far.

Phase One: Local Airport Authorities

GOVERNANCE. The Airport Transfer Act of 1992 authorized the establishment of four local airport authorities (LAAs) at Calgary, Edmonton, Montreal, and Vancouver. The transfer of the federal assets was predated by a federal policy change in 1987. The new policy, announced in *A Future Framework for Airports in Canada*, emphasized the commercial reorientation of airports as the government intended to transfer them to local parties.[3] LAAs are not agents of the Crown. The LAAs were nonshare capital corporations (not-for-profit) incorporated under Part II of the Canada Corporations Act or pursuant to provincial legislation. The boards of directors were composed of representatives of local business and community interests, excluding elected officials and government employees. Directors were appointed by a process acceptable to municipalities and the federal government, and there was no requirement for federal, provincial, or user representation.[4] Collectively, board members were to have skills in specified disciplines (such as air transportation, commerce, law, and engineering).

TRANSPARENCY. The LAAs had few requirements to ensure the transparency of their decisionmaking to users and other stakeholders. The ground lease required that certain documents be made available to the public and that public meetings be held after the end of each fiscal year. The LAAs were not required to make service contracts available for public tender, undertake public consultation, submit business plans to the minister, or disclose remuneration. That is, the LAAs were private companies, not public agencies.

FEES, CHARGES, AND SERVICE LEVELS. The prices set by LAAs were not subject to external review, approval, or appeal processes. The policy made clear that airports had full authority and power to establish charges. The

---

3. Policy statement of the minister of transport, released by Transport Canada, April 8, 1987 (www.tc.gc.ca/programs/Airports/policy/menu.htm).
4. Calgary, Edmonton, and Vancouver each have two federal appointees on their boards.

ground leases prohibited charges on state aircraft, however, and obliged the LAAs to respect Canada's international agreements on aeronautics.[5] LAAs were free to determine service levels within the safety regulatory framework. The ground leases contained a broad requirement to operate the airport "in an up-to-date and reputable manner befitting a First Class Facility and a Major International Airport."

ACCOUNTABILITY. By rights granted by the ground leases, Transport Canada could, at any time, audit the LAAs' financial and other business records and procedures to ensure the LAAs' compliance with the ground lease and the LAAs' and other airport tenants' compliance with other applicable laws.[6] The LAAs were to submit to performance reviews every five years, with the results provided to Transport Canada and nominating entities.

RENTS. LAAs were required to make annual lease payments to the federal government. The basis for the magnitude of rents was never clear. The initial policy stated that rents were to leave the federal government no worse off, which meant that the few airports that had been generating a surplus of revenues over costs were required to pay rents of equal magnitude.[7] Later the policy changed to establish rents on the basis of "fair market value," although what this meant was unclear. Clearly the airports were not going to be charged market values for large tracts of land in urban areas, which would have resulted in annual rents of billions of dollars at some sites. The auditor general ultimately criticized the government for lack of clarity on the basis for establishing airport rents. In addition to the auditor general's criticisms, major disparities arose among the airports in terms of rents paid, which showed no logical basis on either traffic levels or local land values. Rents had components for base rents as well as "participation rents" based on airport gross or net revenues. Some airport rents were capped while others were not. Moreover, the mere fact that airports were or eventually would be charged rents raised issues of reduced competitiveness with U.S. airports, which effectively pay no rent for the lands they occupy.

OTHER. Conflict-of-interest provisions were found in the bylaws of each of the LAAs, and the code of conduct was consistent with the rules set out in the Canada Business Corporations Act. LAAs were free to undertake ancillary activities in Canada and abroad. Nonaviation activities were to be compatible

5. The public service obligations would later be imposed on the Canadian Airport Authorities (CAAs) as well.
6. Calgary and Edmonton have adopted the broader audit provisions applicable to the CAAs.
7. When Transport Canada operated the airports, it had a national schedule of airport fees and charges. Thus the same landing fee was charged at all airports, regardless of the cost or demand conditions.

with the broad socioeconomic interests of the adjacent communities and the province. There was no limit placed on LAA revenues, and LAAs were explicitly exempted from income tax.

Phase Two: The Canadian Airport Authorities

The LAA policy was a voluntary policy. Communities that wished to establish not-for-profit authorities to operate their airports, generally without subsidy, could do so. A change of government led to the next phase in the policy, whereby the federal government indicated it would no longer operate or subsidize any airport and would require communities to establish authorities to take over operation of their airports. In 1994 the National Airports Policy was introduced, which used a variant of the local airport authority governance structure, now referred to as Canadian Airport Authorities (CAAs).[8] The principal differences between the LAAs and the CAAs were in public accountability provisions and in the lease provisions. Neither are agents of the Crown.

CORPORATE STRUCTURE. The CAAs are nonshare capital corporations (not-for-profit) incorporated under Part II of the Canada Corporations Act or pursuant to provincial legislation. Directors must be appointed to the board by a process acceptable to municipalities and the federal government. Unlike the LAAs, there are specific requirements with respect to the composition of the CAA boards. They must include two or more federal nominees, one provincial nominee, and one representative each from the business community, organized labor, and consumer interests, and the majority of the directors must be nominated by the local or regional government. The board itself may name no more than three directors.

TRANSPARENCY. There is a slightly higher degree of transparency mandated for the CAAs than for the LAAs.[9] Price increases, including justification, are required to be published in local media at least sixty days before they are imposed. A Community Consultative Committee, including aviation industry representatives, must meet twice a year "to provide dialogue on matters related to the airport," and a general public meeting must be held after each fiscal year ends. The public is allowed access to more documents than it was with the LAAs, including the airport transfer agreements. Contracts over $75,000 (in 1994 dollars) must be available to competitive tender and exceptions must be disclosed with reasons. The ground lease requires that the annual reports dis-

---

8. Minister of Transport (1994).

9. It should be noted that the four LAAs had generally adhered to principles required of the CAAs, although there was no regulatory or contractual requirement to do so.

close remuneration of directors and salary ranges of senior officers. Like the LAAs, the CAAs are not required to submit business plans to the transport minister. It should be noted that most of the LAAs were already operating with most of the above transparency provisions as a matter of corporate policy, even though they were not required to do so in their lease or legislation.

FEES, CHARGES, AND SERVICE LEVELS. Just like the LAAs, the prices set by CAAs are not subject to external review, approval, or appeal processes. The ground lease prohibits charges on state aircraft, however, and obliges the CAAs to respect Canada's international agreements on aeronautics. CAAs are free to determine service levels within the safety regulatory framework. The ground lease contains a broad requirement to operate the airport "in an up-to-date and reputable manner befitting a First Class Facility and a Major International Airport." Airports must be returned to the government at the end of the lease with no debt or other obligations. This raises the question as to how the airport authorities will be able to sustain a first-class airport to the last day of their lease, yet have no debt.

ACCOUNTABILITY. The ground lease gives Transport Canada the right, at any time, to audit the practices and procedures of each CAA as they relate to the lease, the leased premises, and the CAA's business affairs. Transport Canada may have access to any information or document to determine the extent of a CAA's compliance with the lease and the CAA's and airport tenants' compliance with applicable laws. The CAAs are subject to independent review of their management, operation, and financial performance every five years. The findings are made available to Transport Canada, nominating entities, and, on request, to the public.

OTHER. The CAA director's code of conduct is to be consistent with the rules set out in the Canada Corporations Act. Changes to the code must be approved by the minister of transport. Conflict of interest on contracts is also addressed in the Canada Corporations Act. CAAs are free to undertake ancillary activities in Canada and abroad. CAA revenues are not capped and are exempted from income tax. Table 6-1 compares elements of the governance models of the LAAs and CAAs.

Phase Three: Rent Renegotiation and Conversion of LAAs to CAAs

During the period of federal departmental operation of airports, an annual subsidy of up to $250 million had been provided. By the completion of the transfer of Canada's national airport system to LAAs or CAAs, this subsidy had been eliminated and the airports collectively were paying $300 million a year in rent, with scheduled increases expected to eventually bring annual

Table 6-1. *Governance Models of LAAs and CAAs*

Element	LAAs	CAAs
Enabling legislation	Airport Transfer (Miscellaneous Matters) Act Canada Corporations Act Regional Airports Authorities Act (Alberta)	Airport Transfer (Miscellaneous Matters) Act Canada Corporations Act
Corporate structure	Nonshare capital corporation (not-for-profit) incorporated under Part II of Canada Corporations Act or pursuant to provincial legislation	Nonshare capital corporation (not-for-profit) incorporated under Part II of the Canada Corporations Act or pursuant to provincial legislation
Board composition and nomination process	No fixed formula, other than that directors be appointed by a process acceptable to municipalities and federal government. Board is to be composed of representatives of local business and community interests; collectively, board is supposed to have skills in specified disciplines (such as air transportation, commerce, law, and engineering). Directors must not be elected officials or government employees. Alberta legislation requires board to have between nine and fifteen directors (Calgary authorized to have seventeen directors to accommodate appointment of two directors by federal goverment); Calgary and Edmonton have agreed to public accountability principles.	CAA model retains basic principles applicable to LAAs. In addition, public accountability principles establish specific requirements for CAAs, board must include at least one director to represent the interests of business, organized labor and consumers; up to three directors nominated by federal government; one director nominated by the province; majority of directors to be nominated by local or regional governments; board itself may nominate no more than three directors.
Federal participation on board	No requirement for federal nominee(s); however Calgary, Edmonton, Montréal, and Vancouver now each have two federal appointees on their boards.	Federal government ordinarily nominates two directors but reserves the right to nominate an additional director to any CAA during a period of subsidization by the federal government.
Provincial participation on board	No formal provision for provincial nominee	Provincial government may nominate one director.

rent payments to $1 billion.[10] The present value of lease payments was estimated by the government to be roughly $12 billion as of 2005, in addition to over $1 billion already paid by the airports. Unlike Australia, where the private sector airport operators prepaid their leases, rent payments by Canada's not-for-profit airport authorities were annual payments. This resulted in opportunities for airport authorities and their stakeholders to put significant pressure on the federal government to renegotiate rent payments, something that would not have occurred if leases had been prepaid.[11] Key concerns expressed by the airports and many of their supporters included financial viability, the economic value of airport land, competitiveness with U.S. airports, and inconsistencies in rents charged to different airports. Each of these is discussed in turn.

The financial viability of airports with under 750,000 annual passengers was increasingly becoming a problem. These airports had been operating with an initial "rent holiday," but as dates for rent payment loomed, it was clear to many operators that they could not operate their airports and finance long-term capital requirements. In many cases, lenders indicated that these airports could not be financed for the long term. With the exception of the largest airports, the CAAs were being financed by short-term bank debt and were unable to secure long-term financing for capital programs. In contrast, airports of this size in the United States received grants from the federal government for long-term capital projects, and many received grants from state governments for other support, such as for planning activities. U.S. airports also utilized revenue bonds guaranteed by airlines, but with certain veto powers accruing to airlines over key airport capital investment decisions.

There were significant inequities between the airports in terms of rents paid, both in absolute numbers and in amounts per passenger, per acre, and per million dollars of historical net book value. As an example, Victoria airport was the only airport in its size range paying any rent for the first ten years. It was often stated that the first airports that were transferred were required to pay much higher rents than later transfers. Further, it had been stated to the early transferees that all airports would be treated equitably in terms of rents, which was interpreted by some as suggesting that if airports that transferred later received lower rent schedules, the payments of the initial transferees would be adjusted downward to maintain equity. That did not happen. There were also important differences between the structure of rent

---

10. There was provision for a small annual subsidy to small airports for safety-related investments. This was capped at $39 million, subsequently reduced to $35 million.
11. The tourism industry, provincial governments, and local chambers of commerce were especially vocal in expressing the need for changes to the airport rent policy.

formulas for the LAAs and CAAs, especially with regard to participation rents, rent rates on different types of participation revenues, and rent capping.

An argument was also made that airport land had no economic value. Airport authorities were required to use the land for airport operations or airport-related activities. With no alternative use for the land, the economic value was claimed to be zero. Concerns were also raised regarding competitiveness with U.S. airports. No U.S. airport paid rent to federal, state, or local governments, other than nominal amounts. While Canadian airports make payments or grants in lieu of property taxes, U.S. airports generally pay no property taxes. Further, the U.S. federal grants program was viewed by Canadian airports and their stakeholders as a subsidy to competitor airports, compounded by the fact that many U.S. airport authorities and all airports run by local governments could levy property or other taxes to finance their capital needs.[12] Air carriers put significant pressure on airport authorities and the federal government to reduce airport costs in order to maintain the competitiveness of Canadian air carriers and Canadian air services; airport rents were one of the targets for cost reduction.

The auditor general criticized the government for inconsistencies in rent payment schedules and the lack of justification for the rents charged to individual airports. Rents were not based on fair market values of surrounding land. Nor was there consistency in rents per passenger, even with a gradient for airport size, rents per acre, or any other measure. To many it appeared that the actual rents had no economic justification but were simply based on the relative bargaining power of negotiators, political considerations, and a trend toward lower rents for airports transferred later in the process.

On May 8, 2005, Transport Minister Jean-C. Lapierre announced a program of rent relief for Canada's airports, which reduced rent for each of the twenty-one rent-paying airports in the National Airport System (NAS). The underlying justification for the rent reductions came from Transport Canada's review of rents, which began in June 2001 in response to the comments of the auditor general and complaints from airports and stakeholders such as the tourism industry. The rent reduction announcement essentially indicated that Transport Canada had found that rents paid by the Canadian NAS airports were excessive compared with public utilities and with foreign airports that had been privatized. The scale of the rent reduction was large: a 60 percent reduction in net present value (NPV) of the rents to be paid over a fifty-eight year period—from an estimated $12.9 billion in NPV to $5.1 billion, for

12. For example, the Port Authority of Seattle-Tacoma levies property taxes. The authority indicates that these taxes are used for port investments and not for airport operations, but the power to utilize taxes for airports exists.

a total reduction of $7.8 billion. Figure 6-1 shows the old and new schedules of annual rent payments in nominal dollars. The new rent formula is considerably simpler, transparent, and equitable in the sense that the same formula applies to all airports (table 6-2). It is based on gross revenues, not on local land values, implicitly indicating that airport rents are not based on local land market conditions.[13] Airports with less than $5 million in annual revenues will pay no rents, and the graduated scale of rent payments will keep rents down for most small and midsize airports. The graduated rent scale works much like progressive income tax schedules—as you earn more, the percent you pay increases with each income bracket.

The zero or 1 percent rents for airports with less than $10 million in annual gross revenues is expected to ease the viability problem of airports with fewer than 750,000 passengers. For some of these airports, however, long-term financial viability is still unclear. One aspect of the airports policy is that Canadian government and military aircraft pay no landing or terminal fees and pay no rent for space in airport terminals. A few airports, such as Gander, have disproportionate levels of such traffic that must be served with no compensation, either through landing or terminal fees or through direct government subsidy. Some airports, however, have adjusted various terminal fees so as to cross-subsidize certain services, such as free terminal space, provided to government.

As part of the rent relief, the LAAs were required to modify their governance models slightly to conform to the governance transparency required of the CAAs. The LAAs had generally adopted governance principles that conformed to what was required of the CAAs, but the government wished to formalize these requirements.

The Proposed Canada Airports Act

In 2003 the government introduced the Canada Airports Act, which was intended to impose a detailed governance structure on the CAAs.[14] This bill died with a change in government. In 2006 it was reintroduced with modifications as Bill C-20.[15] The bill consists of 253 sections, making it longer than

---

13. It might be observed that the rent formula is consistent with the view that the airport operators have no alternative use for the lands, and thus airport rents represent something different than land values. Some even suggest that airport rents effectively are disguised taxation.

14. The minister's announcement indicated the objective was to provide "one common, yet flexible, governance structure and a strengthened accountability framework to guide the operators of Canada's major airports." See Transport Canada Press Release H022/03, March 20, 2003.

15. The bill never progressed beyond first reading.

Figure 6-1. *Total Rent, All Canadian Airports, 2004–20*

Millions of Canadian dollars

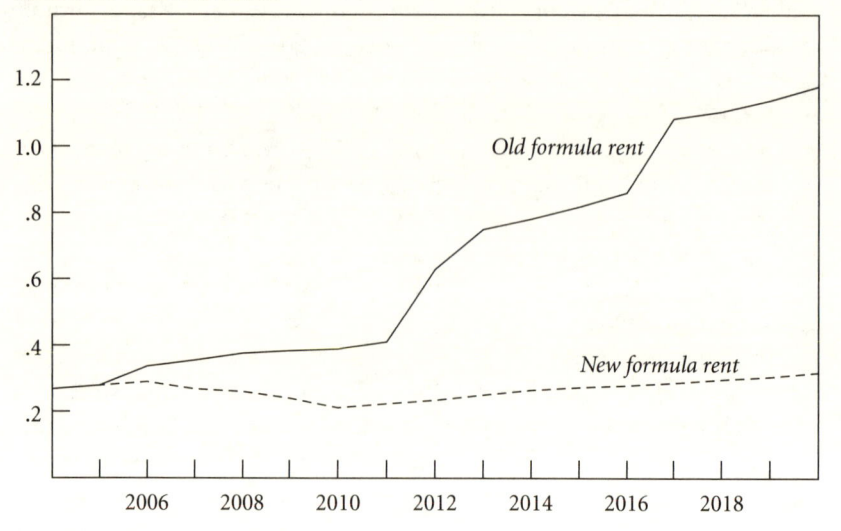

[Line chart showing "Old formula rent" rising from about 0.25 in 2006 to about 1.2 by 2020, and "New formula rent" remaining relatively flat around 0.25–0.3 across the same period.]

Source: Transport Canada, *Airport Rent Policy Fact Sheet, All Airports 2005-09-05*.

the Competition Act and almost as long as the Canada Transportation Act that governs all modes. This bill also died, when the government prorogued Parliament in September 2007.

The proposed act is largely concerned with governance principles, taking a detailed, prescriptive approach to this issue. For example, Section 117 would establish *in law* the conditions under which meetings of the board of directors can be called, and Section 128 would require *in law* that any resolution of the audit committee must be provided to the authority's auditor. That section would further specify the conditions under which a member of the audit committee can call a meeting of the committee—specifically, any one member of the committee can request that a meeting be held.

Locking such provisions into legislation is peculiar, as such a detailed, prescriptive approach is seldom found in Canadian legislation. The Aeronautics Act, for example, empowers the minister to make regulations on a wide range of safety issues. The regulatory approach provides great flexibility, allowing regulations to change as markets, traffic levels, and technology change.[16] Well-

---

16. As an example, the proposed act locks in legislation requiring use of the Internet for certain notices. One wonders what the implications would be today of an act passed twenty years ago, which enshrined in law the need to provide notification by telex.

Table 6-2. *New Airport Rent Formula*

Gross revenue (Millions of Canadian dollars per year)	Rent paid (percent)
On the first $0 to $5 million	0
On the next $5 million	1
On the next $15 million (total $25 million)	5
On the next $75 million	8
On the next $150 million	10
Any amount over $250 million	12

intentioned regulations that do not achieve their intended results can be modified or eliminated by the minister. This is not the case for the proposed Airports Act. If, for example, it is found that some boards have a single member of the audit committee who requests frequent, even daily meetings (perhaps to earn meeting fees, or perhaps as a strategy of harassment) that experience shows is disruptive to the good governance of the authority, only new legislation can make a change to the act's provision that any member of the audit committee can compel a called meeting.

In the area of price regulation, the act grants no powers for regulation of airport charges. This is surprising in some ways, as airlines had complained loudly regarding airport fees and charges. The act contains a number of provisions regarding airport fees. Airports may have discriminatory fees, provided that differences among users are based on objective criteria (other than carrier nationality). Airports must consult users on proposed fees or fee changes, but after consultation the airport is able to impose its proposed fee. The authority need only "consider" any comments it receives. Airport authorities must establish a charging methodology, but there is no economic guidance on the choice of methodology. Fees, such as airport improvement fees, may be imposed on passengers, but generally only for capital investments including land acquisitions. Airport fees must not generate revenues exceeding financing requirements. The latter point is interesting. Not-for-profit entities can only generate equity for financing long-term capital by retained earnings. The paradox of the not-for-profit governance model is that it generally requires authorities to generate a surplus of revenue over costs so as to build retained earnings. The proposed act seems to allow this building of retained earnings.

Although the proposed act does not provide for price regulation of airport authorities, it would allow users to appeal airport fees to the Canadian Transportation Agency. The basis for an appeal is very limited, however, and is largely confined to a complaint that an airport authority does not have a pricing methodology and is not complying with the consultation requirements of the act. Similar provisions applying to Nav Canada, the not-for-profit authority that operates the air traffic control system, resulted in an appeal, but the agency upheld Nav Canada's charges, since it had complied with the transparency and consultation provisions. There is no provision to appeal the substance of a pricing policy, only the process.

The act thus seems to provide for a process for an airport establishing and imposing its fees, but not for price regulation per se. One rationale that has been put forward is that not-for-profit organizations have no objective to seek profits, and thus price regulation would be of limited value.

Airport authorities indicate that the proposed act would impose significant costs on the airports to demonstrate compliance with its 253 sections but would have little or no effect relative to current conditions, including fees and charges. The act does nothing to regulate prices or even to establish pricing principles that would result in a change of established policy at most airports. There are no new access provisions, and the allocation of airport slots would be little different from existing powers of the transport minister.

The Financing Paradox of the Non-for-Profit Governance Model

Canada adopted the not-for-profit governance model for airports at a time when there was little established experience with private sector airport operation. The intent of the policy was to facilitate much-needed investment in airport infrastructure without recourse to the public treasury. The pure private sector approach was rejected as being too risky for Canada to adopt, given the limited precedence and performance record at the time of for-profit private sector operation of airports. The government at the time believed that a for-profit governance format would result in unnecessarily high fees.

However, the not-for-profit model has consequences that also result in higher fees and charges. The financial community made clear that it would not provide airports with 100 percent debt financing or even high-leverage financing. Thus airport authorities could not undertake major capital projects until they had generated sufficient retained earnings. This immediately revealed that the governance models would not be able to quickly achieve the government's policy to facilitate major investments in airport assets—a prime objective of the transfer. It also made clear the paradox that not-for-profit entities had to generate profits in order to create retained earnings to support long-term capital investments.

The first airport to be transferred to a not-for-profit authority, Vancouver International, had immediate needs for major investments in both runway and terminal capacity. Its only recourse to financing this investment was to impose a fee on passengers to finance capital expansion. This Airport Improvement Fee generated revenue with no associated costs, thus creating surpluses (profits) that would become retained earnings for the authority. Effectively, today's users were paying fees for capital assets that would benefit only future users. In contrast, under the for-profit private sector governance model, capital investment would be financed by paid-in shareholder equity, levered with debt capital. Today's users would not face higher charges because equity investors would finance construction without recourse to higher fees and charges today. Tomorrow's users would pay higher fees to cover the costs of newly deployed capital, but they would also benefit from the flow of capital services from the expanded or renewed capital. The not-for-profit model thus has an undesirable intergenerational transfer.

Some airport authorities are beginning to recognize the limitations of the not-for-profit financing model. Some are concerned that large capital programs in the years beyond 2010 may be difficult to finance without large advance passenger fees, which users and the community may strongly resist. A few airport managers are now contemplating the possibility of embracing a for-profit model, with paid-in equity capital, as being a more effective governance model.

Achievement of the Objective: Capital Investment at Canadian Airports

Given that the primary objective of the airports policy was to facilitate much-needed investment in Canada's airport infrastructure, it is useful to look at the actual track record. Table 6-3 provides a listing of the top eight airports, ranked by passenger volume, and the capital investment made since the transfer from Transport Canada operation to airport authority operation.

A legitimate question is how much of this investment would have been made without transfer of the airports to airport authorities. Statistical analysis of historical data is of limited value, as capital investment decisions were largely a matter of political decisionmaking, both in terms of the amount of money available for investment and its allocation to competing demands. As well, investment data by airport for the years before the new policy was implemented are incomplete, inconsistent, and fragmentary. As an alternative, interviews were conducted with airport managers, Transport Canada officials, and a number of ministers of transport. One of the authors participated in the federal transfer process and subsequent operation of airports. Based on these sources, we offer several observations regarding achievement of the financing objectives. These share the common property of confirming that the government policy of

Table 6-3. *Investment in Capital Assets to 2003*
Millions of Canadian dollars

Airport	Investment in capital assets
Toronto	2,300
Vancouver	789
Montreal[a]	1,122
Calgary	566
Edmonton	287
Ottawa	330
Halifax	57
Winnipeg	49

Source: Annual reports.
a. Aéroports de Montréal operates two airports: Mirabel and Trudeau (formerly Dorval).

increased investment at Canadian airports was achieved and can be attributed to the transfer policy.

Vancouver was the first airport authority to undertake a major investment program, including construction of a new runway and major new international terminal. The runway investment ($100 million) would have been made by the federal government if the transfer had not taken place. Transport Canada had completed the environmental authorization process and had budgeted for the investment. But Transport Canada had no plans to make any investment in a new terminal (which cost $350 million). Its ten-year capital plan called for the addition of two gates to the existing terminal, rather than the construction of a new sixteen-gate facility.[17] To the new operator, this was paradoxical as the runway system was capacity constrained and the increased runway capacity was highly likely to result in increased traffic through the terminal. The existing terminal had been built to accommodate 3 million passengers but was processing roughly 10 million passengers with only minor expansion of its terminal capacity. The new runway would have removed an airside capacity constraint that was expected to result in an increase in total passenger volume, requiring a significant increase in terminal capacity. To the Transport Canada officials of the day, as well as to the new airport authority, there was no question that needed capital investment in the terminal would not have been made without transfer of the facility to the airport authority.[18]

17. The new Vancouver International Terminal also "retained" a temporary six-gate facility, which increased net incremental capacity by twenty gates.
18. It should be noted that Vancouver's ground lease, and that of several other airport authorities, required the new operator to make major capital investments, in excess of those

Montreal consisted of two airports, with substantial overcapacity at the international airport, Mirabel. At the time, international services (except for transborder flights to the United States) were allowed only at Mirabel, whereas virtually all domestic and transborder flights operated from Dorval. This system of airports was a chronic money loser and accounted for a large portion of the net annual subsidy to airports. With overcapacity, the new operators made limited investments at first, focusing instead on eliminating the operating deficit. The transfer process implicitly subsidized the Montreal system through rent deferral and other provisions for the initial ten years, but these were phased out, and rents were backend loaded. The major decision of the Montreal authority was to consolidate most traffic at Dorval so as to build the potential for international-to-continental connecting traffic, which in turn would increase the range of services available to the origin-destination market. This decision would decrease operating costs, but as it was implemented, it required the authority to make major investments in upgrading and expanding the terminal. Mirabel airport today largely operates as a cargo and manufacturing facility.

Calgary and Edmonton were the other two airports of the four LAAs. Neither facility required immediate major investments. However, in the second five-year period, both airport authorities undertook major expansions of terminal capacity, which had not been planned by Transport Canada. Both airports experienced dramatic traffic growth fueled by the launch of service in 1996 by low-cost carrier WestJet and by general economic growth. A new terminal was constructed at Edmonton and new terminal wings at Calgary. Although some criticized the Edmonton capital expansion program as being excessive, by the late 1990s the old terminal was approaching a crisis in its ability to handle its burgeoning traffic, which incremental investment would have been unable to accommodate. The new terminal became a necessity.[19] Calgary's traffic growth has been the highest among the major airports in Canada, something that Transport Canada had not anticipated before the transfer.

Transport Canada had planned. The government was locking in the achievement of its objective to expand investment with the new policy. In partial anticipation of the financing challenges for the no-equity not-for-profit authorities, their ground leases and accompanying legislation made clear that the airport authorities would have the right to impose fees in excess of current-year costs, so that they could build equity to finance capital investment.

19. In hindsight, the decision by Edmonton was the right one. The investment led to increased volumes, which showed that constrained demand had existed. Furthermore, increases in the cost of construction in Alberta would have resulted in much higher costs had a portion of the expansion been postponed.

The first of the CAAs, and the largest airport in Canada, Toronto airport was in almost desperate need of new capacity for both runway and terminal services. As in the Vancouver case, Transport Canada would have made a major investment in runway capacity. The terminal situation had reached such a crisis that before transfer of operations to the CAA, the government had chosen a different, private sector solution to investment. In the mid-1980s, the government allowed a private sector developer (Lockheed Air Terminals) to construct a new terminal, because it was unable to allocate the required investment funds through the federal budgeting process and had rejected a Crown corporation governance structure that might have enabled debt-based financing (with full government guarantee of the debt, of course). In the early 1990s the government decided to privatize the two older terminals and awarded a terminal operation and expansion contract to a private sector consortium. This consortium would have replaced the oldest terminal and expanded capacity of the two terminals at an investment cost of $750 million. There were operational challenges with the design, and the design also would have limited the long-term capacity of the airport terminal complex, but it would have resulted in desperately needed capacity that Transport Canada was unable to finance. With a change in government, the privatization contract was canceled, and eventually the two older terminals and runway system were transferred to a CAA. The CAA also purchased the private sector third terminal, thus consolidating the terminal capacity (and eliminating potential terminal-to-terminal competition). The CAA undertook a new design for terminal capacity, which requires a much greater capital investment for only a modestly higher terminal capacity. The new design does increase the long-term capacity potential of the site and solves many of the operational challenges posed by the private consortium's design.[20]

For Ottawa airport, Transport Canada made one of its few capital investments in terminal capacity in the mid-1980s but had no subsequent plans for further investment for the foreseeable future. The Ottawa CAA recognized that at the end of the first ten years of CAA operation, substantial new capacity would be required, and it invested in a major new terminal that had not been anticipated by Transport Canada.

20. The investment in Toronto has contributed to an increase in costs that has been criticized by the airlines. As was shown in the cases of Denver and Osaka, and undoubtedly will be for Miami, airport authorities with the most recent major capital investments initially face high debt loads per passenger, but these decline over time as debt is retired. Beyond this factor, a recent study by InterVISTAS revealed that a number of government fiscal and operating policies also negatively affect costs at Canadian airports in the range of $25 per passenger, a significant amount compared with the average domestic Canadian airfare, which Statistics Canada estimates to have been under $200 in 2006.

Winnipeg and Halifax had no immediate capacity requirements at the time of their transfer, and indeed Halifax was among the last major airports to transfer to CAA operation. Halifax has subsequently made major new investments in terminal capacity to accommodate traffic growth. These investments had not been planned by Transport Canada. Winnipeg is interesting. Its terminal was believed to have adequate capacity to 2015, but operating and rehabilitation costs were so high that construction of a new terminal accelerated by almost ten years, based in large part on justifiable savings in these costs.

For the midsize and smaller airports, conditions varied, but a number of facilities were operating beyond their design capacities and required major investments (relative to the size of the market) that were not anticipated or planned for by Transport Canada. Moncton, for example, operated a terminal that was close to failure on a site that offered extremely limited opportunity for expansion. It invested in a new terminal on a different site with better long-term potential. There seems to be little doubt that Transport Canada would not have made this investment.

A question that could be posed is whether the increased investment at Canada's airports has been excessive. Some theorists have constructed models that claim not-for-profit governance structures have economic inducements to overinvestment. (Models also claim the potential for gold-plating or the capture of rents by management or labor.) On this basis, the increase in investment by Canada's airports could be viewed as either an economically desirable investment outcome or an undesirable consequence of the not-for-profit governance model. It would require analysis well beyond the scope of this chapter to resolve this issue. Certainly, government policy sought (and in many cases required) increased investments. At the same time, one must note criticism of overinvestment or gold-plating at a few airports, even if unverified. Further pursuit of this issue may be worthy of careful analysis.

Conclusions

The primary objective of Canadian airport policy since the mid-1980s has been to facilitate increased investment in Canadian airports without recourse to taxation-based funding. The policy instrument chosen was the transfer of individual airport operations to not-for-profit private corporations. Because the corporations were not for profit, it was decided there was no need to impose a price or access regulatory structure on the airports.

The key policy objective of increased investment has been achieved. However, some challenges in the corporate governance model have emerged. The not-for-profit format lacks paid-in equity, which proved to be a severe constraint on the ability of the governance model to finance needed investment. That is, the governance model itself threatened to undermine achievement of the primary policy objective. This shortcoming was dealt with by giving airports the ability to charge fees on today's users that would result in net income, thereby generating the needed equity capital through retained earnings. However, this approach raises intergenerational issues, whereby today's users are paying fees for the benefit of tomorrow's users. Some airport operators are understanding the financing limitations of the not-for-profit governance model, and there have been some calls for reconsidering the model.

For the model to work, it was necessary to give pricing freedom to the not-for-profit airport operators. While airlines and other stakeholders have raised questions about the pricing powers of the airport authorities, the government has no plans to impose a price regulation system. Legislation that was before Parliament before it was prorogued in 2007 would have improved the transparency of the price-setting process but would not have constrained the ultimate ability of the airports to impose fees and charges that generate annual surpluses or profits to build equity capital.[21]

We conclude that the not-for-profit model is paradoxical in that the only way it can achieve the government's policy objectives is by generating significant annual net surpluses of revenue over expenses, that is, profits. To generate the profits needed to finance capital investment by not-for-profit airport authorities, traditional price regulation controls cannot be imposed. While one may argue that a not-for-profit model would not require pricing controls, or even that the performance of for-profit airport operators might suggest no need for pricing controls, it is nevertheless the case that the not-for-profit model is self-contradictory. Further, there are no limits or constraints on the degree of intergenerational transfer of wealth other than competition between airports, countervailing powers of users, or community responsiveness of the locally based airport authorities. These in turn may limit the ability to finance needed investments. Governments wishing to use the not-for-profit governance model in sectors requiring large capital investments should appreciate the consequences in terms of intergenerational transfers of wealth and the need for substantial pricing freedom for operators.

It should also be observed that these issues around pricing have led to some discontent, especially with airlines, that has resulted in calls for new legislation to constrain the airport authorities. However, current legislation, not surprisingly, does not address pricing issues, other than to provide for sup-

---

21. The proposed Airports Act had not yet been reintroduced in the second session of the 39th Parliament at the time this article went to press.

posedly greater transparency in airport operator pricing decisions. The proposed legislation adopts a detailed, almost intrusive approach to corporate governance and transparency, while avoiding the fundamental paradox of the governance model.

For future policy development in Canada, the analysis suggests that the proposed Canada Airports Act will have little if any impact. It does not and indeed cannot impose a price regulation regime on the airports. Nor does it address the intergenerational transfer concerns. The detailed governance and transparency provisions in the proposed act are highly likely to increase, not reduce, pressures on the government regarding airports policy. Future policy would be better guided by considering a fundamental change in governance structure that would allow access to paid-in equity capital (such as a for-profit private model) accompanied by a flexible price regulation regime, likely some form of a price cap or trigger regulation. Such a change would directly address issues of accountability and transparency, long-term financing, and price regulation if needed to limit impacts on users.

References

McGrath, T. M. 1990. *History of Canadian Airports.* Ottawa: Lugus Publications and Ministry of Supply and Services.

Minister of Transport. 1994. *National Airports Policy* (www.tc.gc.ca/programs/Airports/policy/menu.htm).

PART THREE

China and Developing Countries

7

ANMING ZHANG *and* ANDREW YUEN

Airport Policy and Performance in Mainland China and Hong Kong

China's airline industry used to be a paramilitary organization—before the 1980s the Civil Aviation Administration of China (CAAC) was a department of the air force. The CAAC not only regulated civil aviation but was directly involved in every aspect of the industry, including airline operation, airport management, and air traffic control. Although civil aviation was effectively separated from the air force in the early 1980s, liberalization of the aviation industry began largely in the late 1980s, when the single CAAC carrier was split into six operationally and financially independent airlines and the entry of non-CAAC carriers was encouraged. The CAAC monopoly in the provision of flight services was broken.

The establishment of commercially independent carriers further separated airline operations from airport operations. In the 1980s and early 1990s, major airports were still controlled and operated by the CAAC, and government spending was the main funding source of airport expansion. Rapid traffic growth had placed enormous pressures on airport infrastructure. To encourage local governments to invest in airports, the central government embarked on a program to surrender its airport control to local governments. As the test case, the CAAC in 1988 agreed to transfer operation of the Xiamen airport to the Xiamen Municipal Government. Other airports came under local control over the next several years. A recent policy initiative has been the

---

We would like to thank Cliff Winston, Gines de Rus, two anonymous reviewers, and participants of the conference on "Comparative Political Economy and Infrastructure Performance: The Case of Airports," Madrid, 2006, for very helpful comments on an early version of the paper. We also thank Chunyan Yu for data assistance. Financial support from the Rafael del Pino Foundation is gratefully acknowledged.

introduction of private ownership by floating airport shares in the stock markets. So far, six airport companies, covering seven airports, have been listed on stock exchanges. Given that a major problem for Chinese airports was their low productivity, resulting largely from poor management, the public listing was expected to improve airport efficiency significantly.

This paper discusses these policy developments in detail and examines their impact on China's air transportation industry.[1] We find that the aviation policy liberalization has contributed to a dramatic growth in air traffic and airline productivity and to improved market competition and air safety. Further, the localization program has been successful in encouraging local governments to invest in airport infrastructure. However, it is not clear from our study of twenty-five major Chinese airports whether public listing—a form of airport privatization—has significantly improved airport efficiency. The listed airports appear to be productively more efficient than the nonlisted airports. At the same time, there is little evidence suggesting that the listed airports' productivity has improved significantly after their initial public offerings (IPOs). Furthermore, the productivity of the listed airports grew at less than half the rate of nonlisted airports. Compared with the nonlisted airports, therefore, public listing does not seem to have had a significant impact on the improvement of airport productivity.

We further examine the reasons why the public listing privatization program has not achieved large efficiency gains by taking a closer look at the corporate governance of listed airports. Because the government still holds the dominant ownership in China's listed airports, these airports are still subject to a large degree of government intervention, and the external (market) discipline mechanisms and the internal control system are still not well developed. The current practice of only partially privatizing airports, with the government retaining dominant ownership, may not be an effective solution to the efficiency problem of Chinese airports. For the policy to work effectively, airport corporate governance must be strengthened and perhaps a complete privatization undertaken (with some sort of antimonopoly regulation). Competition must also be increased—our examination of the Hong Kong airport experience suggests that competitive pressure, either from airport users or from competing airports, may play a critical role in improving performance. Finally, our discussion suggests that further regulatory reform may

---

1. In this paper, the word *China* refers to mainland China. So, for example, domestic routes refer to intramainland routes, while nondomestic routes are either international routes with foreign countries or regional routes with the Special Administrative Regions of Hong Kong and Macau.

be needed in the area of air traffic control as travel delays have become a serious problem at some of the major Chinese airports.

Aviation Policy Developments

The reform of the airline industry began in the late 1970s as part of China's general economic reform and "open door" policy.[2] The administrative structure was reformed first in 1979 and then again in 1982; together these two actions effectively separated civil aviation from the air force and made the CAAC a ministry under the State Council. Although the industry took on some aspects of private business, in this initial stage of reform the CAAC was still heavily involved in running civil aviation.

Substantial reforms began in January 1987, when the State Council passed the "Report on Civil Aviation Reform Measures and Implementation." The long-term goal was to separate the CAAC as the regulator from direct involvement in airline and airport operations. Between 1987 and 1989, the single CAAC carrier was split into six airlines that were operationally and financially independent of the CAAC, while the entry of non-CAAC carriers was encouraged. In 1993 the Big Three carriers, namely, Air China, China Eastern, and China Southern, were further awarded the right to:

—Buy or lease aircraft and other transport equipment (after consultation with the CAAC)

—Borrow money from domestic or international financial markets as an independent legal entity

—Appoint managers to most key posts (with the exception of the presidents and vice presidents and their immediate subordinates)

—Set prices according to market demand conditions, subject to maintaining a "base price" on average

—Staff their overseas postings (a right that was normally restricted to senior administrative levels such as provincial governments).

These rights were not extended to the other airlines under the CAAC control. The added discretionary flexibilities made the Big Three more commercially independent. Furthermore, the three airlines were given approval to list on stock markets, which they did in subsequent years. In 2002 the State Council arranged for the three megacarriers to take over fourteen minor carriers (most of which were under the CAAC control), thus fully removing the CAAC from its role of operating and managing the airlines. Further, the airline oper-

2. Taplin (1993); Le (1997); Zhang (1998).

ation was separated from the airport operation, in which the CAAC was still heavily involved in the late 1980s and 1990s.

The reform policy of the late 1980s encouraged the entry of new, non-CAAC carriers, which began to serve domestic routes in 1986 and Hong Kong routes in 1987. These carriers grew quickly, especially in the domestic market. Over the 1986–92 period, for instance, the average annual growth rate of the new entrants was 126 percent, compared with 17 percent growth for the CAAC carriers. The CAAC also simplified its approval procedure in an effort to encourage carriers to open new routes. As a result, the total number of routes in 1992 was more than three times the number in 1980.[3]

The rapid growth in air transportation placed enormous pressure on airport infrastructure. Historically, the CAAC, representing the central government, owned and operated the commercial airports in China. It was the main source, through government fiscal spending, of capacity expansion and equipment purchase. (The other funding source was the policy loans from state-owned banks.) Although the central government had spent a large amount on airports and related infrastructure, the investment did not meet the (unexpectedly) rapid growth in air travel.[4] Although investment in aircraft increased dramatically during the late 1980s and early 1990s, airport infrastructure did not keep pace with the fleet expansion. For most of the 1990s only 10 percent of Chinese airports were able to accommodate large aircraft (B747s and MD-11s). Passenger terminals at major airports operated at 15 percent over capacity on average, whereas air cargo terminals and facilities could handle only 65 percent of potential demand.[5] Moreover, modernization of air traffic control systems was badly needed.

To overcome the shortage of funds and support the infrastructure development, the CAAC began to levy an airport infrastructure fee in 1992. Each international passenger pays a fee of 90 yuan at the airport, whereas a domestic passenger pays 50 yuan (10 yuan for small remote airports). Between 1992 and 2005, the accumulated income from the fee was 29.1 billion yuan (about US$3.5 billion), which was used mainly to ease the congestion problem in eastern China and to fund airport expansion and safety projects in the west.[6] Furthermore, the CAAC established the Fund of Infrastructure Construction for Civil Aviation in 1993. Chinese air carriers contributed to the fund by

---

3. Zhang and Chen (2003).
4. In the 1990s about 110 billion yuan had been spent on airport construction. Forty-five airports were built or expanded, and more than ninety airports were renovated.
5. Zhang and Chen (2003).
6. (www.caac.gov.cn). Moreover, the fee on international passengers also includes a contribution (20 yuan out of the 90 yuan fee) to the Tourism Development Fund.

paying 10 percent of their domestic revenue and 4–6 percent of their international revenue. To compensate, their corporate tax rate was reduced.[7]

Nevertheless, the scale of required capacity expansion meant local and private initiatives were also needed. To encourage local governments to invest in airports, the central government embarked on a program to surrender its airport control to provincial or municipal governments. Operation of the Xiamen Airport, including all fixed and working capital and all personnel, was turned over to the Xiamen municipal government in 1988. Other airports were localized gradually over the next several years. In 1993, for example, Shanghai Hongqiao International Airport—China's third largest airport at the time—was transferred to the Shanghai municipal government. Newly constructed airports were managed by local governments from the outset. The localization program was accelerated in the early 2000s and was completed by 2003, when the CAAC transferred ownership and control of all its remaining airports to local governments. The only exceptions are Beijing Capital International Airport and airports in politically sensitive Tibet; the CAAC still retains both the ownership and operational controls of these facilities. Localization of airports has forced them to look for new financing channels. In particular, local governments are likely to have a strong investment incentive since airports are a major economic engine in their local economies.

As part of the localization program the central government began to phase out its subsidization of airports in 2006. As a result, many airports will find it difficult to sustain their operations and development in the future unless they significantly improve their efficiency. By making the airports more financially accountable—as opposed to the "soft budget" constraint under the central CAAC—it was hoped that the airports would improve efficiency. The airport localization will also make attracting funds from private and foreign sectors more important.

Since 2002 overseas investors have been allowed to invest in the construction and operation of airport terminals and runways, with a maximum equity interest of 49 percent. In April 2005 the Airport Authority Hong Kong (AAHK) agreed to invest 1.99 billion yuan for a 35 percent stake in Hangzhou Xiaoshan International Airport (which is ranked ninth among Chinese airports by the number of passengers handled). After the AAHK's investment in Hangzhou, airports in Ningbo, Guangzhou, Nanjing, Chengdu, Kunming, and several other cities reportedly began negotiating with foreign investors on stake sales. For example, German airport operator Fraport AG (which manages the Frankfurt airport) signed an agreement to buy 25 percent of Ningbo

---

7. Zhang and Chen (2003).

Airport, and the AAHK took a majority stake in Zhuhai Airport after signing a joint-venture management deal. Currently, the CAAC is formulating policies to encourage more foreign participation in airport operation and may even allow majority foreign ownership for some airports, especially newly constructed airports or airports in the western region so long as Chinese nationals have relative control.[8]

In addition, the government has, since the late 1990s, committed to a policy of establishing the so-called "modern enterprise system" for airlines and airports. Here, a major policy initiative was to float shares of state-owned airlines and airports in the stock markets, in hope of spurring an improvement in corporate governance and hence performance. So far, six Chinese airport companies have been listed on stock exchanges in Hong Kong, Shanghai, and Shenzhen. While the state still holds majority ownership, asset management has been transferred to the State-Owned Assets Supervision and Administration Commission (SASAC) under the State Council. Now the CAAC serves predominantly as the regulator of the industry that aims to maintain a fair market environment and protect consumer interests. The aviation reform has thus paved the way for more market-oriented airline and airport management.

Industrial Performance

Since the late 1970s (when the aviation reform started), civil aviation has been the fastest-growing transportation mode in China. Between 1980 and 2005, the number of passengers traveling through China's airports grew at an average rate of 16.8 percent a year, while airport cargo tonnage grew 18.2 percent. This growth outperformed the growth in the 1960–78 period. Air transport has also become a much more important mode in domestic intercity passenger travel: Its proportion of passenger-kilometers of all modes—rail, road, water, and air—rose from 1.7 percent in 1980 to 7.6 percent in 1998, and to 9.0 percent in 2002. In 2004 China ranked third in the world in both passenger-kilometers and freight-ton-kilometers flown, a huge leap from its thirty-third place in passenger-kilometers and thirty-fifth in ton-kilometers in 1980.[9]

Although China's general economic growth since the late 1970s has contributed to the traffic growth, undoubtedly the aviation policy reform has

---

8. Consistent with its airport policy liberalization, China also made important concessions allowing foreign investors to take larger equity stakes in domestic airlines. Since 2002 foreign investors have been allowed to take stakes of up to 49 percent (so long as no single investor holds more than 25 percent), compared with the maximum 35 percent foreign ownership allowed under earlier regulations.

9. ICAO (1981, 2005).

also contributed significantly.[10] For example, the government policy of encouraging carrier entry has facilitated the large expansion of new routes and total traffic. Furthermore, by affecting the market structure at both the carrier and route levels, the reform has been conducive to airline competition.[11] In the mid-1990s, for instance, price discounting (from the official rates) was prevalent, and price competition was so intense that many small airlines suffered significant losses. The CAAC had to reaffirm its price regulation and forbid, after May 1, 1998, any discounts of ticket prices beyond the 20 percent limit for all routes. This fare control was later relaxed, and airlines could set fares as much as 45 percent below the CAAC base rate for most routes; discounts on tickets for tourist destinations were unrestricted. As a consequence of both airline competition and policy relaxation, cheaper tickets became more readily available, which further stimulated air travel demand.

Competition may further explain, at least in part, airlines' rapid improvement in labor productivity, which grew an average of 11.4 percent a year, as measured by revenue-ton-kilometers per employee, for the 1978–2000 period. Moreover, the industry's total factor productivity (TFP) rose significantly in the 1987–92 period, averaging over 4 percent a year.[12] This gain is much higher than the gains found in other Chinese state-owned enterprises: the annual TFP growth of the enterprises in the 1980s and early 1990s ranged from zero to 4 percent.[13]

As indicated earlier, a main objective of the airport decentralization drive was to encourage local governments to invest in airport infrastructure. This objective appears to have been achieved. For example, when Hongqiao Airport in Shanghai started to show saturation in the mid-1990s, the Shanghai municipal government immediately built another airport in Pudong, to which the Shanghai government contributed 10.7 billion yuan (of the 13 billion yuan total cost) for the first phase of the project. A similar situation occurred in Guangzhou: to deal with capacity constraints at the old Guangzhou airport, the Guangzhou municipal government built a new airport, which was opened in August 2004. Both Shanghai Pudong and Guangzhou Baiyun—the second- and third-largest airports in China, respectively—are designed to handle 80 million travelers a

---

10. China's gross domestic product increased fourfold from 1980 to 1998 in real terms, with an average annual growth rate of 8.7 percent, compared with 5.8 percent in the 1970s and 4.0 percent in the 1960s (*China Statistical Yearbook,* 1999). As people's disposable incomes increase, their demand for air travel will also increase, usually by a bigger proportion.
11. Zhang (1998); Zhang and Chen (2003).
12. Zhang and Chen (2003).
13. Woo and others (1994); Chen and others (1988); Jefferson, Rawski, and Zheng (1996); World Bank (1992).

year, making them comparable with the world's largest airports in passenger capacity. Furthermore, between 1986 and 1992, a total of forty-six airports in the country were built, upgraded, or expanded; in thirty-one of these, the local government was the sole or major investor. Altogether local governments accounted for over two-thirds of the 4.4 billion yuan invested in airports during this period. In 1999 investment in civil aviation fixed assets totaled 19.3 billion yuan. Of this, 7.8 billion yuan, or 40 percent, came from the local governments.[14]

Airline Safety

Safety and security are top priorities in air transportation. Safety in aviation has long been emphasized, for example, through policies and procedures to minimize the risk of failure in the design and operation of aircraft and airports.[15] The major regulatory agencies in China involved in aviation safety are the CAAC, which operates the national air traffic control system and reviews the financial fitness and safety qualifications of new carrier applications, and the Office of Aviation Safety, a part of the CAAC, which oversees operational safety. Furthermore, since air safety often attracts national attention, the State Council appoints an ad hoc investigative group after a serious aviation accident, which includes members from the CAAC, the State Administration of Work Safety, the Ministry of Supervision, and other related official departments. In addition, the Civil Aviation Management Institute of China and the newly established Civil Aviation Safety Academy of China provide aviation safety training to CAAC officers and staff in the sector and conduct related research to improve aviation safety in China.

China's civil aviation was once perceived as unsafe; this perception was especially strong among foreign travelers. Given that perception and the observation that consumers are not fully informed about an airline's safety, a major concern of the aviation policy liberalization was to ensure that aviation safety would not be compromised when the government started to withdraw from the management of airlines and airports. Has the liberalization increased accident risk? Here, figures 7-1 and 7-2 may have some descriptive merit. Figure 7-1 shows the time series of both the total accident rate (per 10,000 flights) and the total number of flights since 1950. It indicates that air safety was a serious problem in the 1950s–60s but that the number of fatal flight accidents dropped significantly in the 1970s and has since remained at a relatively sta-

14. Zhang (2000).
15. Security is concerned with deliberate sabotage or other acts to cause harm to air operations and the traveling public. Since September 11, 2001, security has become the highest priority of the global aviation industry and many governments, including China.

Figure 7-1. *Number of Commercial Flights and Fatal Accidents, 1950–2005*

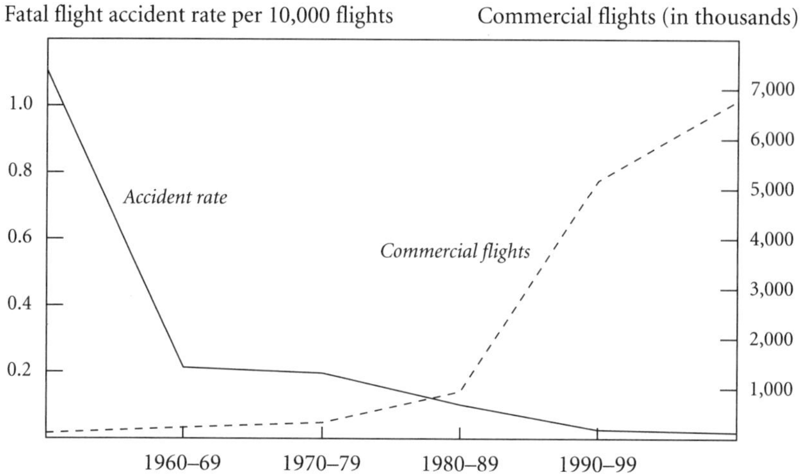

Fatal flight accident rate per 10,000 flights   Commercial flights (in thousands)

[Figure: Line graph showing Accident rate declining from above 1.0 in 1960–69 to near 0 by 1990–99, and Commercial flights rising sharply from near 0 to about 6,000+ thousand over the same period. Y-axis left: 0.2 to 1.0; Y-axis right: 1,000 to 7,000; X-axis: 1960–69, 1970–79, 1980–89, 1990–99.]

Source: Presentation by Ms. Sun Xiaomei, vice president of the Civil Aviation Safety Academy of China, at the Fourth International Aviation Training Symposium, July 2006, Oklahoma.

ble low number. The accident rate has dropped even further since the 1980s, because the number of flights, and thus the number of passengers, has increased dramatically over this twenty-five-year period.[16]

Figure 7-2 shows the aviation incident rate over the past decade (1996–2005).[17] The number of incidents per 10,000 flights dropped significantly between 1998 and 2000—a period when most major Chinese airlines, except Air China and Shanghai Airlines, were listed on the domestic and overseas stock exchanges—and remained stable afterward. These data do not support a claim that liberalization begun in the 1980s has worsened the industry's accident and incident record in any noticeable manner. If anything, the safety record has improved over the period.

This analysis suggests that safety improvement and liberalization may actually go hand in hand. Since the establishment of independent and commercially

16. This pattern is similar to that observed in the industrialized countries with a lag of about ten years: there the number of fatal flight accidents dropped significantly during the 1960s–70s, when commercial jet aircraft were introduced and became popular, tougher safety regulations were imposed, and airline competition was introduced. As a result, while the Chinese accident rates are still considerably higher than the rates for the industrialized countries, the gap has shrunk over time.

17. Aviation accidents include fatal and nonfatal accidents. Fatal accidents involve passenger fatalities and hull losses, whereas incidents involve injuries (usually nonfatal) and damage to equipment. Incidents include serious business interruptions and "near misses."

Figure 7-2. *Incident Rate, 1996–2005*

Incidents per 10,000 flights

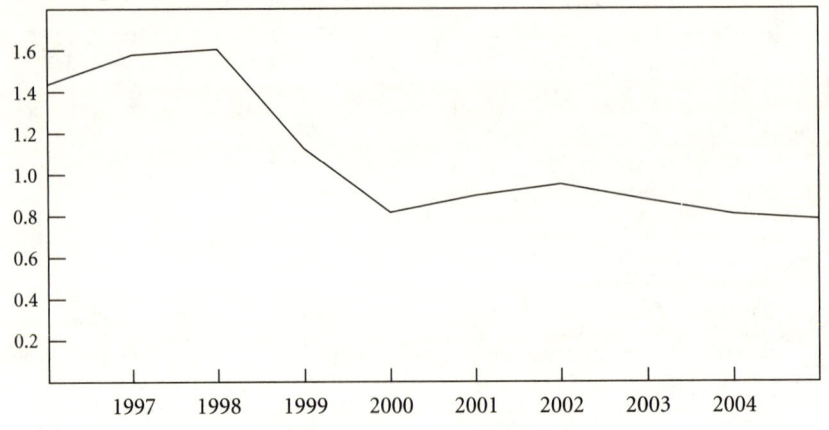

[Figure: Line graph showing incident rate declining from about 1.45 in 1997, peaking near 1.6 around 1998, dropping sharply to about 0.85 by 2000, then remaining relatively flat around 0.8–0.95 through 2004.]

Source: Presentation by Ms. Sun Xiaomei, vice president of the Civil Aviation Safety Academy of China, at the Fourth International Aviation Training Symposium, July 2006, Oklahoma.

oriented airlines, the firms themselves have a strong incentive to maintain safety if only to remain competitive. A good safety record is good for business and for competition. Air travel demand for a carrier drops whenever it has a major air disaster, while tourist demand is strongly influenced by perceived safety and security. Airlines also benefit from a good safety record because they are more likely to pay smaller insurance premiums and to avoid having to pay for costly lawsuits and damage compensation.[18]

Air Traffic Control

Finally, we discuss China's air traffic control management and performance. The CAAC monitors domestic airspace to ensure aviation safety and reduce travel delay. China's airspace is used by both military and civil aviation, and only 30 percent of the airspace is currently available for civil use.[19] The CAAC manages the civilian air traffic control system under a three-level hierarchical structure made up of the CAAC Air Traffic Control Bureau, six regional air traffic control bureaus, and the control centers themselves. The ever-increasing civil aviation demand has made coordination between military

18. Another contributing factor is that safer aircraft are being used. Chinese airlines dramatically increased their use of newer and better aircraft during the period; see, for example, Zhang and Chen (2003).
19. "New Air Route to Cut Flying Time to Europe," *China Daily*, April 12, 2006.

and civil aviation authorities crucial in airspace management. China takes a very tough position on delineating the boundaries between civilian and military airspace, between regions, and between China and other countries. That results in some serious restrictions on the number and position of entry and exit points civilian airlines can use, making it difficult for carriers to design optimal route structures.[20] Furthermore, since the military remains as the "senior" user of the airspace, the military's air traffic control requirements have to be taken into account whenever the civil aviation authority plans to introduce more advanced control specifications and equipment. Two other factors also constrain the traffic control system: private and foreign investors are barred from investing in air traffic control facilities; and safety, security, traffic control, and maintenance positions are severely understaffed. One estimate puts staffing levels at 20–40 percent of the level needed to meet the minimum safety standards.[21]

As a result, the airspace organization and route structure are far from optimal, and airport congestion and delays are becoming a major problem. Daily ceilings on landings and takeoffs have been imposed at Beijing Capital International Airport (1,100) and Shanghai Pudong International Airport (650), the country's two busiest airports.[22] In southern China's Pearl River Delta, which includes Hong Kong and Macau, the airspace congestion has led to increasing delays. It is reported that 2,996 flights departing from Hong Kong were delayed in the first ten months of 2006, compared with 973 in 2004 and 1,733 in 2005.[23] Nearly 70 percent of flights to and from Macau were delayed in May 2006.[24] Although a plan to increase the number of new flight routes in the region has been discussed for a long time among CAAC and aviation officials from Hong Kong and Macau, it has not yet been finalized. These air traffic control congestion issues are exacerbated by the fact that a majority of the region's airspace is allocated to military use.[25]

20. Wu (2005).
21. Wu (2005).
22. On December 1, 2006, the two airports in Shanghai—Pudong and Hongqiao—were temporarily closed without much earlier notice to the airlines, for reasons related to air traffic control, resulting in large flight delays. See "Shanghai Airport Temporarily Closed; Cathay Pacific: Received Military Exercise Notice," *Mingpao*, December 2, 2006.
23. "Inadequate Airspace in Mainland Led to Flight Delays in Hong Kong," *Mingpao*, November 30, 2006. In 2005 Hong Kong connected to 141 destinations in the world, of which 40 were cities in mainland China.
24. Chinese Society of Civil Aviation, *Industry News*, Taipei, June 7, 2006.
25. "The Mainland's Military Department Was the Major Barrier in the Three Regions' Negotiation," *Mingpao*, March 23, 2006.

An Evaluation of the Effect of Public Listing on Airport Efficiency

A major policy reform since the mid-1990s has been the privatization of airports through initial public offerings. As of December 2007, six Chinese airport companies have been listed on stock exchanges: Beijing, Guangzhou, Hainan, Shanghai, Shenzhen, and Xiamen; Shanghai International Airport Ltd. holds both Hongqiao and Pudong airports. Although attracting private funds was a rationale for these IPOs, the principal objective was to improve airport efficiency. The hope was that listing the airports on the stock market would force them to fulfill higher corporate governance standards and to follow stricter capital market discipline, thus improving performance.

That Chinese airports are inefficient has been confirmed by the Air Transport Research Society (ATRS). Its measures of airport productivity—a core aspect of efficiency—are reported for 2004 in table 7-1. In particular, the measure of residual variable factor productivity attempts to correct for factors such as scale, traffic mix, and capital investment that might influence measured productivity and that are out of managerial control. The four Chinese airport companies covered by the ATRS study—Beijing, Guangzhou, Shanghai, and Shenzhen—perform rather poorly relative to Hong Kong and Vancouver (the base case). With the exception of Guangzhou airport, the Chinese airports in the ATRS study also have performed poorly relative to regional comparisons from Asia Pacific, Europe, and North America. As we discuss below, these four airports are actually much more productive than the rest of the Chinese airports. Thus, the Chinese airports as a group are productively inefficient.

This section investigates whether the act of listing a Chinese airport improves economic efficiency of the airport. Lack of data and studies makes an assessment of economic efficiency for Chinese airports difficult. Fortunately, Fung and others calculated productivity of twenty-five major Chinese airports over the 1995–2004 period in the first study ever of efficiency of regional airports in China.[26] The researchers focused primarily on whether airport efficiency was improving and whether productivity among the airports from different regions was converging, and they found positive answers to both questions. We use their data to investigate whether privatization through public listing improves airport performance.

The twenty-five sample airports are listed in table 7-2. These airports accounted for over two-thirds of China's airport passengers in 2004. Among them, Beijing Capital, Guangzhou Baiyun, Shanghai Hongqiao, Shenzhen

---

26. Fung and others (2007).

Table 7-1. *Airport Productivity Comparisons, 2004*
Vancouver airport = 1.0

Airport	Gross variable factor productivity	Residual variable factor productivity
Beijing	0.195	0.487
Shanghai	0.156	0.413
Guangzhou	0.300	0.776
Shenzhen	0.210	0.555
Hong Kong	0.471	0.931
Asia Pacific mean	0.573	0.682
Europe mean	0.350	0.684
North America mean	0.663	0.731

Source: Air Transport Research Society (2006).

Baoan, and Xiamen Gaoqi are held by companies listed on stock exchanges; the rest are unlisted.[27] Table 7-2 also shows the specific region to which each airport belongs.

Fung and his colleagues employed data envelopment analysis (DEA) to measure the productivity level. In its output-oriented approach, the DEA model defines the efficiency score of any firm as the fraction of the firm's inputs necessary for the firm to produce the same output as a firm on the efficient frontier. Firms are said to be on the efficient frontier when their outputs cannot be increased without a corresponding increase in inputs; they are given an efficiency score of unity. Firms with an efficiency score below unity are inefficient.[28] The estimates made by Fung and others are given in table 7-3, which shows the mean efficiency scores of the listed and unlisted airports for each year. As can be seen, the efficiency scores of the listed airports are, on average, higher than those of the unlisted airports during the 1995–2004 period, except for 1997. The pooled mean efficiency score of the listed airports is higher by one standard deviation (or about 0.26 points) than the unlisted counterparts.

The fact that listed airports have, on average, higher efficiency scores does not necessarily mean that they are more efficient, since other factors, such as hub status and demand shocks, also play a role. With respect to hub status, the

27. It is noted that the sixth listed airport, Hainan Meilan, is not included. Also, Shanghai Airport Company controls both Hongqiao and Pudong airports. Hongqiao was listed in 1998 when Pudong was still nonexistent; the latter went into service in late 1999.

28. Detailed descriptions on DEA can be found in Charnes and others (1994).

Table 7-2. *Sample Airports and Listing Status*

Airport	Region	Listing year/ stock exchange	State share in 2003 (percent)	State share in 2006 (percent)
Beijing Capital International	Northern	2000/ Hong Kong	65.0	53.8
Changsha Huanghua	Central and South			
Chengdu Shuangliu International	Southwest			
Chongqing Jiangbei International	Southwest			
Dalian Zhoushuizi International	Northeast			
Guangzhou Baiyun International	Central and South	2003/ Shanghai	60.0	52.4
Hailar Dongshan	Northern			
Harbin Taiping International	Northeast			
Hefei Luogang	Eastern			
Hohhot Baita	Northern			
Jinan Yaoqiang	Eastern			
Kashi	Northwest			
Kunming Wujiaba International	Southwest			
Lanzhou Zhongchuan	Northwest			
Nanning Wuxu	Central and South			
Qingdao Liuting	Eastern			
Sanya Fenghuang	Central and South			
Shanghai Hongqiao International	Eastern	1998/ Shanghai	63.0	57.6
Shenyang Taoxian International	Northeast			
Shenzhen Baoan International	Central and South	1998/ Shenzhen	64.0	54.7
Taiyuan Wusu	Northern			
Tianjin Binhai International	Northern			
Urumqi Diwopu International	Northwest			
Xiamen Gaoqi International	Eastern	1996/ Shanghai	75.0	68.0
Xian Xianyang International	Northwest			

Source: Fung and others (2007); company annual reports.

Table 7-3. *Efficiency Scores for Listed and Unlisted Airports in China*

	Listed			Unlisted		
Year	Count	Mean	Standard deviation	Count	Mean	Standard deviation
1995	0	n.a.	n.a.	25	0.4811	0.2892
1996	1	1.0000	n.a.	24	0.4590	0.2891
1997	1	0.4184	n.a.	24	0.5628	0.3423
1998	3	0.7021	0.3003	22	0.5194	0.3213
1999	3	0.6727	0.3469	22	0.4740	0.3177
2000	4	0.6770	0.2929	21	0.4991	0.2965
2001	4	0.6976	0.2899	21	0.4487	0.3105
2002	4	0.6974	0.2391	21	0.4284	0.3020
2003	5	0.7586	0.2272	20	0.3950	0.2578
2004	5	0.7716	0.2521	20	0.4135	0.2638
Pooled	30	0.7161	0.2471	220	0.4703	0.2985

Source: Fung and others (2007).
n.a. = Not applicable.

sample airports may be classified into international, regional, and nonhub airports. China's three largest airports, Beijing, Shanghai, and Guangzhou, are commonly regarded as the international gateway hubs. These three airports are at the heart of the country's most important economic and industrial zones—Beijing serves the Beijing-Tianjin-Hebei economic ring; Shanghai, the Yangtze River Delta; and Guangzhou, the Pearl River Delta—and have far more international routes than the other airports. Thirty-eight percent of China's air passengers and 55 percent of the country's air cargo passes through these three airports. They are also the bases of the Big Three air carriers. The six regional hubs are Chengdu, Shenyang, Xian, Kunming, Shenzhen, and Urumqi (figure 7-3), with the first three cities being the headquarters of three of the six official regional civil aviation bureaus.[29] Shenzhen and Kunming have strong local traffic and are the country's fourth- and fifth-largest airports respectively, while Urumqi is a gateway for China's western region, especially for traffic to and from Central Asia and Europe, and so has a high proportion of connecting traffic. All other airports in our sample are classified as nonhubs.

---

29. The other three regional civil aviation bureaus are based in Beijing (for north China), Shanghai (east China), and Guangzhou (central/south China). The "chain of command" is a two-level administration system of the CAAC and the six regional civil aviation bureaus. As a consequence, the published aviation statistics, such as those in the *Statistical Data on Civil Aviation of China*, are confined to the six-region division. This division may stem from military considerations in the 1950s.

Figure 7-3. Six Aviation Regions and Major Airports in China

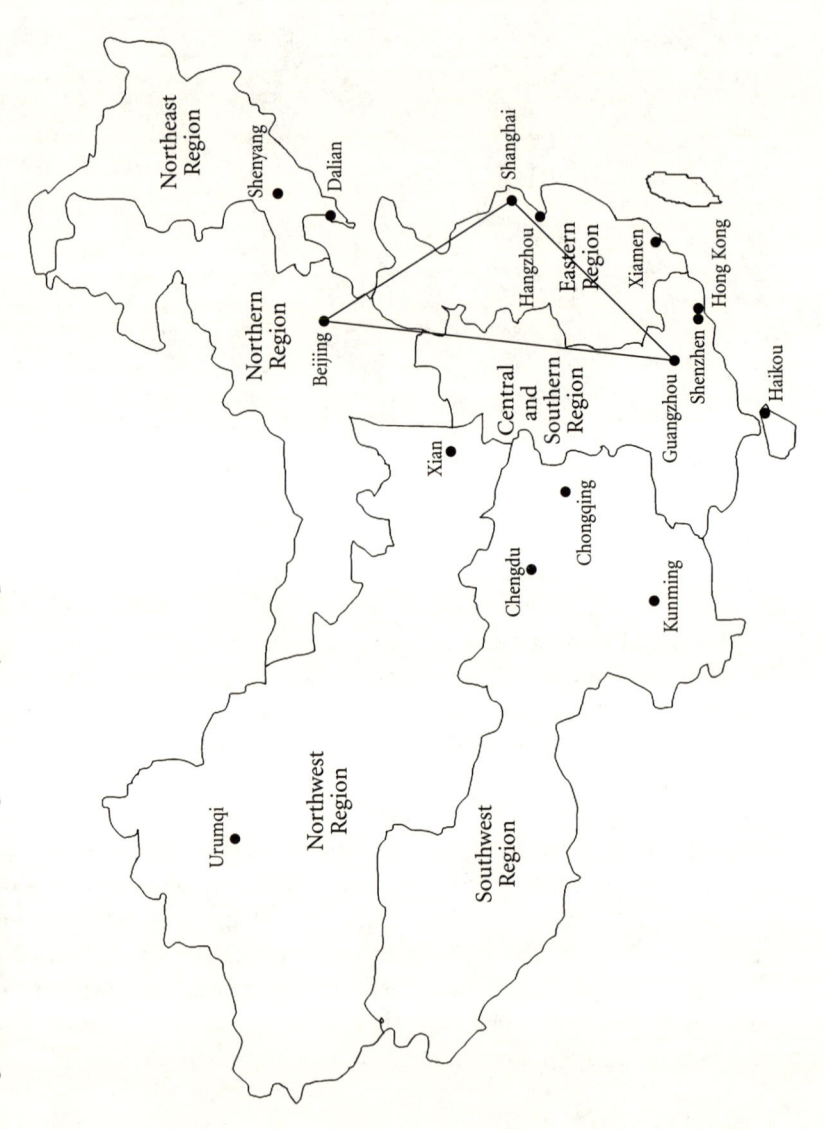

To isolate the effect of public listing on airport productivity, we controlled for the size and location advantages that hub airports possess. As examined in detail in the appendix, the positive relationship between the efficiency and public listing is robust to considerations of hub status, potential demand shocks, and other industrial factors: The listed airports have higher efficiency scores than unlisted airports. The regression analysis reported in the appendix thus shows that the status of public listing is an important determinant of airport efficiency level.

However, this listing effect on efficiency level does not necessarily imply that privatization through public listing improves airport performance. For instance, the positive listing effect might arise because the Chinese government chose the most efficient airports to be listed. In other words, efficiency could be endogenous in the selection of the listed airports. This argument has some merit, because companies were required to be profitable for three consecutive years before they could issue an IPO. (This requirement was dropped when the securities law was revised on October 27, 2005.) According to China's National Audit Office, nine of the twelve major airports and thirty-seven of the thirty-eight secondary airports in China were not profitable in 2001, suggesting that only a handful of Chinese airports were able to meet this listing requirement and that underperforming airports were effectively screened out for listing.[30] As a result, listing, the independent variable in the regression models, may be correlated with the error term; that is, an endogeneity problem exists. In our regression analysis, however, the dependent variable is airport productivity, not profitability. So the endogeneity observation relies on the assumption that high productivity leads to high profits. This assumption appears reasonable, although it might not hold in the context of Chinese state-owned firms such as airports.[31]

Thus, comparing the *efficiency levels* of two types of airports may be insufficient in determining whether public listing improves airport performance. We also need to look at their *productivity growth*, that is, the changes in efficiency level. The growth of productive efficiency as measured by the Malmquist index is given in the appendix. For the five listed airports, overall productivity rose by about 21 percent between 1995 and 2004, which is about 2 percent a year. This growth rate is less than that for the unlisted airports, whose productivity increased by about 34 percent over the ten-year period, or more than 3 percent a year. This differential in growth rates continues to hold after controlling for hub status and other factors, but it becomes statistically

---

30. Li (2002).
31. Zhang, Zhang, and Zhao (2002).

176   Anming Zhang and Andrew Yuen

Figure 7-4. *Malmquist Productivity Change before and after Public Listing*

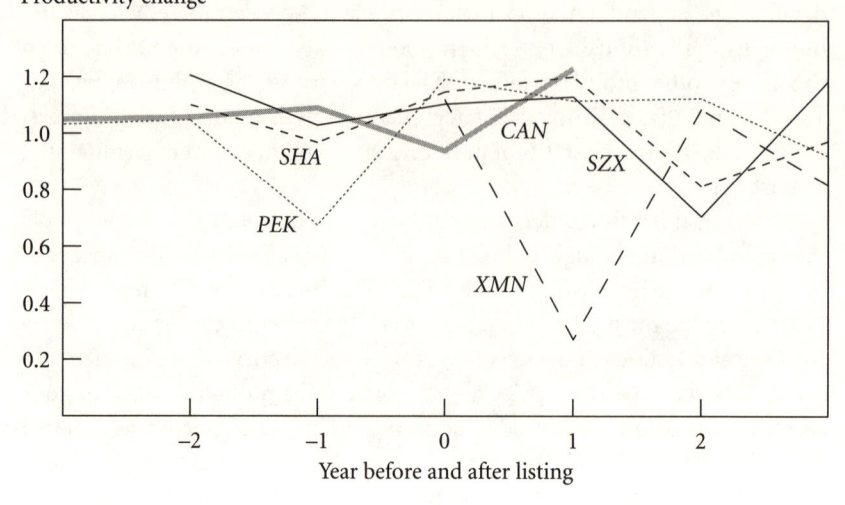

Source: Authors.

Note: XMN is Xiamen Gaoqi International Airport; SHA is Shanghai Hongqiao International Airport; SZX is Shenzhen Baoan International Airport; PEK is Beijing Capital International Airport; and CAN is Guangzhou Baiyun International Airport.

insignificant (see the appendix). Our analysis therefore suggests that the productivity of unlisted airports may have improved, on average, relative to that of the listed airports during the period, although as shown earlier, the efficiency level of unlisted airports was still lower, owing perhaps to their lower starting levels. In other words, public listing may have no significantly positive impact on the productivity growth of listed airports compared with unlisted airports.

An alternative way to investigate whether public listing improves airport performance is to compare the productivity growth of the listed airports before and after their IPOs. Figure 7-4 shows the productivity changes, for each sample airport, for the three years before and the three years after its listing (if the data are available). It shows that with the exception of Guangzhou airport, there does not seem to be a significant growth in productivity after listing. The rather limited data points preclude a very rigorous study, however.

Issues of Corporate Governance and Competition

As noted earlier, one reason given for allowing airports to be listed was to improve their corporate governance—or in Chinese terminology, to establish a "modern enterprise system" for airports, which would then lead to performance improvement. It was widely expected that private investors (domestic and foreign) would require the airports to meet higher corporate governance standards and subject them to stricter capital market discipline. Why does the expectation appear to be unfulfilled? In this section we address this issue by taking a closer look at the corporate governance of listed firms in China.

Dominant State Ownership of Airports

A main reason for the unsatisfactory performance after listing may have to do with the fact that the state (the local or national government) still maintains a controlling interest in all the listed airports (60 percent or more in 2003; see table 7-2). As a result of these *partial privatizations*, the state still has a great influence on their operation and investment decisions. Further, these privatizations have "Chinese characteristics." For example, all the top managers must be approved by the Organization Departments of the local or central Communist Party (which are a part of the local or national government). The government maintains ultimate rights for appointing and changing top management positions.[32]

In general, a dominant position may increase the large shareholder's incentive to monitor management and improve efficiency. As the benefits of monitoring are shared by all shareholders while the costs are borne completely by the monitoring party, dominant shareholders internalize the costs and benefits of monitoring to a greater extent than do small, diverse investors and, therefore, exert more monitoring efforts.[33] However, this argument may not apply to state-owned enterprises in China. As the general public is the owner of the enterprise, the property rights belong to everyone—and yet to no one in particular. For the citizens' interests to be effectively reflected in the policymaking process, a sound political system, one that China is still in the process of developing, is needed. As a result, the "owner" is unable to write an efficient contract with the "agent" (the government) to align the interests of both parties. In general, there are few effective instruments and little incentive for the government to monitor state-owned enterprises so as to improve their efficiency. At the same time, state ownership is likely to create regulatory and management inefficiency.[34] For these reasons, state dominance in listed

---

32. Board members in Chinese joint-stock companies consist mainly of representatives or officials from the State Asset Management Bureau (now the SASAC), local governments, and other state enterprises (Su 2005). On average 90 percent of the board members are government officials and delegates of other state enterprises.
33. Grossman and Hart (1980); Shleifer and Vishny (1986).
34. Winston (2006).

firms may not improve firm efficiency in China. This observation is consistent with empirical findings that the performance of Chinese listed companies is negatively correlated or uncorrelated to state dominance in ownership.[35] For example, Wang finds a sharp decline in post-issue operating performance of IPO firms that are controlled by the state.[36]

Corporate Governance Problems of Listed Companies

External discipline from the capital market plays an important role in monitoring and improving operation of listed companies. For example, investors can punish poor management performance by selling the shares of a listed company. Takeover threats can also be an effective measure to mitigate the agency costs of managerial discretions.[37] For external discipline to work effectively, however, quality of *information disclosure,* that is, the accuracy and completeness of new information that may considerably affect the price at which a listed company's shares are traded, is critical. In China misstatement of financial information is a disturbing issue for the investors as well as for regulatory bodies.[38] Consider, for example, the judicial system. Its role in preventing misstatement is questionable, since it is still treated as part of the government's administrative system.[39] As a consequence, politics and adjudication are often mixed together and there is no effective judicial independence. Chen suggests that although related laws and regulations exist, Chinese courts are reluctant to accept private securities litigation against firms' misstatements, because granting damage compensation in private litigation would amount to the loss of state assets.[40] In September 2001 the Supreme People's Court, facing a wave of private securities litigation, issued a notice in effect directing all lower courts to refuse temporarily to hear private securities lawsuits.[41]

In addition to the external monitoring force, the *internal control system* is also a critical component in the corporate governance system. The statutory power hierarchy of a listed company includes the shareholders' general meet-

---

35. See, for example, Xu and Wang (1999); Chen (2001); Tian (2001); Sun and Tong (2003); Wang (2005).
36. Wang (2005).
37. Shleifer and Vishny (1986).
38. Gu (2006).
39. Chen (2003).
40. Chen (2003).
41. The court's attitude to the issue seems to have changed lately, however. In January 2003 it announced a judicial interpretation on civil compensation concerning breaches of the stock market standards on financial reporting. According to the interpretation, investors can sue not only the companies for compensation, but the information providers, such as the directors, as well.

ing, the board of directors, and, unique to Chinese listed firms, the supervisory board. However, the supervisory boards have done little to uncover misconduct by boards of directors and management. Dahya, Karbhari, and Xiao suggest five reasons for the ineffectiveness of the supervisory board: lack of legal power and responsibilities; lack of independence; technical incompetence; information shortage; and lack of incentives.[42]

For example, the article of association for the Shenzhen airport requires that its supervisory board be composed of three members. Currently, two of the three members are the deputy secretaries of the shareholding company's Communist Party committee, and the third member is the top manager of the company. Furthermore, no member of the board has a professional qualification in law, finance, or accounting.[43] Nor has the board met the legal requirement that one-third of its members be elected by company employees. Hence, it is questionable whether the supervisory board of the company can perform its role independently and effectively.

Finally, as stated earlier, it is widely believed that in general concentrated ownership provides greater incentives to majority shareholders to monitor management. Three separate studies find that corporate performance of Chinese listed companies is positively correlated with concentrated ownership by *institutional shareholders* other than state agencies and is negatively associated with dispersed ownership.[44] Currently, however, the shareholdings of these institutional investors in Chinese listed companies are too low to provide them with sufficient incentives to closely monitor the operation of companies. For instance, among the five listed airport companies, the largest institutional investor was Harvest Fund Management Co. Ltd., which holds about 5 percent of Shenzhen airport.[45]

International Aviation Policy and Airline Competition

Another policy issue is China's international aviation policy, which can have an important bearing on its airport developments. A greater number of international airlines and passengers can positively influence airport corporate governance and performance, as foreign users typically demand more and higher-quality services than domestic users do. Here, a liberal international

---

42. Dahya, Karbhari, and Xiao (2000).
43. According to the Code of Corporate Governance for Listed Companies in China, issued by the China Securities Regulatory Commission and the State Economic and Trade Commission, supervisors shall have professional knowledge or work experience in such areas as law and accounting.
44. Xu and Wang (1999); Qi, Wu, and Zhang (2000); Chen (2001).
45. *Shenzhen Airport Annual Report,* 2005.

aviation policy would be conducive to good governance and efficient operation at airports.

All commercial aspects of international air transportation have been governed by restrictive bilateral air service agreements since the Chicago Convention held in 1944. As part of this bilateral system, China had adopted conservative international aviation policies, resulting in a rather limited number of air traffic rights between China and other countries.[46] Here, physical constraints at major airports in the past were not conducive to a more liberal regime. The centralization of airport control did not help either, as the incentive for liberalization from the airport side was not very high. The lack of airline and airport competition may explain the differential performance between the mainland and Hong Kong airports (see below).

China has been moving toward a more liberal international policy regime for the last five years, in line with its broader trade expansion goals and its accession to the World Trade Organization in December 2001. Among the significant developments have been a rather bold, liberal Sino-U.S. air service agreement, signed in July 2004; a liberal air service arrangement signed with Hong Kong in September 2004; approval for Cathay Pacific Airways (controlled by the United Kingdom's Swire Pacific) to operate flights between Hong Kong and major Chinese cities; the granting of a significant number of fifth-freedom traffic rights to foreign airlines;[47] and the arrangement of an open-skies regime for the resort island of Hainan Province.[48] As a result, the number of international connections has significantly increased for China's airports.

In this move toward a more liberal international aviation regime, airports have played a supportive role, resulting largely from airport localization and expansion. Localized airports tend to pay more attention to their local business and community interests and are more commercially driven than the former centralized airports. For instance, localized airports place high value on the total amount of traffic going through the airport, while paying relatively

46. Zhang and Chen (2003).
47. The fifth freedom is the right to carry traffic between a first foreign country and a second. For example, on a Vancouver-Hong Kong-Bangkok flight by a Canadian carrier, the carrier may be permitted to pick up additional passengers and cargo in Hong Kong.
48. Under the arrangement, the CAAC waives the right to reciprocal air rights in exchange for new services to Hainan and does not require existing bilateral air service agreements to be renegotiated. Further, it does not restrict the country of origin of carriers flying to Hainan and allows both passenger and cargo operations. In addition, the CAAC has adopted a new landing-visa program in Hainan for citizens of all nations; see Annette Chiu, "Hainan to Be Special Zone for Tourism," *South China Morning Post*, July 16, 2003.

less attention to whether the carrier bringing in the traffic is domestic or foreign. In other words, as Chinese airports become more localized, they are more likely to push for a liberal international aviation regime.[49]

Other Recent Policy Relaxations

In an attempt to improve corporate governance of listed firms, the Chinese government in 2001 lifted the stock-investment ban on its social security fund. It has since chosen six domestic mutual fund companies to manage the social security funds. Starting in 2003, these companies were allowed to invest in domestic stock markets. In addition, in December 2002 China implemented the Qualified Foreign Institutional Investors scheme to attract foreign institutional investors to put their money into the Chinese stock markets. As of October 2005, thirty foreign institutional investors were qualified for this program by the China Securities Regulatory Commission (CSRC). These domestic and foreign institutional investors are likely to develop into important participants in the stock market and could become a critical force in the efficiency improvement of Chinese airports.

Finally, important progress has been made in reducing the state ownership share in listed companies. In 2005 the CSRC and the State-Owned Assets Supervision and Administration Commission jointly issued a proposal to promote experiments on a "split share" structure reform, which aims at making the state share and legal-person share tradable in the market.[50] To distinguish them from the previous shares, the new shares are known as G-shares, which include the previous tradable A- and B-shares, and the nontradable state and legal-person shares. More than 80 percent of Chinese firms listed domestically—a total of 1,092—have adopted, or are in the process of adopting, the split-share reform.[51] The four domestically listed airport companies, namely, Guangzhou, Shanghai, Shenzhen, and Xiamen airports, have completed their split-share reforms and the state shares in these airports have

---

49. Another reason for the supportive role of airports is expanded airport capacity and other infrastructures in China since the 1990s; see Zhang and Chen (2003).
50. "China Issues Proposals Promoting Experiments on Split Share Structure," *China Daily*, May 31, 2005. For a typical listed company in China before 2004, there were five major types of shares outstanding: the state share, legal-person share, employee share, and tradable common A- and B-shares. Legal-person shares are controlled by large state-owned enterprises, state banks, and local governments, so they are essentially part of state ownership. Common A- and B-shares are denominated in Chinese and foreign currencies, respectively. Between 1992 (when the domestic stock exchanges started) and 2004, the portion of tradable shares remained almost unchanged at around 35 percent.
51. "State-Share Reform Enters Final Phase," *China Daily*, July 4, 2006.

been significantly reduced, although the state remains the majority shareholder (see table 7-2). In addition, the state share in the Beijing airport, listed on the Hong Kong Stock Exchange, has been reduced.

Hong Kong

Hong Kong International Airport (HKIA) was moved from Kai Tak to Chek Lap Kok in 1998. At its opening, HKIA had one runway, a partially completed terminal, and a capacity of 35 million passengers a year. In 1999 a second runway was put into service, and a new wing of the terminal building was completed. As a result, both passenger and cargo capacities have expanded significantly relative to the capacity-constrained Kai Tak airport. Based on ATRS measures (shown in table 7-1), HKIA performs well compared with the average airport in Asia Pacific, Europe, and North America, and it performs particularly well relative to airports in mainland China. Furthermore, Hong Kong airport charges, which account for 43 percent of the airport's revenue, are quite competitive in the context of world airports after taking the airport location and service quality into account.[52] In 2005 HKIA handled 40.7 million passengers, about six times the number of Hong Kong residents, and 3.44 million tons of cargo, making it the world's fifth-largest in international passengers and first in international cargo (second in all air freight handled, after Federal Express's base city, Memphis).

Several factors have contributed to HKIA's success as a key hub for international aviation, including Hong Kong's geopolitical location as a gateway to China and its long-standing free-market policy. The airport is managed by the Airport Authority Hong Kong, a statutory corporation that was set up under the Airport Authority Ordinance in 1995. The airport has been operated largely on commercial principles and its governance is highly transparent. Nonetheless, it is worth emphasizing that intensive competition has contributed significantly to the HKIA's success, especially compared with the airports in the mainland. Competition is evident on several fronts. First, there is a high degree of airline competition, with about eighty airlines operating at the airport. For several years, Cathay Pacific Airways, as Hong Kong's home carrier, has accounted for around 30 percent of the total traffic (passengers or cargo). This market dominance is weak compared with the market share of other home carriers at other hub airports in Asia.[53] A greater number of airlines can positively influence airport governance and performance.

52. Law, Fung, and Kaw (2005).
53. Cathay's HK$8.22 billon (US$1.05 billion) recent takeover of Dragonair, the second largest Hong Kong airline, will increase Cathay's market share.

Second, HKIA itself competes vigorously with other airports in the region. This competition occurs at two levels: gateway traffic into China's Pearl River Delta, and hub traffic for Asian destinations. Hong Kong has long been the gateway to southern China, to which it is linked by road, rail, and air.[54] Hong Kong's air cargo activity has been predominantly gateway business, with cargo either originating in, or destined for, manufacturing enterprises in the Pearl River Delta. This type of business accounted for 78 percent of Hong Kong's total air-cargo trade in 2000.[55] To maintain this gateway role, HKIA must compete with four other airports in a region that has one of the highest airport densities in the world. Five airports, all newly built, together served more than 80 million passengers in 2005—roughly the same as Atlanta, Chicago, and Tokyo. Hong Kong's competition comes mainly from Guangzhou and Shenzhen. Macau and Zhuhai are considerably smaller in scale and serve niche markets.[56] Over the last several years the regional market has expanded significantly, and both Guangzhou and Shenzhen grew faster than the regional average, while Hong Kong's growth was the smallest of the five airports. As a result, HKIA's traffic share in the region declined from 58 percent in 2000 to 48 percent in 2004. In the near future, Hong Kong's hub role for south China will face a serious challenge when Guangzhou airport gets a greater number of international flights as part of China's more liberalized open-skies policy; the mainland aviation authorities have long intended to make Guangzhou the third Chinese international gateway (in addition to Shanghai and Beijing).

Next consider the airport competition for hub traffic. About one-third of the 40.7 million passengers using HKIA in 2005 were transferring through the airport—arriving from one place outside Hong Kong, staying within the airport, and then departing from the airport by the same or different aircraft. Hong Kong faces competition for this traffic from other Asian hubs like Osaka, Seoul, Singapore, Tokyo, and, lately, Bangkok, Beijing, and Shanghai. Hong Kong's role as a hub between Taiwan and east and north China may also

54. The region covers 42,000 square kilometers and includes Hong Kong, Macau, and the Pearl River Delta Economic Zone. The latter includes Guangzhou, Shenzhen, Zhuhai, Foshan, Jiangmen, Dongguan, Zhongshan, urban districts of Huizhou, Huidong county, Boluo county, urban districts of Zhaoqing, Gaoyao county-level city, and Sihui county-level city.

55. Zhang (2003).

56. Macau and Zhuhai, located on the west bank of the Pearl River, have a small catchment area because most economic activities are located on the east bank (where the other three airports are located). Macau has positioned itself as a tourist destination and a low-cost carrier hub and has been competing with HKIA in the growing Taiwan-mainland passenger market, while Zhuhai has tried to maximize its advantage in funneling cargo traffic from the west bank by forming a joint venture with HKIA in 2006.

dwindle when the two Chinese polities establish direct air links with each other. As for cargo, the market share of hub transshipments in Hong Kong is about 15 percent of its total air cargo, and HKIA faces competition mainly from Seoul, Shanghai, Singapore, and Taipei.[57] These competitive pressures (existing or potential) have played a critical role in improving HKIA's performance. In August 2003 the government announced that it was beginning preparations to privatize the Hong Kong airport, which was wholly owned by the government. The government said its main objectives in the planned privatization were to unlock the airport authority's value by increasing the government's fiscal income and by using private ownership to improve the airport's operational efficiency and its accessibility to capital market fundraising opportunities. Yet with only weak support for the privatization, the government shelved the proposal in late 2005.

Concluding Remarks

We have reviewed China's aviation policy developments and examined their impact on its air transportation industry. We found that the policy liberalization has contributed to the dramatic growth in air traffic and airline productivity and has improved market competition and air safety. Further, the airport localization program succeeded in encouraging local governments to invest in airport infrastructure. However, it is not clear whether airport privatization through public listing has improved airport efficiency. Our examination suggests that the government's current policy of maintaining dominant ownership of the listed airports may not be an effective solution to the efficiency problem of Chinese airports. Although the reform of 2005 has reduced the government's holding, it still maintains a controlling stake in the airports. This practice is likely to remain in the foreseeable future as the central government recently announced that major Chinese airports are considered vital enterprises to national security and should remain under state control. In this case, strengthening corporate governance and introducing competition are vital for the improvement of airport efficiency.

Another issue is management of air traffic. China's civil aviation has access to only 30 percent of the airspace and must clear all of its air traffic control specifications and equipment with the military, which controls the other 70 percent. In addition, funding for air traffic control appears insufficient. Consequently, the current airspace organization and route structure are far from optimal and are contributing to increased airport congestion and more

57. Zhang (2003).

flight delays. Here, further regulatory reform is needed, including better mechanisms for coordinating the use of airspace between military and civil aviation, and permission for the private and foreign sectors to invest in air traffic control facilities.

Appendix

This appendix offers a technical explanation for the regression analysis on the listing-efficiency relationship.

Productivity of Listed and Unlisted Airports

To isolate the effect of public listing on airport productivity, we need to control for the size and location advantages possessed by hub airports. Specifically, let H_i denote the hub dummy with $i = 1, 2$ representing the international and regional hubs respectively. As indicated earlier, there are three international hubs and six regional hubs in our sample. More generally, we run the following regression:

$$(A1) \qquad e_O^t = a_0 + a_1 L_j + \sum_i b_i H_i + \sum_t c_t Y_t,$$

where e_O^t is the efficiency score of airport O in year t, L_j is the dummy variable for pubic listing—being 1 if airport O in year t is publicly listed, and 0 otherwise—and Y_t is the year dummy. To avoid perfect collinearity, the year dummy for 1995 is dropped. Thus, the coefficient estimates of regression A1 are interpreted with reference to unlisted, nonhub airports in 1995. This is the familiar two-stage procedure in productivity analysis: in the first stage, the efficiency scores of the Chinese airports are estimated.[58] In the second stage, we run regressions to examine the effect of public listings on the productive efficiency of airports while controlling for hub and year effects.[59]

Furthermore, airports are a capital-intensive industry and the capital investment in runways and terminals is largely indivisible.[60] This characteristic can affect the role that the yearly efficiency scores play in measuring airport performance. Similarly, demand shocks might significantly alter the efficiency scores through a large output expansion. To control for these potentially external shocks, we extend regression A1 by adding the following input and output indexes:

---

58. The first-stage estimates were made by Fung and others (2007).
59. See, for example, Ali and Flinn (1989); Kalirajan (1990) for other applications of the two-stage procedure.
60. See, for example, Oum and Zhang (1990); Zhang and Zhang (2003).

(A2) $\quad InputI^t(x^t) = \dfrac{x^t}{x^{1995}}, \quad OutputI^t(y^t) = \dfrac{y^t}{y^{1995}},$

where x^t (y^t) is the input (output) level at time t, with $InputI^{1995}$ (x^{1995}) = 1 and $OutputI^{1995}$ (y^{1995}) = 1. The input variables are runway and terminal indexes, whereas the output variables are passenger and aircraft movement indexes.

The results of the above two specifications are reported in columns 3 and 4 of table 7A-1. In addition, the first column (model 1) contains the regression results when the year dummies are omitted from regression A1, whereas the second column contains the results when both the year dummies and Xiamen Airport are dropped from A1. A sharp drop in its efficiency score is noted at Xiamen Airport in 1997 (a year after its IPO). This productivity reduction might be explained by the opening of a new terminal in that year.

All four specifications show that the efficiency scores are positively correlated with public listing and that the coefficients are statistically significantly different from zero. As expected, the impact of hub status—whether airports are international or regional hubs—on the efficiency score is positive and statistically significant. However, no year dummies are statistically significant. Furthermore, based on column 2 of table 7A-1, excluding Xiamen from the analysis does not change the results significantly. In the regression model controlling for the input and output variables (column 4), the results suggest that the efficiency score is negatively correlated with the two input indexes and the coefficients are statistically significant. At the same time, the coefficient of aircraft movements is positive and statistically significant, while the coefficient of passengers is insignificantly negative.

Growth of Productive Efficiency

Now, we turn to productivity *growth*, that is, the change in the efficiency level. The growth of productive efficiency was measured by the Malmquist index,[61]

(A3) $\quad M_O^{t+1}(x^t, y^t, x^{t+1}, y^{t+1}) = \dfrac{D_O^{t+1}(x^{t+1}, y^{t+1})}{D_O^t(x^t, y^t)} \times \left[\dfrac{D_O^t(x^{t+1}, y^{t+1})}{D_O^{t+1}(x^{t+1}, y^{t+1})} \times \dfrac{D_O^t(x^t, y^t)}{D_O^{t+1}(x^t, y^t)} \right]^{\frac{1}{2}},$

---

61. The efficiency growth estimates were done by Fung and others (2007) for each sample airport.

Table 7A-1. *Regression Analysis of Productivity Level*

Models	1	2 (excl. Xiamen)	3	4
Intercept	0.3980**	0.3960**	0.3907**	0.7585**
	(19.9097)	(19.7620)	(7.4898)	(4.7791)
Listing	0.0932*	0.1330**	0.1042*	0.2454**
	(1.7318)	(1.9952)	(1.8669)	(4.2085)
International hub	0.4818**	0.4653**	0.4777**	0.4052**
	(8.9546)	(8.1186)	(8.7529)	(7.5486)
Regional hub	0.1640**	0.1660**	0.1650**	0.1635**
	(4.0118)	(4.0749)	(3.9933)	(4.0963)
Year dummy (base = 1995)				
1996			−0.0046	−0.0140
			(−0.0632)	(−0.2115)
1997			0.0718	0.0821
			(0.9954)	(1.2281)
1998			0.0478	0.0249
			(0.6601)	(0.3671)
1999			0.0042	0.0012
			(0.0584)	(0.0176)
2000			0.0298	0.0335
			(0.4106)	(0.4866)
2001			−0.0092	−0.0186
			(−0.1272)	(−0.2622)
2002			−0.0263	−0.0465
			(−0.3624)	(−0.6370)
2003			−0.0342	−0.0676
			(−0.4687)	(−0.9077)
2004			−0.0168	−0.0960
			(−0.2300)	(−1.1472)
Runway index				−0.4318**
				(−2.8044)
Terminal index				−0.0219**
				(−4.5515)
Passenger index				−0.0224
				(−0.9214)
Aircraft movement index				0.1173**
				(4.1628)
Adjusted R^2	0.3080	0.3230	0.2933	0.4054
N	250	240	250	250

Source: Authors.
Note: *t* statistics in parentheses.
N = number of observations.
**Significant at the 5 percent level.
*Significant at the 10 percent level.

Table 7A-2. *Mean Productivity Change and Components: 1995–2004 Cumulative Changes*

Type of airport	Malmquist productivity	Technical efficiency	Technological change
Listed airports	1.2082	0.8499	1.4215
Unlisted airports	1.3395	1.1045	1.2128

Source: Fung and others (2007).

where D_O is an output distance function of airport O, which is the same as the efficiency score in the output-oriented DEA analysis. The superscripts on D_O indicate the time period within which the efficiency scores are calculated. The superscripts on *x* and *y* indicate the time periods of the data used in the calculation of the efficiency scores.

Note that equation A3 also represents a decomposition of efficiency change from period *t* to period *t* +1. The ratio outside the brackets on the right-hand side measures the change in "technical efficiency" of airport O from period *t* to period *t* +1. Greater (smaller) than unity implies that the technical efficiency has improved (declined) in reference to the production frontier from t to *t* +1. The bracketed term represents the geometric mean of the shift in production frontier. When the value of this term is greater (less) than unity, it implies that the "technology" of the industry has progressed (regressed) from t to period *t* +1. As a measure of the overall efficiency change, the Malmquist index is decomposed into the change in technical efficiency of the airport and the technological change of the industry. Similar to the interpretation of its components, a Malmquist index greater (less) than unity indicates that the overall efficiency of airport O has increased (declined) from *t* to *t* +1.

Table 7A-2 provides the mean Malmquist productivity change and its components cumulated over the period 1995–2004. For the five listed airports, overall productivity rises by about 21 percent between 1995 and 2004, while productivity for unlisted airports increased by about 34 percent during the period. Of this, the improvement in technical efficiency accounted for about one-third, while the remaining two-thirds is due to technological progress. In contrast, while the rate of technological progress of the listed airports doubles that of the nonlisted airports (42 percent compared with 21 percent), the technical efficiency of the listed airports as a group has declined, leading to their slower growth in overall productivity.

This growth comparison has not controlled for factors other than the listing status, however. To investigate the effect of public listing on the growth of productivity, we run the following regression:

Table 7A-3. *Regression Analysis of Productivity Growth*[a]

Models	1	2
Intercept	1.0829**	1.139**
	(46.8068)	(21.2063)
Listing	–0.0307	–0.0488
	(–0.4979)	(–0.8191)
International hub	–0.0165	–0.0109
	(–0.2713)	(–0.1887)
Regional hub	–0.0174	–0.0191
	(–0.3679)	(–0.4278)
Year dummies (base = 1996)		
1997		–0.1634**
		(–2.2079)
1998		0.0079
		(0.1062)
1999		–0.0701
		(–0.9457)
2000		–0.2104**
		(–2.8370)

(*continued*)

(A4) $$M_O^t = a_0 + a_1 L_j + \sum_i b_i H_i + \sum_t c_t Y_t,$$

where the dependent variable is defined by A3 with *t* for year, and the dummy variables for listing and hub defined as in A1. The year dummy Y_t starts with 1996 (rather than 1995 as in the earlier regressions) since we are now concerned with the changes between two adjacent years. To avoid perfect collinearity, the year dummy for 1996 is dropped. Therefore, the coefficient estimates are interpreted with reference to unlisted, nonhub airports in 1996.

The results of regression A4 are reported in the second column of table 7A-3. Column 1 reports, again, the same regression but without year dummies. Both regressions indicate that the coefficients of hub dummies are negative and statistically insignificant. The coefficients of year dummies for 1997 and 2000 are negative and statistically significant. This may be explained by the negative demand shocks in 1997 (Asian financial crisis) and 2000 (the burst of the dot.com bubble). In contrast, the coefficient of the 2004 dummy is positive and statistically significant, reflecting perhaps the strong rebound of demand after the 2003 SARS (sudden acute respiratory syndrome) outbreak.

Furthermore, both regressions show that the productivity growth is negatively associated with public listing. Consider the full regression in column 2. On average, the listed airports have a Malmquist value that is 0.0488 less than

Table 7A-3. *Regression Analysis of Productivity Growth*[a] (*continued*)

Models	1	2
2001		−0.0970 (−1.3043)
2002		−0.0416 (−0.5596)
2003		−0.0732 (−0.9846)
2004		0.1588** (2.1283)
Adjusted R^2	−0.0113	0.0921
N	225	225

Source: Authors' calculations.
N = number of observations.
**Significant at the 5 percent level.
*Significant at the 10 percent level.
a. *t* statistics in parentheses.

that of the unlisted airports. Thus, the analysis suggests that the efficiency of the unlisted airports may have improved, on average, relative to that of the listed airports during the period, although the efficiency level of the former was still lower than that of the latter. Note, nonetheless, that the catch-up effect experienced by the unlisted airports is not statistically significant.

References

Air Transport Research Society. 2006. *Airport Benchmarking Report.* University of British Columbia.

Ali, M., and J. C. Flinn. 1989. "Profit Efficiency among Basmati Rice Producers in Pakistan Punjab." *American Journal of Agricultural Economics* 71 (2): 303–10.

Charnes, A., and others. 1994. *Data Envelopment Analysis: Theory, Methodology and Applications.* Boston: Kluwer Academic Publishers.

Chen, Jian. 2001. "Ownership Structure as Corporate Governance Mechanism: Evidence from Chinese Listed Companies." *Economics of Planning* 34: 53–71.

Chen, K., and others. 1988. "Productivity Change in Chinese Industry: 1953–1985." *Journal of Comparative Economics* 12, no. 4: 579–91.

Chen, Zhiwu. 2003. "Capital Markets and Legal Development: The China Case." *China Economic Review* 14: 451–472.

China Statistical Yearbook. 1985–2005. Beijing: Zhongguo Tongji Chubanshe, National Bureau of Statistics of China.

Dahya, Jay, Yusuf Karbhari, and Jason Zezong Xiao. 2000. "The Supervisory Board in Chinese Listed Companies: Problems, Causes, Consequences, and Remedies." *Asia Pacific Business Review* 9, no. 2: 118–37.

Fung, M., and others. 2007 (forthcoming). "Productivity Changes of Chinese Airports 1995–2004." *Transportation Research, E (The Logistics and Transportation Review)*.

Grossman, S., and O. Hart. 1980. "Takeover Bids, the Free Rider Problem, and the Theory of the Corporation." *Bell Journal of Economics* 11: 42–64.

Gu, Xiaorong. 2006. "How to Prevent Listed Companies from Making Misstatement." Manuscript.

ICAO (International Civil Aviation Organization). 1981, 2005. *Annual Report: The State of International Civil Aviation.* Montreal.

Jefferson, G. H., T. G. Rawski, and Y. Zheng. 1996. "Chinese Industrial Productivity: Trends, Measurement Issues, and Recent Developments." *Journal of Comparative Economics* 23, no. 2: 146–80.

Kalirajan, K. P. 1990. "On Measuring Economic Efficiency." *Journal of Applied Econometrics* 5, no. 1: 75–85.

Law, J. S., M. Fung, and C. K. Law. 2005. *Partial Privatization of the Airport Authority*. APRC submission to the Economic Development and Labour Bureau of the Government of Hong Kong SAR, Aviation Policy and Research Center, Chinese University of Hong Kong (May).

Le, T. T. 1997. "Reforming China's Airline Industry: From State-Owned Monopoly to Market Dynamism." *Transportation Journal* 36: 45–62.

Li, Jinhua. 2002. *Report on Auditing of Central Budgetary Implementation and Other Fiscal Revenues and Expenditures.* Submitted to the National Standing Committee of the National People's Congress by Li Jinhua, Auditor General of the National Audit Office of China. Beijing.

Oum, T. H., and Y. Zhang. 1990. "Airport Pricing: Congestion Tolls, Lumpy Investment, and Cost Recovery." *Journal of Public Economics* 43: 353–74.

Qi, Daqing, Woody Wu, and Hua Zhang. 2000. "Shareholding Structure and Corporate Performance of Partially Privatized Firms: Evidence from Listed Chinese Companies." *Pacific-Basin Finance Journal* 8: 587–610.

Shleifer, A., and R. W. Vishny. 1986. "Large Shareholders and Corporate Control." *Journal of Political Economy* 94: 461–88.

Su, Dongwei. 2005. "Corporate Finance and State Enterprise Reform in China." *China Economic Review* 16: 118–48.

Sun, Q., and W. Tong. 2003. "China Shares Issue Privatization: The Extent of Its Success." *Journal of Financial Economics* 70: 183–222.

Taplin, John H. E. 1993. "Economic Reform and Transport Policy in China." *Journal of Transport Economics and Policy* 27: 75–86.

Tian, Lihui. 2001. "Government Shareholding and the Value of Chinese Modern Firms." Working Paper 395. William Davidson Institute, University of Michigan.

Wang, Changyun. 2005. "Ownership of Operating Performance of Chinese IPOs." *Journal of Banking and Finance* 29: 1835–56.

Winston, Clifford. 2006. *Government Failure versus Market Failure: Microeconomics Policy Research and Government Performance.* Washington: AEI-Brookings Joint Center for Regulatory Studies.

Woo, Wing Thye, and others. 1994. "How Successful Has Chinese Enterprise Reform Been? Pitfalls in Opposite Biases and Focus." *Journal of Comparative Economics* 18, no. 3: 410–37.

World Bank. 1992. *Reform in 1990 and the Role of Planning*. Washington.

Wu, Zhouhong. 2005. "A Chinese Perspective on the Air Proposal." In *Policymaking for an Integrated Transport Market for China, Japan and Korea*, edited by Jae-Hong Kang and Sungwon Lee. Seoul: Korea Transport Institute, and Honolulu: East-West Center.

Xu, Xiaonian, and Yan Wang. 1999. "Ownership Structure and Corporate Governance in Chinese Stock Companies." *China Economic Review* 10: 75–98.

Zhang, A. 1998. "Industrial Reform and Air Transport Development in China." *Journal of Air Transport Management* 4: 155–64.

———. 2003. "Analysis of an International Air Cargo Hub: The Case of Hong Kong." *Journal of Air Transport Management* 9: 123–38.

Zhang, A., and H. Chen. 2003. "Evolution of China's Air Transport Development and Policy towards International Liberalization." *Transportation Journal* 42: 31–49.

Zhang, A., and Y. Zhang. 2003. "Airport Charges and Capacity Expansion: Effects of Concessions and Privatization." *Journal of Urban Economics* 53: 54–75.

Zhang, A., Y. Zhang, and R. Zhao. 2002. "Profitability and Productivity of Chinese Industrial Firms: Measurement and Ownership Implications." *China Economic Review* 13: 65–88.

Zhang, G. 2000. "Construction and Development of China's Civil Airports: An Overview of the Past Fifty Years." Speech by Guanghui Zhang, deputy director general, Department of Capital Construction and Airport Supervision, General Administration of Civil Aviation of China (CAAC), at the 2000 Beijing Airport/Airline Operations Symposium, Beijing, May.

8

KENNETH BUTTON

Air Transportation Infrastructure in Developing Countries: Privatization and Deregulation

The latter years of the twentieth century saw considerable movement toward loosening economic regulation across a wide range of industries. Initiated in higher-income countries, this trend has spread across much of the globe, albeit at different speeds and in a variety of forms. This paper looks at developments in the changing regulatory environments under which airports and associated facilities are provided in developing countries. No firm line is drawn in defining a developing country, but most nations in Africa fall under the rubric, as do many countries in South America and parts of Asia, along with some of the transition states in Europe.[1] The paper covers all forms of economic regulatory change that have occurred,[2] including that of ownership, and sets these within the broader context of the growing importance of air transportation infrastructure to developing countries.[3]

I would like to thank Henry Vega for providing assistance in the preparation of this paper.

1. The World Bank provides a listing of low- and medium-income countries based on per capita income, but this paper sees developing nations as involving an even larger group of countries, and sadly many of the poorest nations can hardly be said to be developing. This is not an unimportant distinction because the evidence suggests that successful privatization depends heavily on country and market conditions (Kikeri, Nellis, and Shorley 1994).

2. A distinction is drawn, however, between economic regulation and social regulation, with the focus here entirely on the former. Social regulation tends to involve such matters as income distribution, racial equity, environmental protection, labor laws, and consumer protection, and there have been major changes in all these fields in recent years. The concern here, however, is solely on matters of pricing, market access, and ownership. There are inevitable overlaps between economic and social regulation, but these are not considered.

3. There is also evidence from Latin America that improved air transportation infrastructure and management in developing countries generates greater cost savings than the freeing up of international airline markets that has been the focus of much policy in recent years (Micco and Serebrisky 2004).

Economic growth is unevenly spread and the econometric evidence indicates that convergence is taking place only very slowly at best.[4] While some parts of the world, especially in Asia, have taken clear leaps forward, many other areas languish in a downward spiral of circular-and-cumulative causation.[5] In particular Africa, which has a population of over 800 million but an aggregate gross domestic product (GDP) lower than Spain's, has seen relatively little economic growth in recent decades, and many nations in Africa have seen their GDPs fall. Initiating more dynamic economic growth paths in poorer countries has proved challenging despite the emergence after World War II of multinational development agencies, such as the World Bank, as well as unilateral initiatives by individual developed nations.

One of the problems encountered in virtually all lower-income countries has been inadequate infrastructure, including transportation infrastructure. Indeed, much of the development aid, as opposed to military or purely humanitarian aid, has gone to enhance the infrastructure of developing countries by investing in better transportation systems.

More recently, development agencies such as the World Bank, as well as scholars, have begun to look not only at the amount and type of infrastructure within a country but also at the way that infrastructure is maintained and the efficiency with which it is being used and managed.[6] This trend may be viewed largely as a demonstration effect emanating from more affluent countries where measures such as regulatory reform and privatization in various forms have generally produced significant economic benefits.[7] The rationale for the change of emphasis is often somewhat different, however, with developed countries trying to squeeze more efficiency from an existing infrastructure as they encounter social and environmental constraints to further expansion, whereas developing countries are dealing with an absolute shortage of infrastructure.

The air transportation sector has been affected by such liberalizing reforms, although most of the changes have involved the operational side of the indus-

---

4. Barro and Sala-i-Martin (1995).

5. While the original circular-and-cumulative causation theory is largely associated with traditional economies of scale, the New Growth Theory of Romer (1990) and others focuses on knowledge creation. In the longer term, the inability of developing countries to integrate fully into the global knowledge economy because of inadequate modern transportation may prove even more of a challenge as they seek to develop. There is a tendency for those involved in knowledge-based industries to make greater use of air transportation than those engaged in more traditional sectors.

6. See, for example, Betancor and Rendeiro (1999); Oum, Adler, and Yu (2006).

7. The intellectual arguments for economic deregulation of markets involving private supplying agents was, at least initially, more compelling than that for privatization of state-owned companies operating under competitive conditions (Kay and Thompson 1986).

try—for example, the privatization of airlines and the deregulation of markets for their services—while other elements in the value chain, such as airports and air navigation services, have so far been less affected.[8] Only 2 percent of the world's commercial airports are managed or owned by the private sector, although where privatization has taken place, the results have been sufficiently encouraging to stimulate further interest by the private sector. In addition, the organizational and management structure of airports that remain in public control has changed significantly, often in efforts to mirror the type of approach a private undertaking would adopt.[9] Such developments tend to be concentrated in developed countries, although they are spreading.

The analysis of air transportation issues in developing countries is relatively sparse. In part this seems to stem from a long-standing focus by agencies such as the World Bank and the Asian, African, and Inter-American Development Banks on surface transportation modes, but it also reflects the relatively small amount of air transportation in many developing countries. As air transportation increases, however, all the major international agencies are now putting more resources into studying it, and national governments are revisiting their own policies. Nonetheless, analysis of the effects of different approaches is still hampered by a dearth of good data and a shortage of good case-study material. Even basic information, if it exists, is often not easily accessible and can be of questionable reliability.

Air Transport and Developing Countries

It is useful initially to consider the particular functions served by air transportation in developing countries and how air transport often differs both in nature and degree from that found in more economically advanced countries. Regulatory structures tend to be conditional, and their effects depend not only on their objectives, parameters, and implementation but also on the background against which they are established. Regulatory changes in airport policy in many developed countries came against a backdrop of successful liberalization of many other markets, strong macroeconomic growth, and fairly well-defined objectives. Such conditions are not always features found in developing countries where command-and-control regimes are only gradually being dismantled and the macroeconomy is not always robust.

---

8. The generic term *air navigation services* is used through out to embrace a collection of activities that includes not only navigation services but air traffic control and weather information systems.

9. DeNeufville and Odoni (2003).

Role of Air Transportation in Developing Countries

The classical view holds that free trade maximizes economic welfare by allowing countries to exploit their comparative advantages. While there are doubts about the prospects of ever meeting all the requirements for a genuinely competitive global marketplace, as well as a lack of clarity about appropriate second-best strategies, continuing efforts are being made at the multilateral level to remove the most severe constraints on trade. Much effort has been paid to removing tariff barriers, a traditional concern of international economists, but more recently it has become clear that the free movements of goods and factors of production are limited by other factors, most notably suboptimally high transportation costs. For a variety of reasons, most prominently the development of containerized freight systems and supply-side logistics, the costs of moving many types of cargoes have fallen, but transportation costs, both internal and external, generally remain high for low-income countries.

It is also slowly becoming appreciated that air transportation has a particular role to play in the long-term economic growth of developing countries. Air transportation offers the possibility for many lower-income countries to exploit some of their comparative economic advantage in producing what are often termed "exotics," generally tropical fruits and flowers that have high value but low volume and weight. An estimated 15 percent of worldwide air cargo flows involve perishables, a sector that is growing at about 7.1 percent a year. From an economic development perspective, up to 80 percent of air cargo exports from South America (340,000 tons to the United States and 150,000 tons to Europe in 2006) and Africa (310,000 tons to Europe) are perishables with extremely short shelf lives. Because these exotics require reliable, high-speed movement to export markets, specialized air transportation infrastructure, together with an institutional setting that minimizes delays and ensures a smooth service flow, is a necessity.

Good air transportation is also a means for developing tourist industries in many developing countries. Rising global incomes, increased leisure time, longer life expectancy, and lower transportation costs are all contributing to the increase of tourism. Developing countries have benefited from this phenomenon, increasing their net earnings from tourism from $6 billion in 1980 to $62.2 billion in 1996.[10] In relative terms, however, areas such as Africa (which had 4.4 percent of all tourists in 2004) and South America (2.1 percent) are still small markets. About 43 percent of tourist arrivals came by air in 2004, and air travel was the main mode of transport outside of Europe. A number of lower-income and smaller island economies in particular have made significant and

---

10. UNCTAD (1998).

successful efforts to build up their tourist industry, which not only can generate foreign income but are also often labor intensive. South Africa, for example, now has over 7 million tourists a year. Nevertheless, the higher-income countries still receive by far the largest flow of tourists; for example, 54.4 percent of all tourists went to European destinations in 2004.

Air transportation is also needed to move the components that sustain many of the extractive industries that developing countries often rely on for foreign exchange earnings. Air transportation has the added advantage of not requiring large amounts of inflexible, fixed-track infrastructure that often involve reliance on links through third-party countries—a particular problem for the landlocked countries of Africa and for movement across the South American continent. The emergence of service-driven activities has not entirely bypassed developing countries, and there is ample evidence that adequate air transportation services are a necessary condition for further growth in this type of economic activity.

Despite these developments, the level of air transportation in less-developed countries is generally poor. Africa is a particular case. The continent accounts for less than 3 percent of the global air market, and forecasts produced by Boeing Commercial Airplanes suggest that without substantial change, growth in passenger-kilometers there will continue to lag behind the global average to at least 2025.[11] While resource constraints are an issue, coordination may be a larger problem. There are fifty-three independent nations in Africa, each with its own air traffic rights, and many of these countries have traditionally chosen to exercise those rights in a very restrictive manner. The market is also very concentrated, with some 65 percent of flight frequencies serving airport pairs in South Africa—the wealthiest nation in sub-Saharan Africa—and the remainder between pairs in central and northern Africa. Much of the traffic involves movement outside of the continent; for example, in 2001 the majority of African cargo traffic was with Europe (65 percent of the tons carried). Only 7 percent was moved within Africa.

Airport Services in Developing Countries

The developing nations are not numerically short of airports. Many of the largest countries in South America, for example, have several airports. The problem is that many of these airports tend to be small and of extremely poor quality and can, at best, provide only very rudimentary commercial air transportation services. Many have no concrete runways or recognizable terminal

---

11. Boeing Commercial Airplanes (2006). The main growth markets are likely to be in Asia. The prediction for all aircraft purchases is that Africa will account for some $40 billion of the $2.6 trillion forecast to be spent on equipment between 2006 and 2025.

buildings and no or very limited tower control or landing aids. Larger airports, often the national hub for domestic services and international operations, vary in quality from country to country. Some are sophisticated, modern pieces of infrastructure that can handle significant flows of tourist traffic, but many more offer only outdated and poorly maintained equipment. Staffing can also pose problems. Activities such as tower control and security and safety oversight require trained staffs that are difficult to retain within a growing global market for their services.

National ownership of air transportation infrastructure is still the norm in developing countries, with a number of larger countries having municipal or regional participation. In some countries with a tradition of a strong military presence, facilities are not run on commercial criteria but rather to meet wider strategic objectives. In many cases airports provide a valuable source of foreign revenue and are treated as something of a cash cow for the exchequer; in other cases subsidies are needed for continued maintenance and operation. In some smaller, frequently island, economies, state provision is often justified because of the importance of ensuring adequate air transportation facilities to boost tourism growth.[12] The picture is thus far from a uniform one.

In the past airports were fitted within a value chain that was highly regulated throughout its length and often contained significant elements of state ownership. Deregulation and privatization of airlines, trends that began in the late 1970s, have affected the economics of airports and air traffic control. The need for airlines to act more commercially has put increasing pressure on other elements in the chain to do the same—it is more difficult now for airports to cream revenues from carriers that are not monopolies and not generally state owned. Airlines can also exercise voice through a variety of channels and organizations that express concerns over the performance of air transportation infrastructure providers. This is as true in developing as developed countries. Equally, the successful privatization of airports and other forms of infrastructure elsewhere makes it difficult for developing countries, or at least those that are open democracies, to maintain arguments that state ownership is preferable. The move toward more private sector participation is nevertheless a slow one.[13]

Wider International Institutional Settings

The Chicago Convention of 1944 established the foundation for the modern, global institutional structure under which international air services are pro-

---

12. Airport facilities are often partly financed in these cases through hotel or tourist taxes, with the complete package of tourist activities being treated as a composite "product."
13. Kapur (1995) provides a picture of where privatization stood in the mid-1990s.

vided. Although not a direct outcome of the convention, the result was some forty years or more of regulated, bilateral air transportation markets. The incentive structure under this regime was a little like sixteenth-century mercantilism, with countries trying to establish a strong transportation industry to reap the benefits of trade in air services in duopoly markets, and airport strategies were part of the game. The fact that the demand for air services is derived from the demands of individuals for mobility and of companies' requirements for market access seldom entered the equation. The open skies initiatives of the United States (first adopted in 1979, but not having a real impact until the mid-1990s) and the creation of the single European market from 1992 moved many developed countries away from this approach. The U.S. initiatives have subsequently been extended to embrace a large number of developing countries and transition economies of Eastern Europe.

Some developing states have also changed their attitudes, and institutionally there have been efforts, for instance, among some African nations, to liberalize their mutual air transportation markets. The 1988 Yamoussoukro Declaration began this process but was largely ineffectual. In 1997 the Banjul Accord, involving six West African states, initiated agreements covering airline operations, infrastructure, traffic rights, safety, and security, and in 1998 the Arab Civil Aviation Commission (ACAC) agreed to the total liberalization of bilateral air service agreements by 2005 (seventeen open skies agreements between ACAC states had been signed by May 2006). A number of subsequent agreements have also sought to open the internal air transportation markets in Africa. Among these are the 1999 Yamoussoukro II Decision and the 2000 Abuja Treaty, which created the African Union, involving forty-four member states, and which has among its aims the creation of a multilateral free trade area in air transportation services.

Taking a wider geographical perspective, many developing countries have signed liberal open skies policies with the United States and less restrictive agreements with other developed nations. Implicitly if they are to benefit from these developments, enhanced airport and air navigation services will be needed.

Externally, there have also been moves both to directly help lower-income countries improve their air transportation services and to bring many of them into line with developments elsewhere. The United States, for example, initiated the Safe Skies for Africa Program in 1998 to help improve the extremely poor safety record of aviation in that continent, and it has fostered open-skies agreements with many countries to allow freer movement of air traffic between them and the United States. The international agencies have also gradually been recognizing the important role that air transportation can play in economic development. The World Bank now gives limited funding to help some countries meet international security commitments; for example, in 2006 two International Development Association credits and two grants for a combined total of $33.6 million went to Burkina Faso, Cameroon, Guinea, and Mali for this purpose.

Airport Policies

Traditionally airports, airlines, and air navigation services were seen as an integrated system that served a public interest. From the outset government involvement was heavy is all three aspects of air transportation, although its degree and nature varied considerably from country to country. Airports and air navigation services, however, were generally viewed as public utilities that should not, for welfare economic reasons, be evaluated only on their financial performance.[14] In addition, monopoly considerations raised questions concerning their potential pricing and investment policies if they were allowed to operate freely in a market context. Policies were also colored by perceptions of the technical nature of airports, which were seen as single entities rather than as composites made up of numerous activities, each of which may or may not be naturally monopolistic or serve a public utility function.

Following the pattern in more advanced economies, airports in developing countries are typically owned by a national, state, or municipal government. They have usually been run through a ministry and partially financed through the exchequer whenever fees and user charges failed to cover costs. The rationale for these subsidies has been the need to finance the necessary infrastructure, or at least the initial investment, through taxation and, on occasion, money from international agencies. Concerns have been raised about the effect on economic development of the potential monopoly power of airports; in most developing countries competition between commercial airports for traffic is limited, and the overall capacity of systems is not large enough to support a multiplicity of facilities that would stimulate competition. A similar pattern emerges for air navigation services, with state-owned and -operated systems being the tradition.[15]

---

14. Kahn (1988) provides an overview of the traditional public policy approach to supplying public utilities, while Train (1991) offers a more modern account of contemporary theory.

15. While the focus of this chapter is on airports, where most of the institutional change has occurred, some developing countries have reformed the way air traffic control services are provided. South Africa, for example has transferred its air traffic control system from state ownership to a not-for-profit, limited liability company (Button and McDougall, 2006).

Constraints on Reform in Developing Countries

Reforming the way that air transportation infrastructure is thought about and supplied has been problematic in developed countries, and the inherent challenges are even greater in most lower-income nations. Intellectually, there are confusions over such things as the economic nature of airports and air navigation services; for example, the degree to which they exhibit public good attributes. Practically, decisionmaking about providing airports and air navigation services has often been subject to a large degree of capture by powerful labor groups such as air traffic controllers, airport management, and frequently the military in developing countries.[16] Such things take time to remedy even where governance is good and resources are sufficiently abundant to withstand any stranded costs associated with change. The situation in poorer countries makes reform even harder—even if the gains are potentially larger.

RESOURCE AVAILABILITY. One of the few cases where Adam Smith advocated public provision was that of large-scale infrastructure, and in particular transportation infrastructure, which he saw as prerequisite for economic growth. His rationale was essentially an institutional one: private finance markets were neither large enough nor sophisticated enough to handle the scale and the long payback period associated with such investments. Ironically, in most developed countries, the modern world sees governments increasingly going to the private financial markets to fund infrastructure investments, either in their entirety or in some form of partnership, because the governments do not have the ability to raise the necessary capital. The sums involved are large. The World Bank estimated in 1995 that airport infrastructure alone would require $350 billion for upgrading and maintenance by 2010, and that was before the additional security systems now needed.[17] Smith's argument, however, may still have some validity regarding lower-income nations where capital markets are poorly developed, risk is high, and access to international funds can be very expensive.

While no work has looked at the direct correlation between the income of countries and their access to funds for airport development, some evidence of the difficulty many countries face can be seen in their ability to meet certain safety requirements, a large part of which is tied to airport activities. Button and

---

16. The literature on regulatory capture is assessed in Stiglitz (1998), and it is clear that many of the conditions leading to capture exist in most developing countries that have sought to reform their airport policies.

17. Juan (1995).

others, in examining compliance with the U.S. International Civil Aviation Safety Assessment program, found a strong link between the economic performance of a country and its ability to meet the requirements of the program.[18]

This lack of resources often means that commercial airports in developing countries are of poor quality and in need of significant injections of capital. (In stark contrast, most cases of privatization in developed countries have involved well-equipped, modern facilities with demonstrably high levels of demand.) The lack of quality in the "product" to be privatized and the need for any investor to take high levels of both commercial and political risk inevitably pushes up the costs of any privatization and influences the subsequent regulatory structure that is put in place.

Other sources of finance also have problems that make them unsuitable vehicles for assisting privatizations. The multilateral aid and development agencies, although certainly not entirely absent from the scene, historically have contributed relatively little in terms of grants and loans to the provision of air transportation infrastructure in developing countries—in the transportation context, roads, railways, and ports have been their dominant concern. These aid and development agencies have not therefore developed the same level of experience in the air infrastructure sector as have public-private partnerships, although this situation is changing somewhat.

GOVERNANCE. Markets do not work in a vacuum; they are contextual. As Ronald Coase pointed out when looking at the particular context of the European transition countries, "These ex-communist countries are advised to move to a market economy, and their leaders wish to do so, but without the appropriate institutions no market economy of any significance is possible."[19] An appropriate institutional structure is thus important as an enabling environment for economic reforms.

Appropriate institutions that combine a reasonable degree of security over property rights to private suppliers and a high level of integrity among government agencies responsible for air transportation infrastructure policy are a normal prerequisite for successful privatization. Political risk is a major consideration when it comes to larger matters of economic development, but it

---

18. Button and others (2004). The U.S. program essentially seeks to see if countries are complying with safety requirements set down by the UN's International Civil Aviation Organization with the intention of both facilitating movement toward meeting these requirements but also limiting access to U.S. airports and airspace when there are significant deviations from the requirements. Because of multicollinearity issues among a large number of right-hand variables, principal components analysis was used to isolate effects. The largest loadings were on a group embracing GDP, imports, and exports.

19. Coase (1992).

also has particular relevance at the micro level for the private sector when investment decisions are made.[20]

In the past political instability in many developing countries has involved not only coups d'état but also the appropriation of foreign assets by existing governments. Such instability has deterred both local private sector investment and inflows of foreign capital. It has reduced the absolute willingness of investors to put money directly into such countries' infrastructure and has increased the costs for those doing so, largely because of the need to obtain political risk insurance. Institutions such as the Multilateral Investment Guarantee Bank (a World Bank affiliate) offer such insurance to cover contingencies involving war, civil disturbance, and breach of contract, but the cost ranges from a low of 0.3 percent to a high of 1.5 percent of the investment, and coverage is limited to 90 percent of equity investment and 95 percent of principal debt up to $200 million. Countries such as India and Peru have drawn upon this type of insurance to facilitate joint public-private ventures in airport privatization. The durable nature of airport infrastructure and the long-term cost recovery of investments in that infrastructure mean that even currently stable countries must demonstrate that their stability is sustainable.

Inevitably policymakers feel a need to regulate airports, most notably where they enjoy a degree of monopoly power. In some cases this regulation may be short-lived, designed to deal with transition issues and to be phased out as competitive forces are allowed to build up.[21] In other cases, regulation may be needed for longer periods.

SOCIAL ATTITUDES. Any form of regime change, including that involving airports, has inevitable distributional consequences—even those changes involving a Pareto improvement.[22] Air transportation in most developing countries—those with a significant tourist industry being a possible exception—has tended to be seen as an elite form of mobility for the wealthy and outside the reach of the vast majority of the population. In democratic states it seems unlikely that a political candidate would gain many votes arguing for improvements in airport efficiency—not only are there far more important concerns, but efficiency may, in the case of an overstaffed airport, mean lower levels of unemployment in the short term, whatever the ultimate outcomes.

---

20. The literature on political risk and its implications for economic development is fairly extensive; see Barro (1991); Alesina and others (1996).

21. The quite widely used price-capping method of regulating airport pricing was initially seen as such an interim measure to the limited short-term monopoly power of incumbent suppliers in the U.K. telecommunications industry (Littlechild 1983).

22. Birdsall and Nellis (2002) provide a survey of much of the generic literature on the topic.

In this sense a large coalition of interests concerned about the efficient provision of airport facilities is seldom created, giving those most closely involved in airport operations—and whose interests seldom involve maximizing allocative or X-efficiency—an opportunity to capture the airport system.

These types of situations differ from those in many developed economies in Europe and North America, where low-cost airlines have brought regular air travel within the reach of a large proportion of the population and where a much larger constituency is interested in optimizing airport service provision. The structure of coalitions of stakeholders and their interests are different, and commercial pressures from the airlines combine with the voice of travelers and air cargo users to increasingly squeeze inefficiencies from the air transportation system.

MILITARY INTEREST. Many developing nations have powerful militaries that often see air transportation infrastructure as part of their domain. For example, before the move to involve the private sector, the Comando de Regiones Aéreas (part of the air force) owned, administered, and operated four hundred airports in Argentina. The Brazilian airport administration, Infraero, although not technically part of the military, had managers from the Brazilian Air Force until 1998.[23] Indeed, in very many cases airports and associated infrastructure serve a dual civilian-military use that makes it difficult to isolate property rights and the determination of priorities.[24]

While military involvement is gradually being reduced and is, in that sense, less of an impediment to privatization and liberalization, important legacy effects can slow the process. In particular, there is a shortage of commercial management skills in many developing countries whose airports were formerly controlled by the military. Such shortages often signal the need for public-private ventures that allow for the introduction of foreign management expertise. It is now relatively common for developing countries to hire foreign consultants to plan their airport development and operating systems; such consultants include Lufthansa Consulting, NACO of the Netherlands, and the LPA Group in the United States.

Indeed, as a more general point, the use of operating concessions that can attract foreign participants can provide a mechanism for overcoming, at least partially, the shortage of expertise and may help explain why developing coun-

23. The Departamento de Aviação Civil (the aviation ministry) is still subordinate to the ministry of defense.
24. Even in Europe and North America the dividing line between the military involvement with airports and air traffic control is one that often poses major problems (Button and McDougall 2006).

tries use them in preference to issuing equity.[25] Much of the equipment and facilities at former military airports may not be fully suited to commercial operations either, and the need for refurbishment capital can make attracting nonspecialist private investors difficult.

Airport Finances and the Nature of Air Transportation Growth

Airports can generate revenues through a variety of market mechanisms, but the availability of those mechanisms differs according to a number of factors, and in many cases developing countries cannot pursue the range of options open to private or more commercial state-owned airports in wealthier nations. This is largely a function of their position in the life cycle of air transportation market growth.

Despite the wide diversity in developing countries and the variation in the nature and quality of their airports, some general patterns separate them from airports in the majority of developed countries. For example, air transportation markets in developed countries appear to be approaching their saturation level, but in developing countries, particularly those in Asia and South America, transportation markets appear to have considerable growth potential. This, combined with the nature of the traffic they carry, suggests that somewhat different business models are appropriate for their airports in the future. Figure 8-1 offers a fairly simple representation of current trends.

Growth in air traffic in and between the developed countries is forecast to be relatively slow over the long term—3.6 percent a year to 2025 within North America, 3.4 percent within Europe, and 4.5 percent between North America and Europe, by one estimate.[26] Slow growth means that major airports in these countries will become increasingly dependent on commercial or nonaeronautical revenues to enhance their revenue stream.[27] That in turn can pose regulatory problems, which have already been seen in the debates over the imposition of price caps in the United Kingdom and elsewhere.[28] Although

---

25. Under a concession, a business is operated under a contract or license for a period of time but ownership of the business is retained by the entity that grants the concession. In the case of an airport concession, a private company enters into an agreement with the government to have the exclusive right to operate, maintain, and carry out investment in all or some specified aspects of the airport. For example, Aéroports de Paris, which has an interest in a number of Cameroon's airports, moved a team of ten experts to the country in 1993 to help run them.

26. Boeing Commercial Airplanes (2006).

27. Additionally, many developed markets have capacity issues that are unlikely, for a variety of reasons including environmental concerns, to be resolved through the provision of additional facilities.

28. Starkie (2001).

Figure 8-1. *A Generalization of Airport Trends in Developing and Developed Countries*

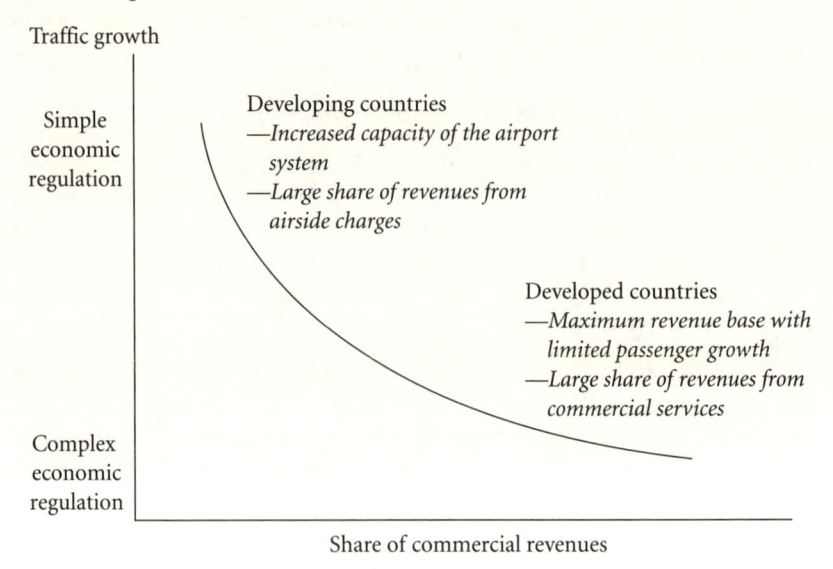

```
Traffic growth
    │
Simple          Developing countries
economic        —Increased capacity of the airport
regulation         system
                —Large share of revenues from
                   airside charges

                            Developed countries
                            —Maximum revenue base with
                               limited passenger growth
                            —Large share of revenues from
                               commercial services
Complex
economic
regulation
    └─────────────────────────────────────
              Share of commercial revenues
```

Source: Adapted from Juan (1995).

their air transportation markets are still relatively small in absolute terms, the projected growth of many of those involving developing countries (for example, 6.9 percent within Latin America, 8.8 percent between Latin America and the Asia-Pacific region, and 8.7 percent between Latin America and Africa) offers the potential for increased airside revenue in situations where there are potentially fewer social constraints on building additional capacity or where capacity is already adequate. The scope for raising significant commercial income is much smaller.[29] In such situations the regulatory regime overseeing a privatized airport system can be less sophisticated because it has to deal only with airside issues. The potential for various forms of regulatory capture, a phenomenon not unknown in many developing countries, is thus reduced.

The problem for many of the poorest developing countries, however, is that even though their traffic flows may in aggregate be growing, they still seldom

---

29. This is not to say that nonaeronautical revenues are always small in developing countries—they account for about 57 percent of total revenues in Latin American countries—but the potential remains for larger increases in aeronautical revenues, and there are persuasive arguments that the private sector may also be more effective in stimulating nonaeronautical sources of revenue.

generate sufficient revenue to cover the full costs of operations—airports are essentially decreasing cost entities where cost recovery can be difficult especially where competition from other airports makes price discrimination difficult even if it were permitted under international agreements.[30] This makes pure privatization options less tenable and the need for outside assistance from aid agencies more relevant.[31]

Nature of Change

Large-scale economic reforms to the ways that air transportation infrastructure is provided notwithstanding, many developments have been more limited, affecting particular activities rather than an entire entity—outsourcing being the clearest example. Although reforms can take place in a multiplicity of ways, specific approaches to reform have emerged almost regionally in developing countries. In part this pattern stems from the starting points of the various countries concerned, but it also has been affected by their wider approaches to economic reform and their overall political, social, and economic proclivities. The problem with assessing reforms globally is that, for a variety of reasons, most of the analysis to date has been focused on developments in Latin America. Analysis of the cases in Africa is limited, and potentially major reforms put forward in India and several other Asian counties have taken time to come to fruition.

Whatever the form, in overall terms, the World Bank has estimated that more than one hundred private sector contracts have been signed to provide some aspect of airport capacity for poorer countries, amounting to about $18 billion between 1990 and 2005.[32] The level of activities has varied over time, in part because of shocks such as the September 11, 2001, terrorist attacks in the United States, and from region to region (figure 8-2). Until 2001 most of the reform activity involved Latin America and East Asia, which accounted for about 75 percent of private investment in airport infrastructure in developing countries between 1990 and 2001. After 2001 Latin America has continued to be the most active region, but the transition economies of Eastern Europe and Central Asia have shown increased interest in private sector

---

30. Button (2005).
31. The International Air Transport Associated (IATA) has also argued that in some cases, such as Uruguay's move to a concession system for its international airport of Laguna del Sauce in 1996, privatization has led to dramatically higher user fees for airlines with potential adverse effects for traffic. IATA did not offer any alternative methods to finance the facility other than existing subsidies.
32. Andrew and Dochia (2006).

Figure 8-2. *Private Sector Investment Commitments in Airports*[a]

Investment commitments in billions of dollars

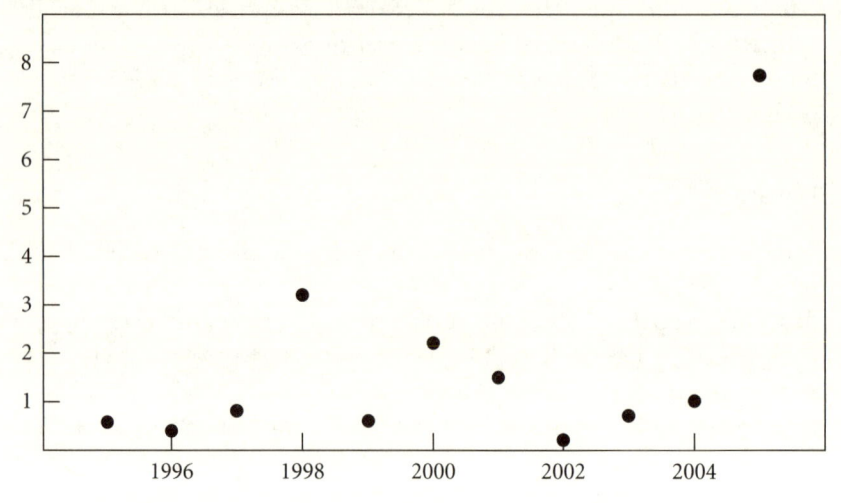

Source: World Bank data from Private Participation in Infrastructure Project.

a. The data contain some contracts under renegotiation, such as the 1998 Argentine airport network concession that was significantly revised after it was first adopted. The large increase in 2005 is attributable primarily to new concession arrangements involving Budapest and Atatürk airports.

involvement, accounting for 60 percent of airport investment flows in developing countries in the 2002–05 period. South Asia has also seen an upsurge of private sector activity, with large private investments of various types at airports in Bangalore, Delhi, Hyderabad, and Mumbai in India.

Certainly the approach favored in Europe—using divestiture, usually through the equity market, as the medium for privatization—is far from the norm in developing countries. The limitations of local stock markets in these countries are the most obvious, but not the only, reason that the European model is not used.[33] In addition, differences in the motivation for privatization seem to affect the approach to privatization. Most actions in Europe, Australia, New Zealand, and other developed countries have focused on efficiency enhancement. Low-income countries, although not entirely unconcerned with efficiency, have often been more interested in privatization as a vehicle for financing new investment—some 20 percent of private sector air-

---

33. Some of the European transition economies that have relatively efficient capital markets have employed a combination of traditional and market mechanisms to develop their airport capacity. Domodedovo, the second-largest airport in Russia, for example, is partly owned by an airline, and 75 percent of Vnukova Airport, the third-largest, is held by the private sector (Hammond 2003).

port investment commitments in developing countries over the past fifteen years have involved new facilities. In many cases concessions have been used as a mechanism for generating continuous revenue flows for the exchequer. The interest in securing revenue has, if anything, been heightened as the need to meet new and enhanced international safety and security arrangements has emerged in recent years.

Some indication of the priorities set by various developing countries can be seen from the nature of private sector involvement in airport infrastructure. World Bank data for 1990 to 2005 indicate that about half of the money injected by the private sector was used to purchase existing, state-owned businesses.[34] This type of investment may be seen simply as a method of revenue raising, but it also injects more commercial experience and objectives into the management of the infrastructure. The remaining 50 percent has gone into new facilities, new airports, upgrading, and modernization.

Concessions are now a widely used mechanism for injecting private finance into air transport infrastructure and for distancing management from political processes.[35] While concessions in general are growing in many sectors, airports are particularly suited to this form of private sector involvement because the demand for their services is relatively inelastic—airports often enjoy a degree of monopoly power, and airport fees are a small part of overall air fares and cargo rates. Concessions have accounted for about 60 percent of investment commitments since 1990, and 73 percent of private investment in airports in developing countries in the 1990s, since their initial use in South America and sub-Saharan Africa.[36] Concessions are increasingly used in Central and South Asia, Eastern Europe and more recently in Hungary, India, and

---

34. The World Bank data may slightly understate the proportion going to acquiring existing facilities because it does not include all concession or lease fees in Bolivia, Costa Rica, Honduras, and Peru.

35. The underlying idea of a concession is that efficiency is produced where there is no natural competitive pressure through the creation of mechanisms that generate competition "for the market" rather than "competition in the market." Theoretically, the tendering process is designed to reveal the supplier that would act most efficiently, with all economic rent going to the government (Demsetz 1968). In practice, setting up the tendering process is not easy and designing appropriate auctioning mechanisms has proved both theoretically and practically difficult. In some cases such as Argentina, it soon became clear that the tendering produced an unrealistic outcome, suggesting that all parties involved saw the tendering process as the first stage in a larger set of bargains, with no parties expecting the concessions arrangement to be durable. Guasch (2004) offers a general critique of the use of concessions in developing countries, and Button (2007) provides an overview of the types of challenges that are encountered in the context of landing-slot auctions and that can be extended to airport concessions.

36. This compares with 17 percent of transactions between 1990 and 2001, and 10 percent between 2002 and 2005, that involved divestiture. Even here, most of the divestures involved sales of minority, noncontrolling stakes in the airports.

Table 8-1. *Airport Concessions in South America in 2003*

Country	Concessions	Planned concessions
Argentina	32	1
Bolivia	3	0
Brazil	0	2
Colombia	3	1
Ecuador	0	2
Paraguay	0	2
Peru	1	1
Uruguay	1	1
Venezuela	1	1

Source: Bosch and García-Montalvo (2003).

Turkey. In some cases, such as Hungary and India, the government has taken a stake in the concession holder, seemingly weakening any effort to distance management from the development of the facilities and their operations.

Concessions are the usual way to involve the private sector in airports in South America (table 8-1). They were initiated largely because of what was felt to be an inherent political need both to retain national ownership and to follow fairly well-established regimes of regulation that had been used in other sectors. On the supply side, the use of concessionary arrangements has grown as more specialized airport contractors have emerged. These are internationally oriented companies, such as Spain's ACS group and Aeropuertos Españoles y Navegación Aérea, France's Aeroports de Paris, and Australia's Macquarie Airports. With these have also emerged more innovative ways of structuring private financial arrangements, often involving high debt-asset ratios. These arrangements make more funds available but could pose problems in the future if major, unforeseen shocks hit the air transportation market.

These concessions take a variety of forms that involve different ways of sharing commercial risk, the length of the concession, and the nature of regulation over the behavior of the private concern. The extent of South American airport concessions in 2003 is depicted in table 8-1 (it should be noted that not all of the anticipated concessions have materialized, and some of the actual ones have encountered trouble).

In Latin America, systems concessions are widely used as a means of privatization, and this includes airports. The first such airport concession was initiated in Argentina in 1998, when the government gave a thirty-year concession, with a possible ten-year extension, to a single consortium, Aeropuertos Argentinia 2000, that includes the right to run thirty-two of Argentina's main airports.[37] To obtain the concession, the consortium had to commit to major investments in the system and agree to make an annual, inflation-adjusted payment to the government. Economic regulation of airside charges was established and is monitored by a specific agency,[38] but other revenue-raising activities were left outside the regulatory regime. The consortium has had difficulty meeting both the required annual payment ($171 million in 1998 prices, adjusted annually for inflation) and its investment commitment at the approved fee levels and the current level of demand.[39]

Similar concessions have been granted in Bolivia and Peru. In Bolivia three airports, La Paz, Cochabamba, and Santa Cruz, were privatized in 1996 under twenty-five-year concessions to the Servicios Aeroportuarios Bolivianos S.A., with a regulatory agency, the Superintendencia de Transportes, overseeing fares and service quality.[40] The regulatory agency is also charged with guaranteeing competition in the industry, which also includes thirty-four state-owned airports managed by the Administración de Aeropuertos y Servicios Auxiliares de la Navegación Aérea. In 2001 Lima Airport Partners, SRL, a consortium of Bechtel Enterprises International Ltd., Flughafen Frankfurt Main AG, and Cosapi S.A., obtained a thirty-year concession contract to develop, manage, and operate the Jorge Chavez International Airport in Lima. Over the concession period Lima Airport Partners plans to finance and build a second runway and a new terminal complex, expand the commercial and retail strategy, and develop new air cargo facilities to support development of other export activities. Under the terms of the agreement, Lima Airport Partners will share revenues with the government and will reimburse the government for its costs in the privatization process.

A narrower, build-operate-transfer option provides a more limited approach to concessions in that it is often restricted to only part of a facility's capacity.[41] These are essentially long-term concessions for private companies

37. Some other airports outside of the main Sistema National de Aeropuertos were also concessioned out to another group, London Supply.
38. The Organismo Regulador del Sistema Nacional de Aeropuertos is within the Department of Economy and Infrastructure and has the remit to set airside fees and charges, approve development plans, and oversee the quality of service provided by the airports.
39. Bosch and García-Montalvo (2003); Lipovich (2008).
40. TBI, a U.K.-based airport company, had managed operations of these airports since 1999 but was taken over by Spain's ACDL (Airport Concessions and Developments Limited) in 2005. This brought about some changes in managerial structure.
41. Jamaica adopted a variant on this approach for Sangster International Airport at Montego Bay that entailed a series of arrangements including a forty-nine-year leasing agreement for the existing terminal.

to build new capacity or significantly upgrade existing capacity in return for having control over the airport's operations for a defined period. Colombia used this method in the mid-1990s to finance the construction of additional runway capacity at El Dorado Airport in Bogotá, the largest cargo and third-largest passenger airport in South America.[42] Under the contract, the construction companies were to recoup their costs from landing fees over a twenty-year period; the period was subsequently shortened to fifteen years in 1998 when the administration of the airport changed. The country has also sought to extend this same type of concession, with some variation, to Cartagena and Cali airports.[43]

Subsequently, the terminal facilities at El Dorado were also put up for concession when the government decided it did not have the resources for necessary expansion that would allow economies of scale to be reaped and costs recovered. The concession auction had five participants that each had to commit to invest $650 million over twenty years and to stimulate both passenger and cargo traffic demand in exchange for ceding a percentage of revenues to the government. The outcome, in 2007, resulted in the second highest bidder, OPAIN, offering 46.75 percent of gross income for the concession. The auction process was very reminiscent of a Vickrey auction, which has the double intent of ensuring a high return to the government coupled with sufficient revenue retention by the winner for it to follow through on its commitments.[44]

In some countries, such as Venezuela, the responsibility for airports has been transferred from central to state governments, which have then tried to bring in private finance. The initial Venezuelan experiments began in 1992 when three airports in Zulia state were privatized but then subsequently taken back by the governor after a change in the state government. More recently the Instituto Autónomo Aeropuerto Internacional Maiquetia, a semicorporatized agency, has operated Simón Bolívar Airport in Caracas with the ultimate

---

42. This concession arrangement dealing only with runways was unique for South America at the time; the others all involved entire airports or terminals.

43. Despite potential moral hazard issues, the government's willingness to guarantee the revenue flow made the Cartagena concession, as with El Dorado, an attractive commercial proposition for a private company. Similar initiatives involving Cali airport encountered problems when such guarantees were not made. The Cartagena airport concession also ultimately proved problematic, mainly because there was no timetable for committed investments, and the concession was subsequently transferred (Pardo 2003). The method of guarantee for El Dorado required the regulatory agency, the Colombia Civil Aeronautics Department, to establish a trust fund equivalent to 30 percent of annual landing fee revenue to cover the guaranteed revenue flow.

44. Vickrey (1961).

intention of concessioning to an international consortium so that the airport may be upgraded.

Increasingly, concessions are awarded for a network of airports in developing countries rather than for single facilities. (Fifty-eight airports in South America were concessioned as networks between 1990 and 1999; outside of South America only Cameroun, Madagascar, and South Africa gave concessions for single airports.) The aim is to foster the cross-subsidization of facilities, a move that is seen as socially necessary for integrating remote areas into the larger economy. (Cross-subsidization can also occur when concessionary revenues from a single or group of profitable airports are used to subsidize unprofitable airports.) These types of systems can also reduce the transaction costs of concession granting and monitoring and stimulate economies of scale in management. Little analysis has been undertaken, however, on the lost efficiency that results from inevitably having suboptimally high fees at the profitable airports or on the additional problems encountered by private companies in financing networks that include unprofitable airports.

The approaches adopted by African states to privatization and regulatory changes have varied substantially. Often there has been more talk than action. Some countries have pursued concessions akin to outsourcing, whereby parts of an airport's activities are turned over to the private sector. Cameroon, for example, created the Aéroports de Cameroun as a company to operate seven of its airports, including the new international facility at Yaoundé, for fifteen years. Aéroports de Paris has a significant share holding in the company in conjunction with the Cameroon Airlines and banking interests. Regulatory requirements allow the company to vary charges but only after consultation processes.

Effects of Regulatory Reforms

The analysis of the implications of deregulation and privatization involving air transportation, and particularly those involving airlines, has created its own mini-industry. Considerably less work, however, has been done on airports and air navigation services, especially in developing countries. The more recent nature of such changes, the plethora of other political and industrial changes that are occurring in many developing counties, and the paucity of reliable data are perhaps the main explanations for this lack of analysis. There are also challenges in trying to define appropriate counterfactuals. Those looking at the U.S. domestic airline market have been particularly lucky in having ongoing federal time series data collection and an explicit formula used in the days of regulation that can serve as a reference point; such data are not collected in most other countries. Comparative cross-sectional analysis of U.S. and European systems was possible throughout the 1980s because the economies involved were broadly similar and political structures stable. Such conditions are rare in developing countries.

Even where work on airport reforms in high-income countries has been highly sophisticated, the analysis has tended to be only partial, focusing largely on the effects of reforms on the airport or airport system of immediate concern rather than on the impact across the entire airport network. For example, the privatization and price-capping regime adopted for BAA in the United Kingdom has clear trade-diversion effects (affecting major continental European airports, for example), but only the trade-creation effects of the regime have been the focus of attention. Airports are part of a network, as are airlines, but much of the analysis tends to treat them as stand-alone entities. The tendency in developing countries, for example, to offer concessions for networks of airports adds to the difficulties of making comparisons with events in the United States and Europe.

A quantitative examination of the impacts of recent regulatory reforms has been made possible by a number of important methodological advances, both in econometrics (for example, making it easier to estimate total productivity measures) and in programming (most notably the development of data envelopment analysis, or DEA). These new methodologies allow changes in economic efficiency to be more carefully assessed and have been employed in a variety of airport studies in higher-income countries, where they have permitted more systematic quantification of effects of institutional change.[45] Their use in assessing the outcomes of reforms in developing countries has been far more limited, however. Data limitations, including useful statistics on prereform trends, and the recent nature of many regulatory changes in developing countries have curtailed their usefulness in this context. In addition, many developing countries simply do not have the expertise available for such analysis. Nevertheless, several studies, not all including strict quantitative assessments, that embrace ex-post analysis of reforms in airport structures have been completed, and some of these are listed in table 8-2. Most relate to Latin America, where much of the activity has been focused and time series information, albeit often for a short period, is available. Not all these studies are free from political bias.

45. *Transportation Research Series E, Logistics and Transportation Review* 33, no. 4 (1997), provides a special issue on this topic.

It is not altogether transparent what one can conclude from these studies. Despite valiant efforts, data limitations and the short time span over which the experiences were assessed reduced the ability of most to produce anything but tentative results. The studies do suggest, however, that a learning process is taking place and that many of the dire consequences sometimes predicted by opponents of change have not materialized. It seems that many of the difficulties developing countries are facing as they pursue privatization strategies are similar to the difficulties found in developed countries. The Argentine example illustrates the difficulties of having a structure of "bidding" that produces realistic offers on the part of the private sector, and, where renegotiations take place, of ensuring that the incumbent does not simply manipulate its position to extract excessive terms from the government. In this respect, Colombia's more recent concessionary agreements seem to reflect a learning experience both from its own earlier activities and from what has happened in other countries.

It is also clear that the regulatory and institutional environment in which reforms take place, both with regard to the airports themselves and with related sectors such as the airlines, affect the outcomes of privatization initiatives, as do any subsequent changes to these environments. The ability to take the provision of airport services completely away from the political arena seems a particularly challenging issue. Additionally, most of the studies deal with concessions rather than full privatizations, and the common motivation for adopting this approach, a concern on the part of government to retain ultimate ownership, reflects an underlying political philosophy that does not pertain to many of the privatizations that have taken place in developed counties. Thus comparing a concession in South America with a privatization in Europe, for example, is unlikely to be very insightful.

The dearth of innovative actions outside of South America can be explained in part by the political climate that exists in many developing countries where direct state control is still seen as the norm. The transaction costs of change can also be considerable for a poor country—concessionary structures are not costless either to initiate or to monitor. The lack of innovation elsewhere also seems to reflect the network nature of the air transportation sector. South America is a large air market that is relatively well developed and growing. There are network externalities from attracting more airline business with other efficient airports. Essentially, an airport can be viable only if it has other airports to interact with. Such a network does not exist on this scale in, for example, much of Africa, and thus the incentive to take actions to make individual national airports more efficient through commercialization is reduced.

Table 8-2. *Studies of Institutional Changes Involving Airports in Developing Countries*

Study	Case	Topic	Findings
Juan (1995)	Ten case studies	Institutional comparison of approaches to privatization adopted by ten countries including six lower-income countries	Privatization is more efficient than corporatization; different approaches are needed for dealing with profitable and unprofitable airports; the specification of concession contracts needs to be carefully thought through.
U.S. General Accounting Office (1996)	Assessment of privatization of airports in fifty countries including developing nations	Looking for lessons for U.S. privatization	Limited evidence regarding performance although privatized facilities generated more revenue
Serebrisky and Presso (2002)	Argentinian airport privatization	Considers the vertical integration between airport and airline in a concession arrangement	Vertical integration can lead to market distortions in the absence of appropriate regulations to control monopoly powers.
Hooper (2002)	Asian airport privatization	Financial aspects of privatization	Appropriate sets of controls must be established before airports are privatized.

Bosch and García-Montalvo (2003)	Airport privatization in Latin America	Review of issues of nondiscriminatory access to airports using secondary sources	The problems of Latin American airports are ultimately similar to many of those being encountered in the European Union.
Hanaoka and Phomma (2004)	Partially privatized airports in Thailand	Comparison of fully state-owned and partially privatized airports	No clear-cut difference in productivity attributable to ownership
Pacheco, Fernandes, and Peixoto de Sequeire Santos (2006)	Brazilian privatization	Used DEA to look at efficiency of managerial changes in the lead-up to privatization	The performance of Infraero improved as it prepared for privatization.
Andrew and Dochia (2006)	Global privatization initiatives	Statistical analysis of airport privatization in low- and medium-income countries	The preferred institutional structure involves concessions rather than divestiture.
Lipovich (2008)	Argentinian airport privatization	Concession issues	Difficulties emerged in the concession allocation process that led to an unrealistic financial structure.
Low and Tang (2006)	Asian airport outsourcing	Degree of factor substitution as outsourcing takes place	Outsourcing has allowed airports to become more adaptive to price changes.

Conclusions

As in the developed countries, many lower-income countries have moved to liberalize the institutional environment in which air transport infrastructure services are delivered. The motivations of the two sets of countries for acting are often slightly different, however, and the methods used in developing countries generally fall short of measures such as full privatization or market allocation. As might be expected, individual countries vary in the nuances of their reforms, and such things as broader matters of regulatory philosophy, the physical and economic state of their air transportation infrastructure, and the quality of governance in the country can also influence their exact nature. Unlike most privatizations and regulatory reforms in developed countries, equity markets have not been widely used but rather outsourcing and concessions have been the norm.

To date, relatively little formal analysis has been done on the changing institutional structures of airports and of air navigation service providers in developing countries, let alone a substantive body of work assessing the implications of these changes. This makes it difficult to generalize and to draw any hard conclusions other than that the process has proved a problematic one in many cases. Most of the countries that have undertaken significant reform efforts, rather than simply spouting rhetoric, have been in Latin America, and these are generally not the poorest nations in the world. Many of these countries have relatively sophisticated financial systems, have taken measures of privatization and liberalization in other sectors, and have relatively stable political structures, compared with many other parts of the world. They also often have large air transportation networks that transcend their national borders. The experiences of South America may well not carry through to other parts of the world where conditions are different.

One point does emerge: while airport privatization in developed countries has not always generated all the benefits that one would have liked, it has nevertheless resulted in systems that are no worse, and in many cases are far better, than the state-dominated structures that preceded them and that still exist in many other developing countries. However, to fully participate in the global air transportation market, minimum standards of service, safety, and security are needed. Indeed, achieving these standards was the reason the Chicago Convention decided in 1944 to create the International Civil Aviation Organization, now a part of the United Nations. Without private finance and expertise, which is often available only from outside sources, it is impossible for most developing countries to meet these standards. The gradual emergence of specialist airport construction and management companies, stemming in part from demands in the liberalization of markets in developed nations, provides a much firmer basis for developing countries to move forward with privatization in whatever form meets local institutional conditions. In the past, lack of such pools of expertise meant that reliance on local skills and financial resources made meaningful privatization extremely challenging at best.

References

Alesina, A., and others. 1996. "Political Instability and Economic Growth." *Journal of Economic Growth* 1: 189–211.

Andrew, D., and S. Dochia. 2006. "The Growing and Evolving Business of Private Participation in Airports: New Trends, New Actors Emerging." Gridlines Note 15. Washington: World Bank.

Barro, R. J. 1991. *Economic Growth in a Cross Section of Countries*, NBER Working Paper 3120. Cambridge, Mass.: National Bureau of Economic Research.

Barro, R. J., and X. Sala-i-Martin. 1995. *Economic Growth.* New York: McGraw-Hill.

Betancor, O., and R. Rendeiro. 1999. "Regulating Privatized Infrastructure and Airport Services." Washington: World Bank.

Birdsall, N., and J. Nellis. 2002. *Winners and Losers: Assessing the Distributional Impact of Privatization.* Working Paper 6. Washington: Center for Global Development.

Boeing Commercial Airplanes. 2006. *Current Market Outlook.* Seattle.

Bosch, A., and J. García-Montalvo. 2003. *Free and Nondiscriminatory Access to Airports: Proposal for Latin America.* Washington: Inter-American Development Bank.

Button, K. J. 2005. "The Economics of Cost Recovery in Transport." *Journal of Transport Economics and Policy* 39: 241–57.

———. 2007. "Auctions—What Can We Learn from Auction Theory for Slot Allocation?" In *How to Make Slot Markets Work*, edited by A. Czerny and others. German Aviation Research Seminar Series 3. Burlington, Vt.: Ashgate.

Button, K. J., and G. McDougall. 2006. "Institutional and Structural Changes in Air Navigation Service-Providing Organizations." *Journal of Air Transport Management* 12: 236–52.

Button, K. J., and others. 2004. "Conforming with ICAO Safety Oversight Standards." *Journal of Air Transport Management* 10: 251–57.

Coase, R. H. 1992. "The Institutional Nature of Production." *American Economic Review* 82: 713–19.

Demsetz, H. 1968. "Why Regulate Utilities?" *Journal of Law and Economics* 11: 55–65.

DeNeufville, R., and A. Odoni. 2003. *Airport Systems: Planning, Design, and Management.* New York: McGraw-Hill.

Guasch, J. L. 2004. *Granting and Renegotiating Infrastructure Concessions: Doing It Right.* Washington: World Bank.

Hammond, J. 2003. "Russian Civil Aviation and Airports—Legal and Financial Issues." In *Business Briefing: Aviation Strategies,* pp. 58–61. Montreal: International Civil Aviation Organization.

Hanaoka, S., and S. Phomma. 2004. "Privatization and Productivity Performance of Thai Airports." Paper presented at the 8th Air Transport Research Society World Conference, Istanbul.

Hooper, P. 2002. "Privatization of Airports in Asia." *Journal of Air Transport Management* 8: 289–300.

Juan, E. R. 1995. *Airport Infrastructure: The Emerging Role of the Private Sector, Cofinancing and Financial Advisory Services.* Washington: World Bank.

Kahn, A. E. 1988. *The Economics of Regulation: Principles and Institutions.* MIT Press.

Kapur, A. 1995. "Airport Infrastructure: The Emerging Role of the Private Sector." Technical Paper 313. Washington: World Bank.

Kay, J. A., and D. J. Thompson. 1986. "Privatization: A Policy in Search of a Rationale." *Economic Journal* 96: 18–32.

Kikeri, S., J. Nellis, and M. Shorley. 1994. "Privatization Lessons from Market Economies." *World Bank Research Observer* 9: 241–72.

Lipovich, G. A. 2008 (forthcoming). "The Privatization of Argentinean Airports." *Journal of Air Transport Management.*

Littlechild, S. C. 1983. *Regulation of British Telecommunication's Profitability.* London: Department of Industry.

Low, J. M. W., and L. C. Tang. 2006. "Factor Substitution and Complementarity in the Asian Airport Industry." *Journal of Air Transport and Management* 12: 261–66.

Micco, A., and T. Serebrisky. 2004. "Infrastructure Competition Regimes and Air Transport Costs: Cross-Country Evidence." Working Paper 510. Washington: Inter-American Development Bank.

Oum, T. H., N. Adler, and C. Yu. 2006. "Privatization, Corporatization, Ownership Forms and Their Effects on the Performance of the World's Airports." *Journal of Air Transport Management* 12: 109–21.

Pacheco, R. R., E. Fernandes, and M. Peixoto de Sequeire Santos. 2006. "Management Style and Airport Performance in Brazil." *Journal of Air Transport Management* 12: 324–30.

Pardo, G. V. 2003. "Airport Concessions in Colombia: An Overview and Perspectives." In *Business Briefing: Aviation Strategies,* pp. 50–52. Montreal: International Civil Aviation Organization.

Park, Y. 2003. "An Analysis of the Competitive Strength of Asian Major Airports." *Journal of Air Transport Management* 9: 353–60.

Romer, P. M. 1990. "Endogenous Technical Change." *Journal of Political Economy* 98: S71–S102.

Serebrisky, T., and P. Presso. 2002. "An Incomplete Regulatory Framework? Vertical Integration in Argentine Airports." Paper presented at the 37th Meeting of the Argentine Political Economy Association, Tucuman.

Starkie, D. 2001. "Reforming UK Airport Regulation." *Journal of Transport Economics and Policy* 35: 119–35.

Stiglitz, J. 1998. "The Private Uses of Public Interests: Incentives and Institutions." *Journal of Economic Perspectives* 12: 3–22.

Train, K. E. 1991. *Optimal Regulation: The Economic Theory of Natural Monopoly*. MIT Press.

UNCTAD (UN Conference on Trade and Development). 1998. *International Trade in Tourism-Related Services: Issues and Options for Developing Countries*. Geneva.

U.S. General Accounting Office. 1996. *Airport Privatization: Issues Related to the Sale or Lease of U.S. Commercial Airports*. Washington.

Vickrey, W. 1961. "Counter-Speculation, Auctions, and Competitive Sealed Tenders." *Journal of Finance* 16: 8–37.

CLIFFORD WINSTON *and* GINÉS DE RUS

9
Synthesis and Conclusions

The ultimate question raised by this book concerns the desirability of privatizing aviation infrastructure. Generally, the largest improvements in economic welfare from privatization of public facilities are likely to be generated in environments where privatized entities are subject to intense competition that leads to lower costs and more rapid technological advance. Because many of their air transport corridors experience a large volume of traffic, the United States and continental Europe have the greatest potential for such competition in aviation infrastructure. But surprisingly these regions have shown relatively little interest in privatization—preferring a network of airports and an air traffic control system that in the case of the United States is almost entirely publicly owned and operated and in the case of continental Europe is predominantly publicly owned and operated. In contrast, Australia, New Zealand, Canada, the United Kingdom, and even China and some developing countries have experimented with various approaches to privatizing their aviation infrastructure.

This book has not focused on the political forces that explain these varied approaches toward privatization, although it has noted that each country's stakeholders, including the government, have taken policy positions that advance their interests. Instead, the book has "exploited" differences in policy to shed some light on how institutions affect aviation infrastructure performance. For example, the substantive design of regulation clearly matters, as indicated by the seeming trade-off between productivity and investment efficiency under light regulation in Australia and by the incentive for excessive investment under regulation in the United Kingdom. And, of course, the nature of airport and air traffic control ownership matters, as indicated by local airport authorities in the United States that receive federal support with little regard for economic efficiency and by state-owned airports in much of the developing world that seek private investment to improve their operations.

It would be misleading to claim that the evidence from the privatization experiments that have been conducted to date is sufficiently positive to make a strong case for more extensive and widespread privatization of aviation infrastructure. Nonetheless, the experiments are compelling because they have shown that privatization has not had an adverse effect on an air transportation system's performance and because they have focused attention on the large costs of allowing the public sector to operate or regulate airports and air traffic control.

Vast inefficiencies have accumulated in the U.S. air transportation system because publicly owned and operated airports and air traffic control are mispriced, subject to suboptimal investment, and slow to exhibit technological advance. These problems are not as well documented in continental Europe, but it is clear that travelers and carriers in the region experience costly inefficiencies attributable to delays that are similar to those experienced by travelers and carriers in the United States. Moreover, neither region has shown an ability to reform its infrastructure significantly under the current institutions.

Privatization experiments have shown that institutional change makes positive reforms possible. Airports in Australia and the United Kingdom have lowered their costs because they have been forced to become more commercially oriented. Similarly, Canadian and U.K. air traffic control systems have become more efficient and responsive to users without compromising safety.

It is also important to realize that the current drawbacks of fully and partly privatized systems and constraints on further improvements are largely attributable to regulations that are promulgated and enforced by the public sector. Australia has avoided inefficiencies created by heavy-handed price regulation, but vague guidelines by the government appear to be contributing to airports' excessive investments. The United Kingdom has maintained inefficient price and ownership regulations that discourage, if not prevent, airports from instituting congestion pricing to reduce delays while encouraging them to make excessive investments. Airports in Canada charge excessive prices because they are prohibited from raising equity from the private sector.

Inefficient residual regulations not only undermine competition but also tend to encourage users and suppliers to squabble over their share of the pie instead of encouraging them to cooperate and resolve their differences over pricing and investment policies. Absent such regulations, airports and airlines in Australia and users and decisionmakers at Nav Canada have negotiated charges—and demonstrated that mutually beneficial cooperation is possible.

The unpredictable dynamics of market competition—and the enormous social benefits resulting from innovations that emerge from the competitive process—make it problematic for a government to micromanage privatized entities with intrusive regulation. In the case of aviation infrastructure, a trade-off is likely to exist between static inefficiency, during the inception of privatization when certain airports and air traffic control may not be subject to competitive pressures, and dynamic efficiency, when competitive pressures and cooperation develop and static inefficiencies begin to erode. The challenges for governments throughout the world are how and when to withdraw their intervention to optimize this trade-off.

Contributors

Robert Andriulaitis
*InterVISTAS Consulting Inc.,
  Vancouver, Canada*

Kenneth Button
George Mason University

Peter Forsyth
Monash University, Australia

David Gillen
University of British Columbia

Anne Graham
*University of Westminster,
  United Kingdom*

Steven A. Morrison
Northeastern University

Hans-Martin Niemeier
*Bremen University of Applied Sciences,
  Germany*

Ginés de Rus
*Universidad de Las Palmas de Gran
  Canaria, Spain*

Michael W. Tretheway
*InterVISTAS Consulting Inc. and
  University of British Columbia*

Clifford Winston
Brookings Institution

Andrew Yuen
University of British Columbia

Anming Zhang
University of British Columbia

Index

AAHK. *See* Airport Authority Hong Kong
Aberdeen (U.K.), 102
Abuja Treaty of *2000*, 199
ACAC (Arab Civil Aviation Commission), 199
ACCC. *See* Australian Competition and Consumer Commission
Accountability: in Canada, 139, 141; in U.S., 28
Adelaide (Australia): aeronautical revenues in, 86; airport investments in, 77, 84; charges in, 86, 89; location constraints in, 68; ownership patterns in, 76
ADI, 106
ADP. *See* Aéroports de Paris
ADS-B (Automatic dependent surveillance-broadcast), 15
AENA (Spain), 39
Aeronautics Act (Canada), 146
Aéroports de Cameroun, 213
Aéroports de Paris (ADP): in developing countries, 210, 213; and EU, 39, 42, 44, 47, 48
Aeropuertos Argentinia *2000*, 211

Africa: air cargo exports from, 196, 197; air transportation in, 197; concessions in, 209, 213; economic growth in, 194. *See also* Developing countries
African Union, 199
AIP. *See* Airport Improvement Program (U.S.)
Airline safety, 2, 166–68. *See also* Air traffic control
Airport and Airway Trust Fund (U.S.), 11, 14, 25
Airport Authority Hong Kong (AAHK), 163, 164, 182
Airport Development and Investment Limited (ADI), 106
Airport Development Program (U.S.), 10–11
Airport Holding Kft, 42
Airport Improvement Fee (Canada), 149
Airport Improvement Program (AIP, U.S.), 11, 20
Airport infrastructure fee (China), 162
Airport operators: in Canada, 140–45; in China, 159–60, 163, 166, 184; in EU, 41–44; in U.K., 122–23, 131

227

Index

Airports Act of *1986* (U.K.), 104, 105, 108
Airports Act of *1996* (Australia), 83
Airports Act (proposed, Canada), 145–48, 155
Aeroporti di Roma, 39
Airport slot coordinator (ASC, EU), 49–50
Airports Policy (U.K. white paper), 108
Airport Transfer Act of *1992* (Canada), 138
Air traffic control: air route traffic control centers (ARTCCs), 14; in Australia and New Zealand, 66; in Canada, 137; in China, 162, 166, 168–69, 184; in U.K., 100, 111; in U.S., 14–16, 24–27, 32–33
Air Traffic Control Bureau (China), 168
Air Traffic Organization (ATO, U.S.), 8, 25, 26, 32
Air Transport Association, 19, 21
Air Transport Research Society (ATRS), 69, 170, 182
Amsterdam (Netherlands), 117
ANA (Portugal), 39
Andriulaitis, Robert, 136
Ansett, 84–85, 86
Arab Civil Aviation Commission (ACAC), 199
Argentina, 210–11, 215
ARTCCs (Air route traffic control centers), 14
ASC (Airport slot coordinator, EU), 49–50
Atlanta, 19
ATO. *See* Air Traffic Organization (U.S.)
ATRS. *See* Air Transport Research Society
Auckland (New Zealand), 68, 73, 74, 77, 93, 94
Auditing. *See* Monitoring
Australia, 65–99; competition between airports in, 75–76, 95; efficiency in, 67, 78–82, 96; financial and economic performance in, 67, 69–72, 94–95, 96; light-handed regulation in, 65, 66, 77–94, 95–97; monitoring in, 85–91, 95–96; overview, 67–69; ownership patterns in, 65–66, 73–75, 94; price cap in, 67, 82–85, 95–96; privatization in, 66, 72–73, 94; reform in, 67, 91–93, 96; regional development and strategies in, 76–77, 94, 95
Australian Competition and Consumer Commission (ACCC): dispute resolution through, 83, 90, 91, 92; efficiency determinations by, 87; investment determinations by, 83, 84; as monitoring system, 85; and price caps, 82
Australian Productivity Commission, 76
Austria, 43
Avalon (airport), 75
Averch and Johnson effect, 80, 90

BAA airport group: and airport development, 104; common ownership by, 128–31, 132; and designation of airports, 124, 127; and dual-till regulatory system, 115; efficiency of, 114; and Heathrow Terminal 5, 112; investment incentives for, 119, 122; market share of, 101; as NATS shareholder, 111; performance of, 109–10; privatization of, 101, 105; regional airports owned by, 106; and regulation, 120, 121; and regulatory review process, 122, 123; Scottish airports owned by, 102, 132. *See also* British Airports Authority
BA (British Airways), 112
Banjul Accord of *1997*, 199
Beijing Capital International Airport, 163, 169
Belfast City (airport), 132
Belfast International (airport), 132

Bilateral air service agreements, 180
Birmingham-Nottingham East Midlands (airport), 102, 106, 121
Bolivia, 211
Boston, 19
Bridgepoint (private equity firm), 106
Brisbane (Australia): charges in, 85; competition between airports in, 75–76; direct flights from, 77; environmental constraints at, 69; losses in, 84; ownership patterns in, 73; privatization of, 72; productivity in, 70, 71, 89
Brisbane Port Corporation, 73
Bristol (U.K.), 132
British Airports Authority, 101, 105. *See also* BAA airport group
British Gas, 128
British Telecommunications, 128
Brueckner, Jan K., 18
Brussels (Belgium), 48–49, 74
Burkina Faso, 200
Bush, George W., 9
Button, Kenneth, 193, 201–02

CAA. *See* Civil Aviation Authority
CAAC. *See* Civil Aviation Administration of China
CAAs (Canadian Airport Authorities), 140–45
Cairns (Australia), 67, 87
Calgary, 151
Cameroun, 200, 213
Canada, 136–55; airport authorities in, 140–41; Airports Act, proposed, 145–48, 155; capital investment in airports, 149–53; conversions of LAAs, 141–45; conversions to CAAs, 141–45; financing in, 148–49; local airport authorities in, 138–40; not-for-profit airport governance model, development of, 137–45; rent renegotiation in, 141–45

Canadian Airport Authorities (CAAs), 140–45
Canberra (Australia), 82, 84, 86
Capacity constraints, 49–54
Capital investment. *See* Investment incentives
Cardiff-Bristol (airport), 102
Cardiff (U.K.), 101
Cargo. *See* Freight traffic
Carlin, Alan, 17
Charges. *See* Fees and charges
Chen, Zhiwu, 178
Chew, Russell, 25
Chicago Convention of *1944*, 180, 198–99, 218
Chicago Midway, 31
Chicago O'Hare, 19
China, 159–92; airline safety in, 166–68; airport efficiency, effect of public listing on, 170–76, 185–89; air traffic control in, 168–69, 184; competition issues in, 177–78, 179–81; corporate governance in, 178–79; industry performance in, 164–69; international policy of, 179–81; localization program in, 159–60, 163, 166, 184; policy developments in, 161–64; public listing, effect on airport efficiency, 170–76; reform in, 179–82; state ownership in, 177–78
China Securities Regulatory Commission (CSRC), 181
Christchurch (New Zealand), 68, 73, 74, 93, 94
Civil Aeronautics Act of *1938* (U.S.), 10
Civil Aviation Administration of China (CAAC): and air traffic control, 168–69; as paramilitary organization, 159; and policy developments, 161–64; price regulation by, 165
Civil Aviation Authority (CAA, U.K.): and designation of airports, 126, 127, 133; and dual-till regulatory system,

115, 117, 131; in efficiency-promoting role, 114; regulation approach of, 107–08, 120, 121; and regulatory review process, 110–11, 122, 123, 124; and service-quality incentives, 109; and Stansted complaint about pricing levels, 119
Civil Aviation Management Institute of China, 166
Civil Aviation Safety Academy of China, 166
Coase, Ronald, 202
Colombia, 212, 215
Commerce Commission (New Zealand), 93
Common use gate leases, 21
Community Consultative Committee (Canada), 140
Compensatory charging system, 11–12
Competition: in Australia, 75–76, 95; Canadian vs. U.S. airports, 144; in China, 160, 165, 177–78, 179–81; in EU, 53; in Hong Kong, 182–84; in New Zealand, 75–76, 95; rail system as, 38; and safety, 168; in U.S., 29–30
Competition Authority (EU), 53, 56
Competition Commission (U.K.): investigation of BAA group by, 117, 122, 130; and Northern Ireland services, 132; and ownership patterns, 129; regulatory expertise of, 123; and regulatory review process, 110, 124; system funding favored by, 120
Concessions and developing countries, 213
Conflict of interest: LAA provisions for, 139; in regional development, 76; in U.K., 76
Congestion pricing model, 28
Copenhagen, 47, 74
Corporate structure and governance: in Canada, 140; in China, 160, 178–79. *See also* Ownership patterns

Cost-based airport regulation (EU), 45–46
Cost-plus basis airport charges, 45
Cost recovery, 79–80, 87
Countervailing power, 76, 95
CPI-X caps, 82, 83
CSRC (China Securities Regulatory Commission), 181

Dahya, Jay, 179
Darwin (Australia), 86
Data envelopment analysis (DEA), 114
Deadweight loss, 79–80
Delays: in China, 169; and infrastructure investments, 2; in U.S., 7–9, 17, 33
Denmark, 38
de Rus, Ginés, 1, 222
Designation of airports in U.K., 108–09, 124–28, 133
Developing countries, 193–221; airport policies in, 200–07; airport services in, 197–98; air transport growth in, 205–07; air transport in, 195–200; changes in, 207–13; economic issues in, 205–07; and globalization, 198–200; governance in, 202–03; and military interests, 204–05; reform in, 201–05, 213–17; resource availability in, 201–02; and social attitudes, 203–04. *See also specific countries*
Disclosure and corporate governance, 178. *See also* Transparency
Doncaster Finningley, 102, 125
Dual-till regulatory system: ACCC use of, 82; adoption of, 131; arguments for, 117; differences in opinion over, 123; efficiency of, 81; in EU, 45; merits of, 115; revenues calculated in, 110. *See also* Single-till regulatory system
Dublin, 47
Düsseldorf, 47

Eastern Europe, 207
easyJet, 124
ECAA (European Common Aviation Area), 41
ECJ (European Court of Justice), 105
Edinburgh, 102
Edmonton, 151
Efficiency: in Australia, 67, 78–82, 96; in China, 170–76, 185–89; in U.K., 114–18
Environmental impact standards and airport expansion, 12, 19
Environmental Protection Agency, 12, 28
European Commission, 37, 53
European Commission Treaty, 41
European Common Aviation Area (ECAA), 41
European Court of Justice (ECJ), 105
European Union (EU), 36–61; airport industry in, 38–41; capacity constraints in, 49–54; cost-based airport regulation in, 45–46; freight traffic in, 41; ownership patterns in, 41–44; price-cap airport regulation in, 46–49; privatization in, 41–44, 56; regulation environment in, 44–49; slot allocation in, 49–54, 56; traffic levels in, 38. *See also specific countries*
EU-U.S. open-skies agreement, 36, 55
Exclusive gate leases, 20
Exeter (U.K.), 132

FAA. *See* Federal Aviation Administration (U.S.)
FAC (Federal Airports Corporation), 72
Federal Airport Act of *1946* (U.S), 10
Federal Airports Corporation (FAC), 72
Federal Aviation Act of *1958* (U.S.), 14
Federal Aviation Administration (FAA, U.S.): AIP funds allocation by, 11; and air traffic control, 8, 24; creation of, 14; and federal grants, 12, 20; and flight delays, 33; and Nextgen, 16, 27;

reform constraints of, 27–28; and slot allocation, 18–19
Fees and charges: in Canada, 138–39, 141; in China, 162; in EU, 44–45; in U.S., 11, 17, 25; weight-based, 46
Ferrovial, 105, 106, 122
Finnish Airports, 39
Forsyth, Peter, 65
France, 38, 42
Frankfurt, 47, 117
Fraport AG, 163–64
Freight traffic: in developing countries, 196; in EU, 41; in Hong Kong, 183–84
Fund of Infrastructure Construction for Civil Aviation (China), 162–63
Fung, M., 170, 171
A Future Framework for Airports in Canada policy statement, 138
"The Future of Air Transport" (U.K. white paper), 104

GAO. *See* General Accounting Office (U.S.)
Gate leases: common use, 21; exclusive, 11, 20; preferential, 20–21
Gate utilization (U.S.), 20–22
Gatwick: airport-airline dialogue with, 132; and CAA regulation, 120; charges at, 119; and designation of airports, 127; efficiency of, 114; growth at, 103; operating margins at, 102; ownership patterns at, 31, 128; and price caps, 109; price regulation at, 108; and regulatory review process, 123; runways at, 104; and Stansted, 121; traffic to, 101. *See also* London
General Accounting Office (GAO, *now* Government Accountability Office, U.S.), 15, 27
General aviation, 24–25
Germany, 37, 38, 42, 48
Gillen, David, 36

Giuliani, Rudolph, 8–9
Glasgow, 102
Globalization, 1, 198–200
Gold Coast (airport), 75
Goldman Sachs, 106
Gold-plating and capital investments, 153
Gold-plating effect, 118, 119, 121, 126
Government's Better Regulation Task Force (U.K.), 122
Graham, Anne, 100
Grandfather provision for slot allocation, 50–51, 56–57
Grants, 12, 20, 202
Gray market for slots, 52–53
Greece, 38, 42
Ground-based radar systems, 1, 14, 15
Ground leases, 138–39, 140–41
Guangzhou Baiyun Airport, 165–66
Guide to Community Legislation in the Field of Aviation (EU), 41
Guinea, 200

Halifax, 153
Hangzhou Xiaoshan International Airport, 163
Harvest Fund Management Co., 179
Heathrow: airport-airline dialogue with, 132; and CAA regulation, 120; capacity at, 112; charges at, 116–17, 119; and designation of airports, 127; efficiency of, 114; growth at, 103; operating margins at, 102; ownership patterns at, 31, 128, 129; price regulation at, 108, 109; quality of service at, 130; and regulatory review process, 123; runways at, 104; and Stansted, 121; and Terminal 5, 104, 112, 118; traffic to, 101. *See also* London
Homeland Security, Department of (U.S.), 22, 28

Hong Kong International Airport (HKIA), 182–84
Hubs: in Australia, 76–77; in China, 171–73; and competition, 183; in EU, 39, 55; in Hong Kong, 182–83; in U.K., 127; in U.S., 12–13, 18
Hybrid price caps, 47

IATA. *See* International Air Transport Association
ICAO. *See* International Civil Aviation Organization
India, 203, 208
Information disclosure and corporate governance, 178
Infratil, 74
Initial public offerings (IPOs), 170
Institutional shareholders, 179
Intergenerational transfer, 149
Internal control system, 178
International Air Transport Association (IATA), 49, 56, 81
International Civil Aviation Organization (ICAO), 45, 218
International Civil Aviation Safety Assessment program, 202
International Development Association, 200
International gateway hubs, 173
Investment incentives: in Australia, 67; in Canada, 148–53; in China, 163, 169; in U.K., 118–22; in U.S., 26. *See also* Private sector investment
Ireland, 38, 42
Israeli airport security model, 23

Jetstar, 75

Karbhari, Yusuf, 179

LAAs. *See* Local airport authorities
Labor productivity, 165, 170

LaGuardia, 22
Lapierre, Jean-C., 144
Late handbacks of slots, 53
Latin America, 207, 210–11, 214. *See also* Developing countries
LAX. *See* Los Angeles Airport
LCCs. *See* Low-cost carriers
Leases: gate, 20–21; ground, 138–39, 140–41
Leeds Bradford (airport), 106, 125
Levine, Michael E., 17
LFV (Sweden), 39
Light-handed regulation in Australia and New Zealand, 65, 66, 77–97; and efficiency in airports, 78–82; and monitoring in Australia, 85–91; New Zealand approach, 77–78, 93–94; and price cap in Australia, 82–85; and reform, 91–93
Lima Airport Partners, 211
Liverpool-Manchester (airport), 102, 125
Local airport authorities (LAAs, Canada), 138–40, 141–45
Localization program in China, 159–60, 163, 166, 184
London City (airport), 101, 106. *See also* London
London: air traffic control in, 111; capacity of airports in, 104, 112, 129; demand for airports in, 120; economic distortions at airports in, 131; investment in airports in, 118; market share of airports in, 103; and system pricing, 110, 119; traffic through, 101. *See also* Gatwick; Heathrow; London City; Luton; Stansted
Los Angeles Airport (LAX), 19, 29
Los Angeles Airport Commission, 21
Low-cost carriers (LCCs): in Australia and New Zealand, 68, 75; in EU, 38; facilities and services standards for, 123; and fare competition, 121; and ownership patterns, 129; in U.K., 100, 101, 102–03
Luton, 101, 106, 119, 120, 121, 125. *See also* London

Macquarie Airports, 73, 74, 106, 210. *See also* Sydney
Macquarie Bank, 73–74
Malev, 112
Mali, 200
Malmquist index, 114
Manchester (U.K.): and designation of airports, 108, 125, 126, 127, 133; efficiency of, 114; market share of, 102; ownership patterns in, 106; services and infrastructure at, 132; traffic to, 105; unit costs at, 119
Manston (airport), 102
Marginal-cost pricing model, 25
Maryland Aviation Administration, 21
Mayer, Christopher, 18
Melbourne (Australia): charges in, 86; competition between airports in, 75–76; direct flights from, 77; environmental constraints at, 69; pricing regulations in, 85; privatization of, 72, 73
Midlands. *See* Birmingham-Nottingham East Midlands (airport)
Military interests: in China, 168–69; in developing countries, 198, 204–05; and landing and terminal fees, 145
Modern enterprise system (China), 164, 177
Monitoring: in Australia, 85–91, 95–96; in Canada, 139, 141, 144, 146–47; in China, 168, 177, 178–79
Monopoly power, 30, 160, 200, 209
Montreal, 151
Morrison, Steven A., 7, 17, 18, 19, 26

Multilateral Investment Guarantee Bank, 203

National Airports Policy (Canada), 140
National Airport System (NAS, Canada), 144
National Air Traffic Controllers Association (U.S.), 19, 27
National Audit Office (China), 175
National Business Aviation Association (U.S.), 27
National Plan of Integrated Airport Systems (U.S.), 12
NATS (*formerly* National Air Traffic Services, U.K.), 111
Nav Canada, 32, 148
Necessary new investment (NNI), 82–83
Newcastle (Australia), 67
Newcastle (U.K.), 106
New Zealand, 65–99; competition between airports in, 75–76, 95; financial and economic performance in, 69–72, 94–95, 96; light-handed regulation in, 65, 66, 77–78, 93–94, 95–97; overview, 67–69; ownership patterns in, 65–66, 73–75, 94; privatization in, 66, 72–73, 94; regional development and strategies in, 76–77, 94, 95
NextGen air traffic control (U.S.), 15–16, 26
Niemeier, Hans-Martin, 36
Night curfews, 68, 69
Ningbo Airport, 163–64
NNI (necessary new investment), 82–83
Noise issues, 68, 72, 73, 100
Nonaeronautical revenues, 70, 90, 110, 116
Northern Ireland, 132
Norway, 38
Norwich (U.K.), 121
No-shows and slots, 53–54

Office of Aviation Safety (China), 166
Office of Fair Trading (OFT, U.K.), 126, 127, 129, 130, 132, 133
Olympic Games (*2000*), 83
Open skies initiatives, 199
Oster, Clinton V., Jr., 26, 32
Ottawa, 152
Ownership patterns: in Australia, 65–66, 73–75, 94; in EU, 41–44; in New Zealand, 65–66, 73–75, 94; in U.K., 100, 101, 105–06, 107, 128–31, 132–33. *See also* State ownership

Paris, 117
Parker, D., 114
Park, R. E., 17
Partial privatizations, 177
Participation rents, 139, 144
Part IIIA. *See* Trade Practices Act of *1974* (Australia)
Passenger facility charges, 11
Peel Airports, 106
Perth, 72, 76, 82, 85, 86
Peru, 203, 211
Peters, Mary, 9
Planning: in U.K., 100, 101, 112–14, 131; in U.S., 10, 16
"Planning for a Sustainable Future" (U.K. white paper), 113
Political risk, 202–03
Portugal, 42
Preferential gate leases, 20–21
Price caps: in Australia, 67, 82–85, 95–96; in EU, 45, 46–49; in U.K., 109–10, 114–18, 124, 125, 131
Pricing: in Canada, 140–41, 147, 154; in China, 165; in developing countries, 205; in EU, 43, 44–45; in U.K., 110, 119, 120, 121, 123; in U.S., 24–26. *See also* Price caps
Private sector investment: and airport privatization, 31; in developing

countries, 207–08. *See also* Investment incentives
Private securities litigation, 178
Privatization: in Australia, 66, 72–73, 94; in China, 160, 177; in EU, 41–44, 56; in Hong Kong, 184; and monopoly power, 30; in New Zealand, 66, 72–73, 94; in U.K., 101, 103–05, 128, 132; in U.S., 10, 28–33; as vehicle for financing new investment, 208–09
Privatization pilot program (U.S.), 31
Productivity Commission (Australia), 84, 85, 86, 87–89, 90–91, 92
Productivity growth, 175–76. *See also* Efficiency
Public listing and airport efficiency, 160, 170–76
Pure price caps, 47

Qantas, 74, 75, 76, 77, 86–87
Qualified Foreign Institutional Investors program (China), 181
Queensland (Australia), 77

RAB. *See* Regulated asset base
Radar systems. *See* Ground-based radar systems
Rafael Del Pino Foundation, 3
Rail system as competition, 38
Ramsey pricing, 80
Rate-of-return basis airport charges, 45
RDFs (route development funds), 103
Reform: in Australia, 67, 91–93, 96; in China, 179–82; in developing countries, 201–05, 213–17; in U.K., 101, 124–31, 133; in U.S., 27–28
Regional development and strategies: in Australia, 76–77; in China, 172–74, 183; in EU, 41; in New Zealand, 76–77; in U.K., 101–03, 125, 132
Regional hubs, 173
Registered traveler program, 13–14, 23

Regulated asset base (RAB), 109, 110, 118, 122
Regulation: in Australia and New Zealand, 65, 66, 77–94, 95–97; in China, 165, 178; in EU, 44–49; in U.K., 100, 101, 106–11, 131–32, 133
Regulatory review process in U.K., 122–23, 133
Rents: in Canada, 139, 141–45; in U.S., 11. *See also* Leases
"Report on Civil Aviation Reform Measures and Implementation" (China), 161
Residual charging system, 11
Revenue-sharing agreements, 47–48
Review-sanction model, 91–92, 95, 96
Route development funds (RDFs), 103
$RPI +/- X$ regulatory mechanism: in EU, 46–47; U.K., 109, 110, 114, 118, 122
Runway investment: in Australia, 72, 73; in Canada, 150, 152; in China, 163, 185; in developing countries, 211, 212; in U.K., 104, 119, 120, 122; in U.S., 19–20
Ryanair, 119

Safe Skies for Africa Program, 199
Safety, 2, 166–68
St. Louis, 19
SASAC. *See* State-Owned Assets Supervision and Administration Commission
Satellite-based air traffic control, 1, 15–16
Scottish Islands and Highlands, 105
Seattle-Tacoma airport (Sea-Tac), 22
Secretary of State (U.K.), 127
Securities litigation, 178
Security issues, 12–14, 22–24
Shanghai Hongqiao International Airport, 163, 165
Shanghai International Airport Ltd., 170

Shanghai Pudong International Airport, 165–66, 169
Show-cause-price inquiry mechanism, 92, 96
Sinai, Todd, 18
Single-till regulatory system: argument for, 116; criticism of, 81; differences in opinion over, 115, 123; in EU, 45; at London airports, 131; retained by CAA, 117; revenues calculated in, 110. *See also* Dual-till regulatory system
Sino-U.S. air service agreement, 180
Slot allocation: in Australia, 81; in EU, 49–54, 56; grandfather provision, 50–51, 56–57; gray market for, 52–53; in New Zealand, 81; transfers of, 50–52; in U.K., 101, 112, 117–18, 131; in U.S., 18–19
Slot hoarding, 53
Slovak Republic, 43
Smith, Adam, 201
Social attitudes and airport policies, 203–04
South Africa, 197
South America, 196, 209, 210. *See also* Developing countries
South Asia, 208
South Australia, 77
Southend (airport, U.K.), 105
Southhampton (U.K.), 105
Spain, 42
Split-share reforms, 181–82
Stand-alone pricing, 110, 119, 120, 121, 123. *See also* System pricing
Stansted: capacity at, 104; charges at, 114; and designation of airports, 108, 125–26, 127, 133; investment at, 118, 119, 122; ownership patterns at, 31, 120, 128, 129; and regulatory review process, 123; traffic at, 101. *See also* London

State-Owned Assets Supervision and Administration Commission (SASAC), 164, 181
State ownership: in China, 160, 177–78, 182; in developing countries, 198, 210; in EU, 39, 42
Stiglitz, Joseph, 27
Strong, John S., 26, 32
Subsidies: in Canada, 141–42; in China, 163; in developing countries, 198
Supervisory board, 179
Supreme People's Court (China), 178
Sweden, 38, 42
Sydney: aeronautical revenues in, 86; charges in, 87, 90; competition between airports in, 76; as international flight hub, 77; investment in, 72; location constraints in, 68; ownership patterns in, 73; peak problems at, 79; price caps in, 83, 85; productivity in, 69–70, 71, 89. *See also* Macquarie Airports
System pricing, 120, 121. *See also* Stand-alone pricing

TBI, 106, 132
Technology adoption, 26–27
Terminal radar approach facilities (TRACONs), 14, 26
TFP (Total factor productivity), 165
Thatcher, Margaret, 103–04, 105
Toronto (Canada), 137, 152
Total factor productivity (TFP), 165
Tourism, 196
TRACONs. *See* Terminal radar approach facilities
Trade Practices Act of *1974* (Australia), 83, 85, 87, 90, 91, 92
Transparency: in Canada, 138, 140–41, 145; in EU, 48–49, 53; in Hong Kong, 182; in U.K., 120, 124
Transportation Agency (Canada), 147

Transportation Security Administration (TSA, U.S.), 8, 13, 22
Transport Canada, 137, 139, 141, 144, 150, 152
Transport Research Laboratory, 117
Transport Select Committee (U.K.), 127
Tretheway, Michael W., 136
TSA. *See* Transportation Security Administration (U.S.)

United (airline), 112
United Kingdom (U.K.), 100–135; airport operators' role in, 122–23, 131; air traffic control in, 100, 111; background of airport industry in, 101–03; designation of airports in, 108–09, 124–28, 133; efficiency and price-cap regulation in, 114–18; investment incentives in, 118–22; ownership patterns in, 100, 101, 105–06, 107, 128–31, 132–33; planning process in, 100, 101, 112–14, 131; privatization in, 101, 103–05, 128, 132; reform in, 101, 124–31, 133; regulation in, 100, 101, 106–11, 131–32, 133; regulators' role in, 118, 123–24, 131; regulatory review process in, 122–23, 133
United States (U.S.), 7–35; airport performance in, 16–22; airport system in, 10–12; air traffic control in, 14–16; competition with Canadian airports, 144; economic assessment of, 16–27; gate utilization in, 20–22; overview and evolution of current policy, 10–16; pricing in, 17–20, 24–26; privatization in, 28–33; reform in, 27–28; runway investment and pricing in, 17–20; security in, 12–14, 22–24; and Sino-U.S. air service agreement, 180; technology adoption by, 26–27

Vancouver (Canada), 137, 148–50
Venezuela, 212–13
Victoria (Australia), 77
Vienna, 48
Virgin Blue, 74, 76, 90

Wang, Changyun, 178
Wellington (New Zealand), 68, 69, 73, 74, 93, 94
Winnipeg, 153
Winston, Clifford, 1, 7, 17, 18, 19, 26, 222
World Bank, 200, 201, 207, 209
World Trade Organization (WTO), 180

Xiamen Airport, 159, 163
Xiao, Jason Zezong, 179

Yamoussoukro Declaration of *1988*, 199
Yamoussoukro II Decision of *1999*, 199
Yokomi, M., 114
Yuen, Andrew, 159

Zhang, Anming, 159
Zhuhai Airport, 164

BROOKINGS The Brookings Institution is a private nonprofit organization devoted to research, education, and publication on important issues of domestic and foreign policy. Its principal purpose is to bring the highest quality independent research and analysis to bear on current and emerging policy problems. The Institution was founded on December 8, 1927, to merge the activities of the Institute for Government Research, founded in 1916, the Institute of Economics, founded in 1922, and the Robert Brookings Graduate School of Economics and Government, founded in 1924. Interpretations or conclusions in Brookings publications should be understood to be solely those of the authors.

Board of Trustees

John L. Thornton
Chair
Strobe Talbott
President
Robert J. Abernethy
Liaquat Ahamed
Alan R. Batkin
Richard C. Blum
Geoffrey T. Boisi
Abby Joseph Cohen
Arthur B. Culvahouse Jr.
Alan M. Dachs
Kenneth W. Dam
Steven A. Denning
Vishakha N. Desai
Paul Desmarais Jr.
Thomas E. Donilon

Mario Draghi
Kenneth M. Duberstein
Alfred B. Engelberg
Lawrence K. Fish
Cyrus F. Freidheim Jr.
Bart Friedman
David Friend
Ann M. Fudge
Jeffrey W. Greenberg
Brian L. Greenspun
Glenn Hutchins
Joel Z. Hyatt
Shirley Ann Jackson
Kenneth M. Jacobs
Suzanne Nora Johnson
Philip H. Knight
Harold Hongju Koh

William A. Owens
Frank H. Pearl
John Edward Porter
Edgar Rios
Haim Saban
Sheryl K. Sandberg
Victoria P. Sant
Leonard D. Schaeffer
Lawrence H. Summers
David F. Swensen
Larry D. Thompson
Andrew H. Tisch
Laura D'Andrea Tyson
Antoine W. van Agtmael
Beatrice W. Welters
Daniel Yergin
Daniel B. Zwirn

Honorary Trustees

Leonard Abramson
Elizabeth E. Bailey
Zoë Baird
Rex J. Bates
Louis W. Cabot
James W. Cicconi
A. W. Clausen
William T. Coleman Jr.
D. Ronald Daniel
Robert A. Day
Bruce B. Dayton
Charles W. Duncan Jr.
Walter Y. Elisha
Robert F. Erburu
Henry Louis Gates Jr.
Robert D. Haas
Lee H. Hamilton
William A. Haseltine

Teresa Heinz
F. Warren Hellman
Samuel Hellman
Robert A. Helman
Roy M. Huffington
James A. Johnson
Ann Dibble Jordan
Michael H. Jordan
Vernon E. Jordan Jr.
Breene M. Kerr
Marie L. Knowles
James T. Lynn
Jessica Tuchman Mathews
David O. Maxwell
Donald F. McHenry
Robert S. McNamara
Mary Patterson McPherson
Arjay Miller

Mario M. Morino
Maconda Brown O'Connor
Samuel Pisar
Steven Rattner
J. Woodward Redmond
Charles W. Robinson
James D. Robinson III
Warren B. Rudman
B. Francis Saul II
Ralph S. Saul
Henry B. Schacht
Michael P. Schulhof
Joan E. Spero
Vincent J. Trosino
John C. Whitehead
Stephen M. Wolf
James D. Wolfensohn
Ezra K. Zilkha